The Teacher Development Series

Children Learning English

Jayne Moon

MACMILLAN
HEINEMANN
English Language Teaching

Macmillan Education

Between Towns Road, Oxford OX4 3 PP, UK

A division of Macmillan Publisgers Limited

Companies and representatives throughout the world

ISBN 0 435 24096 X

Text © Jayne Moon
Design and illustration © Macmillan Publishers Limited 2000
Heinemann is a registered trademark of Reed Educational and Professional Publishing Limited

First published 2000

Designed by eMC Design, Bromham
Illustrated by Richard Duszczak
Front cover illustration by Viktória Hadnagy (8 years) Àldás Primary School, Budapest, Hungary.
Back cover illustration by Törös Bálázs (10 years) Tantitokepzo Foiskola

The authors and publishers would like to thank the following for permission to reproduce their material:

Macmillan Press Ltd for the extracts on p36 from English Club Student's Book 1 (Heinemann 1992) and on p89 from Big Red Bus 1 Pupil's Book and Teacher's Book (Heinemann 1993); Pearson Education on behalf of John and Julie Clarke for the extract on p72 from Stepping Stones Pupil's Book 1 and on p80 from Stepping Stones Activity Book 1, © J. and J. Clarke 1989, originally published by Collins ELT.
The extracts on pp 102, 103 and 155 respectively are reproduced by permission of Oxford University Press from:
Project English 1 Student's Book by Tom Hutchinson
© Oxford University Press 1985
Project English 1 Teacher's Book by Tom Hutchinson
© Oxford University Press 1985
Fanfare Teacher's Book by M. McHugh & G. Occhipinti
© Oxford University Press 1993.

Printed in China

2004   2003   2002
10   9   8   7   6   5

Contents

About the author

I am a lecturer in the School of Education, University of Leeds, where I have taught for 13 years on postgraduate and short courses for experienced TESOL teachers, teacher trainers and material developers from all over the world. One of the most rewarding aspects of my work is the opportunity to work with TESOL teachers and trainers from many different international contexts, and to recognize both our shared concerns as well as our differences. Before I came to Leeds, I worked for many years in different parts of Asia, such as Hong Kong, the Maldives, Nepal, Bhutan, Indonesia, initially teaching and then later working as a teacher trainer and a curriculum developer. I am very interested in children's second language development, and, in particular, how children develop their ability to write stories and other texts in English. I would like to dedicate this book to all the children, teachers and trainers I have worked with around the world, from whom I have gained immense insights about teaching and learning. They come from Bangladesh, Bhutan, Colombia, Hong Kong, Hungary, Iceland, Indonesia, Malta, Malaysia, Nepal, South Africa, Spain, Sri Lanka and many other countries.

Author's acknowledgements

Many people have contributed in different ways to this book. I would like to thank all of them:
Dugald for supporting me through the whole process, Marilyn for giving me the initial push, Adrian Underhill (series editor) and Jill Florent (commissioning editor) for their helpful and insightful comments in the early stages of the book, Lynne Cameron, Jenny Jarvis, William Gibbs, Gary Knamiller and Angi Malderez for commenting on early drafts of chapters, Alyson Maskell, who has come in with a fresh eye and done a wonderful job on the final editing of the book. Last, but not least, I would like to thank all the teachers I have worked with in different countries and my students at Leeds, in particular, B.A. Tesol teachers from Malaysia, who have contributed in different ways to the development of my ideas for this book.

The Teacher Development Series

TEACHER DEVELOPMENT is the process of becoming the best teacher you can be. It means becoming a student of learning, your own as well as that of others. It represents a widening of the focus of teaching to include not only the subject matter and the teaching methods, but also the people who are working with the subject and using the methods. It means taking a step back to see the larger picture of what goes on in learning, and how the relationship between students and teachers influences learning. It also means attending to small details which can in turn change the bigger picture. Teacher development is a continuous process of transforming human potential into human performance, a process that is never finished.

The Teacher Development Series offers perspectives on learning that embrace topic, method and person as parts of one larger interacting whole. We aim to help you, the teacher, trainer or academic manager to stretch your awareness not only of what you do and how you do it, but also of how you affect your learners and colleagues. This will enable you to extract more from your own experience, both as it happens and in retrospect, and to become more actively involved in your own continuous learning. The books themselves will focus on new treatments of familiar subjects as well as areas that are just emerging as subjects of the future.

The series represents work that is in progress rather than finished or closed. The authors are themselves exploring, and invite you to bring your own experience to the study of these books while at the same time learning from the experiences of others. We encourage you to observe, value and understand your own experience, and to evaluate and integrate relevant external practice and knowledge into your own internal evolving model of effective teaching and learning.

Adrian Underhill

Other titles in the Teacher Development Series

Inside Teaching   Tim Bowen and Jonathan Marks

Learning Teaching   Jim Scrivener

Sound Foundations   Adrian Underhill

Readings in Teacher Development   Katie Head and Pauline Taylor

The ELT Manager's Handbook   Graham Impey and Nic Underhill

Introduction to *Children Learning English*

Who is the book for?

I have written this book for teachers. It will be suitable, in particular:

- for those of you already teaching English to children, who want to consider your teaching in new ways
- for those of you who are general primary teachers in your own countries, but are now going to teach English as well
- for those of you who are already specialist English language teachers of secondary school students or adults, who are now going to teach English to children.

What is the book for?

I have written this book because of my interest in teaching languages to children. I would like to share with you something of my own fascination and enjoyment in working with them. But this real interest took time to develop. When I first began teaching, I was busy trying to survive and cover the syllabus. My focus was on the subject matter, the methods and keeping the children quiet. It was only gradually that I began to understand the importance of observing what children do and talking to them. It was only later that I began to see them as real people with preferences, ideas and views of their own. As I responded to them as human beings, they responded to me. As I observed them closely, I realized what an amazing capacity they had for learning and how many abilities they already had which I could draw on in the classroom. These changes in my understanding and beliefs led to changes in my practice and also made me feel much more excited about and involved in teaching children.

In this book, I want to help you to examine your own teaching and beliefs about teaching in the context of teaching English to children. Change can only take place if we become more aware of the assumptions and beliefs which underpin our practice. This new awareness may lead to change. I hope that the book will provide you with different ways of doing this.

- The new challenge (for some of you) of teaching children English may provide an opportunity to re-examine your practice and the reasons for your practice.
- Learning from children, observing what children do and say, and talking to them as people rather than pupils in a class can influence your teaching in new and exciting ways.
- Considering the points of view of specialists and of other primary teachers may help to give you new ideas or different perspectives to consider so that you have more options to think about in your teaching.

I hope that this book will enable you to feel excited about teaching English to children, both professionally and personally.

What is the book about?

This book focuses on the teaching and learning of English as a foreign language (EFL) – that means where English is a subject taught at school and where the child generally does not use English outside of school. However we have also included examples from second language (ESL) teaching situations where this helps to illuminate the way children's language develops. The book is concerned with children from six to twelve years of age but it also includes examples from older children where this seems relevant, to illustrate the way children's language and attitudes to language develop and change.

It is a book:

- which provides insights into the special characteristics, abilities and attitudes children bring to the classroom
- which helps you to think about how you can learn from children and make use of this information in planning your teaching and your work with children
- which offers you ideas and frameworks for teaching English as options to consider carefully in relation to your own context
- which encourages you to develop yourself as a teacher.

It is **not**:

- a book of teaching tips, though it does contain teaching ideas for you to consider and try out
- a book for beginning teachers
- a book which recommends a universal method for teaching children.

There are many ways of teaching children, but these need to be considered in relation to your own context and the needs of your pupils. Teaching situations around the world vary considerably, and yours may differ from the ones I describe in this book. However, I hope that no matter what your teaching situation is like, you may acquire ways of examining your own teaching contexts and beliefs which will help you to see your own teaching and your pupils in new ways.

Finding your way through the book

The book is organized into two parts. In the first three chapters, the focus is on children and their special characteristics, and how they think and learn. From Chapter 4 onwards, the focus is on teaching English and how teachers can assist and support children's language learning.

The book can be used in different ways. It is possible to work through the chapters in sequence. It is equally possible to focus only on the chapters which interest you. There are cross references in the text so that you can find other chapters which may deal with the topic again, eg managing groupwork. Reader tasks are included to help you to reflect on and actively engage with the material in the book.

Starting points

Changing the level at which you teach from adults to children or beginning to teach a new subject, eg moving from teaching general primary subjects to teaching English, can be quite stressful. In this situation it is natural to have secret fears or worries about whether you will be successful. So it can help to begin by writing down all the things you can do already (credits) and think about which of these things you can make use of or adapt for the new teaching situation (credit transfers).

You may be quite pleasantly surprised to find that there are many skills or abilities which you can make use of in your new teaching situation. Try writing down your credits, as in the example below from Abdulgader, a Libyan teacher who had previously taught adults.

Credits   *Credit transfers*

Knowledge or experience of children, eg relatives, your own children	Teaching English	Teaching children	Which credits can be transferred /adapted?
My young cousin: 1 He is curious. 2 When it comes to playing, he is very creative. He creates games that are suitable for the place he is in and the resources available. 3 He likes going to new places. 4 He likes stories. 5 He plays a lot.	My experience is with adults: 6 Language is best learned when learners attempt to use it to communicate something. 7 A focus on form in a meaningful way does help interlanguage development. 8 The teacher needs to accommodate students' explicit needs as they have a clear vision of what they want to learn. 9 Adults like to feel rapid progress in learning. 10 The language we teach to adults is sometimes specific (work related). 11 We need to help learners to learn how to learn.		• I was thinking of adults as different from children. But now I am puzzled! Differences now seem a matter of degree. Many aspects of adult teaching have similarities to teaching children, eg points 6 and 7. • My knowledge of children in 1–5.

Many of the examples given in this book are taken from real classrooms and from teachers I have worked with. Other examples are drawn from real classroom data but have been altered in some way, eg names, contexts, etc to preserve anonymity or to illustrate particular points. There are examples from all around the world to show that you belong to an international community of English teachers who share many common concerns.

Chapter 1 Children learning English

Children as language learners

The child in the example here[1] speaks English as his first language. But we can tell that he is still learning by the errors in his speech. By about four and a half years of age, however, he will have acquired the basic grammar system needed for everyday communication, though there will be some more complex aspects of grammar, eg sentence connectors, which he will only finally acquire in his teens. Children learning English as a foreign language also make errors which can be seen as a sign of active learning. These errors give us evidence that both first and second language children are not just imitating what they hear like parrots, but are working out how the language system operates. The errors give us windows to look through and see what they have discovered about language so far.

But there is one important difference between children learning their first language and children learning a second language at school: second language children have already learned one language. So they bring with them to the language classroom a great deal of experience of language, of life and many other natural abilities which help them to learn and to learn English. As teachers, we need to make use of and build on these abilities and characteristics. In this chapter, we will consider:

1 **Contexts for learning English**
2 **Children as language learners**
3 **How teachers' beliefs about learning affect their teaching**
4 **Ways of observing children's language learning**

The aim of this chapter is to help you to reflect on your own teaching so that you can consider to what extent you take account of the ways in which children learn and learn languages.

1 Contexts for learning English

Many teachers I have talked to believe that the ideal situation for children learning a second language is to live in the country where the language is spoken, to be surrounded by it and to acquire it naturally through using it every day.

If we analyse this suggestion, we can identify a number of different conditions which are associated with this ideal learning situation:

- *Time*
  Children will have plenty of time for learning English and it can be spread over several years.
- *Exposure*
  They are exposed to English all around them, both in and outside of school.
- *A real need for English*
  They have a need to use English in order to survive on a daily basis, eg to make friends, to study in school, to shop, to travel, etc.
- *Variety of input*
  They are exposed to a wide variety of uses of English, eg spoken and written, English for thinking, for interacting, for getting things done, for imagining.

1

● *Meaningful input*
They will receive plenty of meaningful language input through experience of English not as a subject to be learned, but as a means of communication, where the focus is on the meaning not the form of the language.

Task 1   Comparing situations

Here are three different situations for learning English. Which situation is closest to the one in which you teach?

Junko is an eight-year-old Japanese girl. Her parents are working in England. She attends a Japanese school. After one year, she has picked up quite a lot of English from the au pair girl who works for the family and from the children who live next door. She can chat away quite happily with other children and she often translates for her mother when they go shopping to the market. Her mother finds it difficult to speak English.

Rosa is an eight-year-old girl who lives in Colombia in South America. She learns English at school. She does not hear or use any English outside school. She is not sure why she is learning English, except that her parents think it is important. At the end of one year of English, she knows a few words of English.

Dorji is an eight-year-old boy from Bhutan in the Himalayas. He is in Class 2 and he is learning all his subjects through English. Outside school, he will see some shop signs in English and he may watch English films at home on his video with his parents. By the end of two years, he already knows a lot of English and can use it to communicate with his teachers, who speak to him in English.

■ Compare the three situations and tick the chart to show which points in the left column apply to each learning situation.
■ Which situation do you think is the most favourable for language learning for young learners and why?
■ Which situation is the least favourable and why? Can you identify three ways in which it could be made into a more favourable environment?

	Situation A (Junko)	Situation B (Rosa)	Situation C (Dorji)
Plenty of time for English			
Exposure to English inside/outside school			
Need to use English			
Exposure to a variety of different uses of English			
Meaningful input – focus on meaning and communication			

Commentary ■ ■ ■

These three situations represent different opportunities for learning English. Situations A and C seem the most favourable for learning English because they allow more exposure to English and more opportunities for using it.

Compared to situations A and C, situation B offers:
- a limited amount of time spent on English
- no need or reason for using English
- a formal learning environment with the focus mainly on correctness
- a limited and controlled language input.

However a great many children learn English successfully in school contexts like B. So we need to consider the best way of making the classroom a positive learning environment. Our role as the teacher is likely to be very important in doing this.

Here are some suggestions for how to create a more favourable environment in the classroom. Which ones can you use in your classroom? What other ideas do you have?

- Make your classroom a lively place through the use of attractive wall displays, displays of pupils' work, a book corner, etc.
- Motivate pupils to want to learn English by using interesting and enjoyable learning activities, eg project work, games, drama.
- Create a warm and happy atmosphere where teacher and pupils enjoy working together.
- Help pupils to develop personal reasons for learning English, for example by encouraging out-of-school class activities, eg pen friends, projects, reading story books.

In order to be able to create the right conditions for language learning in your classroom, you need to develop an awareness of how children learn foreign languages. You may already have many ideas gained from your own experience, from your reading or from training. It may be helpful to re-examine these ideas in order to develop your teaching further. ■

2 Children as language learners

In this section we will consider some of the natural abilities and characteristics children possess which help them to learn a foreign language. We will begin by examining teachers' beliefs about how children learn languages.

Task 2 Examining teachers' beliefs about how children learn languages

- How do you think children learn a foreign language?
- How far do you agree with the views below?

Children learn a foreign language ...

> '... *in a natural way, the same way they learn their own language.*'
> '... *through being motivated. It depends on the teacher's style. If the teacher motivated them they would learn fast or quicker.*'
> '... *by listening and repeating.*'
> '... *by imitating the teacher. They want to please the teacher. They feel embarrassed when they make mistakes.*'
> '... *by doing and interacting with each other in an atmosphere of trust and acceptance, through a variety of interesting and fun activities for which they see the purpose.*'
> '... *through translating sentences into their own language.*'

Quotes from teachers attending an international summer school

The following examples are taken from real classrooms or teaching situations around the world, in both foreign and second language learning contexts. As you read and work through them, consider whether they support or conflict with your views.

Teacher is indicated by the letter T, Pupils are indicated by Pps and individual pupils by P1, P2, etc.

Example 1   Using language creatively

The example below shows how pupils' language can give important clues about how they learn languages.

A class of Bhutanese children (Year 3) has just prepared a set of simple written instructions *(Read and draw)* and tried them out with some younger children. Here is an example of the instructions which one pupil produced.

> Draw three nice flowers.
> Draw a flower on the ground.
> Draw nine leaves round the flower.

The younger children (Year 2) had to read the instructions and draw. The teacher is now having a discussion with the Year 3 pupils to evaluate how successful the younger children were and what problems they had in doing the *Read and draw* activity.

T What's the problem?
P They [Year 2 children] do not know how to write [the child means *draw*] leaves. They are writing on the ground.
T Where did you ask them to draw the leaves?
P In the flower's stick.[The child means the stem of the flower.]
T Oh yes, that's right. *(smiles)*

Task 3

■ Do you think the pupil has been taught the phrase 'the flower's stick'? If not, where has it come from?
■ What does this example tell us about how children learn English?

Commentary ■ ■ ■

This example shows a child using language creatively. She is using a phrase she has not heard or been taught before. She has made up the phrase *flower's stick* to express her own meaning by using previously learned language (*flower* and *stick*), but recombining it in a new and creative way. It shows that she already has knowledge of the language system, eg that we show possession through using apostrophe + s. She is *trying out* her knowledge by using it to express her message.

This example shows us that pupils actively try to experiment and work out the rules of the language in their heads, though they may not be aware of doing this. The activity which the pupils carried out in this classroom and the discussion afterwards allowed them the freedom to be creative and go beyond what they had learned. For example, the teacher's question *What's the problem?* invited pupils to say what they felt. When the pupil spoke, the teacher showed interest *(Where did you ask them to draw the leaves?)* and was supportive *(Oh yes, that's right)*. So the pupils felt confident enough to try to use the rules of the language they already knew to experiment. This is also a nice example of how a classroom can provide opportunities to use English in more varied ways (a pupil explaining and commenting) and create a real need for children to use the language.

One implication of this example is that children need opportunities to try out and experiment with language, but they also need feedback to confirm or modify their hypotheses. ■

Example 2   Going for meaning

Children are able to draw on many of the abilities which they have made use of in learning their first language. One of these is the ability to make sense of what is happening in a situation.

In this example, the (ten-year-old) pupil is looking at a picture of a man who is sleeping. Two men are trying to steal his drum. The teacher is asking him questions about the picture.

₁ **P**   The man is sleeping.
 T   And then?
 P   The mango is fell down.
 T   Then?
₅ **P**   Two men is taking his drum.
 T   Two ...
 P   Two men is taking his drum.
 T   You say *two men ... (stresses the words 'two men')*
 P   Two meen men ... *(tries changing the pronunciation)*
₁₀ **T**   No. *(The pupil still does not provide the answer the teacher wants.)*
 P   ... is taking his drum.
 T   Again, do you say *is*?
 P   Two men are taking his drum. *(The pupil finally realizes that the teacher is concerned about subject/verb agreement.)*

Task 4

■ There is a breakdown in communication between the pupil and teacher from line 6 onwards. What is the reason for it?
■ What does the example tell you about how pupils learn a foreign language?

Commentary ■ ■ ■

The pupil is trying to explain what is happening in the picture, whereas the teacher is concerned for the pupil to get the grammar right. The pupil focuses on the meaning, while the teacher is concerned with the form of the sentences. Finally the pupil realizes what the teacher wants.

This example shows that children have a good instinct for interpreting the *sense or meaning of a situation*. They do this through using their knowledge of everyday life and the clues provided by the situation, or the picture, as in this example. They work out the meaning first and tend not to pay attention to the words that are used to express the meaning. As children get older, they begin to pay more attention to the words. This ability to *go for meaning* is a very useful one in language learning as it allows children to work out what is happening in a situation, eg a story, a video, a conversation, and this then helps them to attach meaning to the words used. The use of communication games, drama, project work, story telling and practical activities in teaching, all allow children to make use of this ability to go for meaning. However, teachers need to respond initially in ways which build on children's natural instinct for meaning, and not ignore it as in this example. Accuracy is, of course, important, but it can be dealt with later once children are familiar with the meaning. ■

Example 3   Using 'chunks' of language

Children use a variety of strategies to learn a foreign language. This example, recorded by Linda Ventriglia[2] with two Spanish-speaking children who are learning English in America, shows how children make use of ready-made phrases of language.

The children find a group of wooden blocks which are lying in a cardboard box.

Miguel: Vamos a hacer un tren fantastico con estos bloques.
          (Let's make a pretend train with these blocks.)
          Pon el mas grande acqui.
          (Put the biggest one here.)
Maria: Pero necesitaremos mas bloques grandes. No podremos haccrlo con los pequeños.
          (But we will need more large blocks. We will not be able to make it with the small ones.)
Miguel: Claro que si. We have the technology.
          (Yes, we can.)

Task 5

- Notice the phrase the pupil says in English. Where did he learn it? Is he using it appropriately?
- Have your pupils used any whole phrases or sayings like this? How can using whole phrases help children's language learning?

Commentary ■ ■ ■

The conversation is entirely in Spanish until the last sentence, which is said in English: *We have the technology.* The pupil has possibly heard the phrase in school or on TV and picked it up as a complete phrase (chunk) or formula learned as a whole. He uses it appropriately for the situation.

Children learning a foreign language often use complete phrases of language they have picked up from someone else, eg *I don't know, Knock it off, Come on, Goodbye.* These are sometimes called chunks of language because they are learned and used in speech as whole phrases. Children may not have been taught these chunks formally, but they help them to communicate when they have very little language. Later they may begin to break down these phrases and recombine the words in new ways. For example, in the beginning a child may just use the phrase *I don't know.* Later he/she may begin to realize that this can be combined with other bits of language, eg *I don't know his name, I don't know spelling.* Later he/she may begin to change other parts of the phrase, eg *We don't know, They don't know* and at a later stage he/she may begin to realize that the verb changes according to the subject, eg *He doesn't know.* It is useful to observe when children begin to break down a phrase in this way as this is a sign of language development. We can help to encourage this by getting children to notice common or recurring elements in phrases. ■

Teaching children chunks may be very helpful in the early stages of language learning to enable them to take part in conversations. They can *take over* and use for themselves ready-made bits of language so that they can join in. By joining in, they get more exposure to input for language learning and more practice. The use of songs, rhymes, poems, drama and classroom routines all help to give children access to ready-made bits of language so they can begin to communicate.

Example 4   Having fun

Children have a great capacity to enjoy themselves. When they are enjoying themselves, they are usually absorbed by the activity and want to continue with it. They are not always aware that they are learning language.

In this example, children in their first year of learning English (six to seven-year-olds) in Croatia[3] are playing a game with their teacher. They have obviously played it before.

T   Let's start. Oh what's that up there in the sky? *(sounds surprised)* Oh my goodness, you know I can see seven helicopters in the sky.
Pps No, no. Yes. Yes ... No... *(pupils laugh disbelievingly)*
T   You don't believe me. Have a look there. *(gives one pupil a pair of binoculars)*
Pps What can you see?
P   I can see three monkeys. *(sounds very surprised)*
Pps No, no you can't. *(smiling)*
P   Have a look. *(gives binoculars to another child)*
Pps What can you see?
P   I can see a spaceship in the sky.
Pps No, no, you can't. Yes? *(sound disbelieving)*

Task 6

■ What activity are the children involved in?
■ Do you think they are enjoying themselves? How do you know?
■ How do you think this will affect their language learning?

Commentary ■ ■ ■

The class in Croatia is playing a chain game which involves imagining you can see something interesting or unusual in the sky when you look through the binoculars. The rest of the pupils have to express disbelief. This leads to the pupil who made the claim inviting someone to check for themselves and so the game continues. It allows pupils the opportunity to use their imagination fully.

They seem to be really enjoying themselves and entering fully into the spirit of the ritual exchange between the person who makes a claim and the rest of the class who express disbelief. The pupils are laughing and seem keen to take part even though they have obviously played the game before.

If pupils enjoy the learning activities, they will be more involved and this may increase their desire to continue. This is very positive for language learning, because if children want to continue with an activity for some time, it will give them more exposure to language input and more chance to practise the language. They will also develop more positive attitudes towards English as they will associate it with something enjoyable and pleasing. The game also involves the use of language patterns, eg *I can see a* ... , which assists the building up of their underlying language system. ■

Example 5   Joining in the action

Children are naturally curious and active. They eagerly explore their environment and interact with people, which helps them to construct their understanding of the world they live in. An important way in which they do this is through physical activity and experiencing things at first hand. Let's see how this helps them in learning a foreign language.

In this example, a teacher from Croatia[3] has been doing an action rhyme with (six to seven-year-old) children involving their fingers *(Put your finger on your toes, etc)*. Children have enjoyed this and have even requested her to do it again. Now she has invited children to come out and give instructions to their friends. They listen and then carry out the instructions.

P1 Put your finger on your hand. *(The last word was not clear and some children are not clear where to put their finger.)*

T Well, once again you have to be precise. Where do put ... where do you want them to put ...

P1 Put your finger on your *hand. (stresses the word 'hand' and pupils put their fingers on their hands)*

T *(asks pupils)* Where is your hand?
All right.

P1 Put your finger on your neck. *(pupils obey)*
Put your finger on your knee.

T OK that was very good. Next? *(another child volunteers)*

P2 Put your finger on your nose.
Put your fingers on your head.

Task 7

■ How is the language linked to the physical activity?
■ Why is this type of activity (action game) likely to be very helpful for language learning?

Commentary ■ ■ ■

In the first part of the lesson, the teacher and children did the actions together as they said the words. So the actions helped to make the meaning of the words clear. In the later *listen and do* activity, pupils listened to the instructions as their classmates told them what to do and then demonstrated their understanding of it through a physical action.

Physical activities, eg making things, action songs, games, rhymes and drama provide excellent contexts for language learning. The language is closely related to what is happening in the situation, and so children can get clues about the meaning from the activity which accompanies the language. *They learn through doing.* There is also a clear and meaningful purpose for them in using the language. The *listen and do* activities are particularly useful for beginners, as children's listening abilities may be far ahead of their speaking abilities. This type of activity allows pupils to be actively learning and participating, but does not force them to speak or produce language till they are ready. It provides them with exposure to meaningful input. ■

Example 6   Talking their heads off

If we watch children speaking in their first language, we notice how much they enjoy talking. If you visit a primary school, children quickly come up to talk to you and will ask you questions and tell you about themselves without any prompting. What happens to this desire to communicate when children learn another language?

In this example, Ram is introducing (six to seven-year-old) pupils in their first year of learning English to the concepts *same* and *different*. He has placed a pile of objects in the middle of the room, eg bottle tops, match boxes, fir cones, etc and the children are sitting round in a big circle.

T Give me two that are the same. *(pupil looks at the pile of objects)* Give me two the same: matching ... *(pupil picks up two bottle tops)*
Very good, very good, boy. *(teacher pats pupil on the shoulder)*
Right.

Pps *(clap loudly)*

T Very good, boy. Go now. *(sends him back to his place and chooses another pupil called Gembo)*

Pps Yes, yes, Gembo. *(pupils agree with teacher's choice)*

T   Now you go and give me two different ... different things.
P   Gembo Dorji *(says pupil's name, possibly to help teacher who is new and does not know all the names)*
Pps Different ... *(pupils try to prompt Gembo)*
G   Different ...
Pps No. *(Gembo picks up two similar objects and pupils tell him that he is wrong)*
Pps Different – no. *(pupils tell teacher that the objects are not different)*

Task 8

- Do the children in the example above show any desire to communicate in English?
- Is there likely to be any difference between age groups (eg between six to eight-year-olds and 12 to 14-year-olds) in their desire to communicate?
- How will children's desire to communicate help them to learn a foreign language?

Commentary ■ ■ ■

The pupils show a lot of eagerness to participate and express their ideas even though, as near beginners, they have very limited language. They use the limited phrases they have to communicate, eg *Different – no.*

Children are likely to vary considerably even among the same age group, with some children being much quieter than others. In general, younger children (five to ten-year-olds) tend to be more enthusiastic and willing to talk in class than older children. As children reach puberty, they get more embarrassed about talking in front of others. Peer approval becomes very important and they are very concerned not to make a fool of themselves publicly.

Children's desire to communicate is very powerful and this carries over into foreign language learning. If they are engaged in an interesting activity, they will *talk their heads off* happily. This is very useful for language learning because it means that pupils will get plenty of practice in using the language. This may be one reason why in natural situations, children often seem to do better than adults, ie their strong desire to communicate means that they immediately try to use the new language and so get more practice. Adults usually want to study it formally in classrooms first. We need to think how to activate this desire in the foreign language classroom through the teaching methods and resources we use. ■

Example 7   Feeling at home

Friday 31st march
Mrs
I feel better when MRs
B   says allright then
who can help Rowan.
Then people put up thier *their*
hands and tell me the
answer. I can understand
alot more than I could
before I came to this
school. That is a way that
helps me. Another thing
that helps is once some-
body Lets tells me the
answer I keep on saying
it in my head

We should not underestimate pupils' feelings. If they are happy and secure, they are more likely to enjoy and benefit from their language learning[4]. This example is taken from a diary written by a nine-year-old British child who has been learning French as a foreign language for a year.

Task 9

- How does the pupil feel about learning French?
- What support does he receive from the teacher and pupils?
- What effect does this have on him?
- What can we learn from this example about pupils' feelings and the way this affects language learning?

9

Commentary ■ ■ ■

The pupil does not seem very confident about his own abilities.

The teacher is aware of his need for support and asks other pupils to help.

The support he receives makes him feel more confident and secure. As a result, he feels that he has made some progress since he came to the school.

This example shows that pupils have feelings about language learning. They often feel quite frightened, embarrassed or insecure about learning a new language. In this case, the teacher has understood the pupil's need for support, and this has helped him to gain confidence. As teachers, we need to be very sensitive to pupils' feelings as this may affect their motivation and attitude to learning the language. If they feel *at home* in the classroom, they are more likely to participate and take risks. ■

The examples above may have confirmed your own experience or may have raised questions that you want to explore further. We have seen that children do not learn just in one way. The points made by teachers on page 3 represent many different ways in which children learn, not just by repeating or imitating or translating.

Here is a summary of some of the important abilities which our pupils are able to make use of in learning a foreign language and which indicate the active nature of their learning.

USING LANGUAGE CREATIVELY

JOINING IN THE ACTION

GOING FOR MEANING

TALKING THEIR HEADS OFF

USING 'CHUNKS' OF LANGUAGE

FEELING AT HOME

HAVING FUN

Creating conditions which support language learning

Children will only be able to make use of these abilities if we create the right kind of learning environment in which they can draw on them. This means we need to consider how to:

● create a real need and desire to use English
● provide sufficient time for English
● provide exposure to varied and meaningful input with a focus on communication
● provide opportunities for children to experiment with their new language
● provide plenty of opportunities to practise and use the language in different contexts
● create a friendly atmosphere in which children can take risks and enjoy their learning
● provide feedback on learning
● help children notice the underlying pattern in language.

3   How teachers' beliefs about learning affect their teaching

Often we are not aware of our own beliefs until we hear someone express an opinion which we agree with or disagree with. We may not be aware of how our beliefs affect the way we respond to other people or the way we do our work or the way we teach. For example, I recently talked to some primary teachers in Bangladesh. They felt that it was very difficult for young children to learn English at primary level. So they used translation as their main teaching method to make things easier for children. They could not imagine how a pupil could learn without translation.

Let us look at some examples of how teachers' views about learning may affect the way they teach.

Task 10   How beliefs affect teaching

Here are outlines of two lessons on prepositions for eight to nine-year-old children.

- How does Teacher A think pupils learn language?
- How does Teacher B think pupils learn language?
- Which lesson provides most opportunities for pupils to make use of the natural abilities and characteristics which they bring to language learning?

TEACHER A

1 Presentation

The teacher presents each preposition through showing a concrete example and then modelling the sentence, eg

The ruler is in the box.

The ruler is under the table.

The ruler is on the table.

Ruslan is standing near the table.

2 Whole class repetition

Pupils repeat the sentence after the teacher several times.

3 Group drill

The teacher points to objects in different locations and gets groups to describe them in chorus, eg

T Group C, where is the ruler? *(puts it under the table)*

C The ruler is under the table.

T Group B, where is the ruler?

B The ruler is under the table.

T Where is the ruler? *(puts it on the table)*

TEACHER B

1 Warm-up game/revision

The teacher calls out six children (in pairs) to the front of the class to carry out some instructions, eg *Stand in front of your partner. Stand behind your partner,* etc. The rest of the class have to guess which pair will be fastest in following the instructions.

2 Dialogue

The teacher draws pictures of two girls and builds up a dialogue on the blackboard with the pupils' help. One of the girls has to draw a plan of a classroom for homework and needs help from her friend to find out where pupils are sitting. With the pupils' help, the teacher elicits questions and answers, eg *Where is Asna sitting? She is sitting on the left of Aishah.* Pupils practise the dialogue in pairs.

3 Communication game

Pupils work in pairs to fill in the missing names of children on a picture of a birthday party. There are two versions of the picture so Pupil A has names that Pupil B does not have and vice versa.

Commentary ■ ■ ■

The way teachers plan and organize their lessons reflects their beliefs about teaching and learning. It gives some idea about what the teacher thinks is the most appropriate way to help pupils to learn.

Teacher A seems to believe that:

- pupils need to understand the meaning of new language, and so, for example, she demonstrates as she introduces the new language
- pupils need a lot of repetition in order to learn
- pupils' language needs to be controlled so that mistakes are reduced
- pupils should not be exposed to language that they have not been formally taught
- pupils may not have enough language to work together in pairs or groups independently of the teacher
- the teacher provides the main source of language input.

Teacher B seems to believe that:

- pupils need to understand the meaning of new language
- pupils need a variety of activities
- pupils need activities which are enjoyable and stimulating
- pupils learn through using the language more freely for a communicative purpose
- pupils benefit from being actively involved
- pupils benefit from practising together independently of the teacher.

Although there are many apparent differences between the teachers, there are also some similarities. They both seem to believe that …

- pupils need plenty of practice
- pupils need to understand the meaning of what they are learning
- focusing formally on the rules of grammar would not be appropriate for children.

Although both lessons provide opportunities for language learning, Teacher B's lesson seems to provide more opportunities for pupils to make use of the abilities which they bring with them to the language classroom. For example, the games will appeal to their sense of fun and arouse their interest. The communication game gives them a real purpose for using language and provides opportunities for them to use language more freely and to experiment. Pupils' desire to talk is also catered for in the dialogue activity and the communication game. In general, Teacher B's lesson gives more opportunity for children to try out their language. However Teacher A's lesson does highlight the importance of repetition in learning. Children need opportunities for repetition, but it needs to be done in an interesting and meaningful way. Mechanical repetition, eg as in the chorus drills in Teacher A's lesson, where children do not need to pay attention to the meaning, has limited value for language learning.

Of course, it is difficult to know in reality which teacher's class would be most effective for language learning. It would depend on how they were carried out, as both lessons can be well or badly done. It may be that the teacher's relationship with his/her pupils is more important in the end than the particular teaching method used. And this brings us back to beliefs again, for our beliefs about learning and teaching will affect the kind of relationships we build with pupils. ■

4   Ways of observing children's language learning

Task 10 has shown that our beliefs about learning can affect the way we plan our teaching and the way we respond to young learners. If you want to develop your teaching further, you need to become aware of the beliefs which influence your teaching. Development is only possible if you can become aware of these beliefs by trying to articulate them to yourself or to others.

Maybe like Teacher A above, you believe that pupils' language should be carefully controlled. *Why do you believe that? What would happen if you gave your pupils some freer activities occasionally? How would it affect pupils?* To answer those questions, you need to think about the reasons for what you do and to think about how and why pupils respond in the way they do by observing them closely. If you become better at watching and learning from pupils and relate what you learn to your beliefs, you will have a good basis for developing your own ideas about teaching and learning. Here are some ideas:

MONDAY 21

Class 2

Lily made a joke today when we were playing the game **Simon says**. I told everyone to stand up & David didn't want to. So Lily said jokingly `he's grandfather'.

Really interesting to see that children can joke even using limited English. Must listen out for other examples. Maybe they could try and write jokes in English.

1   Keep a diary

Keep a diary or observation note book and start to write down interesting things you observe children say or do. You can then use this information in planning future lessons or providing specific help for individuals.

2   Tape record children's pair or group interaction

Tape record a pair or group of children doing a particular language-learning activity. Focus on some particular aspect of the activity, eg the way they work together and interact to do the activity. Use the recording to consider how successfully the children were interacting to do the task.

Here is an example recorded by Rod Ellis[5] of two children learning English in the UK. P1 is holding a picture and giving instructions to P2 how to draw it. P2 cannot see the drawing.

P1   Draw big red circle.
P2   Big red circle. *(pupil draws as instructed)*
P1   And a small blue circle.
P2   In here? *(pupil indicates circle he has already drawn)*
P1   I don't know. *(pupil is not sure how to explain)*
P2   A big?
P1   I don't know. A square in a circle.
P2   Big or small?

When we examine the dialogue we see that the children manage some level of communication mainly because P2 takes charge. P2, with a limited amount of English, is skilful at supporting P1's attempts to give instructions. He confirms what has been said in line 2, asks questions of clarification in line 4, tries to prompt in line 6, asks for clarification in line 8. These strategies provide more opportunities for P2 to use his English. They also support P1's initial attempts to communicate by structuring the interaction and giving prompts of the kind of information needed.

The recording suggests that P1 may need additional language input and practice to build up the language required for giving instructions. It also shows that strategies for managing the interaction, as P2 demonstrates, are an important help in communication. So it may be useful to spend time on raising children's awareness about these strategies and demonstrating how to use them.

Summary

In this chapter, you have considered:

- *the different contexts in which children can learn English* and how these affect the quantity and quality of language input which children get. In a foreign language situation, children will depend almost entirely on the school environment for input. So you, as their teacher, may be the only source of language, which makes your role in children's language learning very important.
- *the variety of ways in which children learn* and the natural abilities and characteristics children make use of in learning another language, eg the desire to communicate, the ability to work out the meaning, creativity, the need for security, etc. Children do not learn in just one way, but use all the different ways mentioned by teachers. However children can only make use of these means if you develop the right kind of learning environment – one in which they have plenty of exposure to a variety of meaningful input, feel free to take risks and experiment, want to use the language to communicate with you and other class mates and get feedback on their learning.
- *how teachers' beliefs about teaching affect the way they teach.* The way you create the conditions for learning through your planning, your management and your responses to pupils is determined by your beliefs and assumptions. So if you want to be responsive to what you learn from observing and working with your pupils, you need to examine those beliefs constantly and be prepared to change them if necessary.
- *some ideas for observing children* which may help you to become better at watching and understanding their learning. You can use the information you gain from observing to examine your own beliefs and classroom practice so that the actions you take are based on beliefs supported by evidence from children's learning. You can make use of this information to plan more effectively for children's future learning.

One of the implications from the discussion in this chapter is that children learning a second or foreign language will use similar processes. However a key difference lies in the type and amount of language exposure. In a second language situation, children gain input both from inside and outside school. They are not totally dependent on the school environment. But in a foreign language situation, they depend almost entirely on the school for input. That puts you in a powerful position to make their learning of English a positive, stimulating and successful experience. In the rest of the book, we will explore how this can be achieved.

References

1 Wells, G. 1986 *The Meaning Makers.* London: Hodder & Stoughton
   A readable account of a research project which followed a group of children learning their first language from their first words to the end of primary school.
2 Ventriglia, L. 1982 *Conversations with Miguel and Maria.* New York: Addison Wesley
   A description of the strategies children use as they acquire a second language.
3 Film based on a project in Croatia to introduce English to children of six years of age. More information can be found in Vilke, M. and Vrhouac, Y. (eds.) 1993 *Children and Foreign Languages.* Zagreb: University of Zagreb, Faculty of Philosophy
4 Gregory, A. 1996 *British Primary School Children's Attitudes to Learning French.* (unpublished M. Ed. thesis. School of Education, University of Leeds)
   This diary was collected from a primary school near York.
5 Ellis, R. 1984 *Classroom Second Language Development.* Oxford: Pergamon Press
   An interesting academic account of L2 acquisition in the classroom.

Chapter 2   Do you like learning English?

Pupils' attitudes to learning English

Children do not come to their English lessons like blank sheets of paper. They already have views about and attitudes towards learning English, as the two quotes from ten-year-old Spanish children show. These attitudes are formed by the social environment in which they grow up and by the people around them. It is important to be aware of these attitudes as they can influence pupils' desire and motivation to learn and ultimately their success in learning English.

How are pupils' attitudes formed? What influences their attitudes towards English and learning? In this chapter, we will consider:

1 **Pupils' attitudes to learning English and what influences them**
2 **Finding out about pupils' attitudes**
3 **Ways of developing positive attitudes towards English**
4 **Teachers' attitudes to their own English**

The aim of this chapter is to develop your awareness of pupils' attitudes towards learning English and how these may affect language learning. It may also encourage you to examine your own attitudes to English and teaching English and consider how your attitudes may affect your pupils' attitudes.

1   Pupils' attitudes to learning English

Task 1   Do you like learning English?

- What are some of the things your pupils say about learning English?
- In your opinion, what are the most important factors which influence pupils' attitudes to learning English?
- Now study these comments below in translation from a group of 13-year-old Spanish children. They give reasons why they like or dislike learning English. What may have influenced their attitudes?
- Compare what your pupils say with the Spanish children's comments.

Do you like English?

YES, because …	NO or not much, because …
It is good to learn another language and to go to work to other countries in the world.	Sometimes one gets all mixed up. It's very confusing.
It is not complicated and is a beautiful language.	My English is poorish. I feel a bit behind.
It is nice and can be useful later on.	It is very difficult.
It is a language of great relevance in the world.	Only a bit. I am not very enthusiastic about it, but I think it will be useful.
That way I have more culture. I can understand computers and game instructions.	At the beginning I didn't like it much, but when you know a bit more and attend classes, you end up liking it.

Commentary ■ ■ ■

It is difficult to know exactly what has influenced pupils' attitudes but we could guess from the comments that pupils are influenced by:

- teaching methods *(It is difficult, I feel left behind)*
- seeing a need for English outside school *(work in other countries, useful later on, understand game instructions, world language)*
- personal preferences, interest in languages *(It is a beautiful language)*.

Pupils vary widely in their attitudes, as the chart above shows. It is also likely that their attitudes change or can be changed by their experiences. For example, one pupil clearly developed a liking through gaining knowledge of the language, which perhaps contributed to his/her sense of confidence. Some of the pupils above may have found English very difficult because of the way it was taught and a change of method could stimulate their interest. Others may have experienced an early lack of success which could have contributed to their negative feelings. Achieving some success could make all the difference to their feelings. In your answers, perhaps you have included other influences on pupils' attitudes like parental views and peer group pressure. ■

Pupils' attitudes seem to change as they get older, perhaps in response to internal developments and different experiences in their environment. It is interesting to consider differences in attitudes between age groups and also differences in the factors which influence their attitudes.

Task 2 Differences in attitudes between age groups

- What factors are likely to influence the attitudes of younger children aged six to ten?
- Compare the attitudes of a group of Spanish pupils aged seven to eight below with the older pupils above.

> *I like it and it is fun.*
> *I play in English and I learn a lot.*
> *Es muy chuli! (It is cool!)*
> *It depends on the teacher.*
> *I'm with my friends.*
> *It is interesting.*
> *I like to speak in English and my mother likes it.*
> *I like how it sounds but sometimes it is a 'pain'.* (translated from Spanish)

Commentary ■ ■ ■

Younger children tend to be influenced by their feelings for their teacher, the general learning atmosphere in the classroom, the methods used and by their parents' opinions.

Two of the most important reasons for pupils liking English appear to be *teacher* and *teaching methods*. This suggests that your role as the teacher is very important in selecting appropriate learning materials, planning interesting learning activities and in creating a positive learning environment. However, parental and peer influences are also important and need to be considered in trying to develop positive attitudes. Parental influences may be more important in younger children, while peer influences may become more important as children approach their teens.

>> Chapter 7
>> Chapter 4

The main difference between the older and younger Spanish pupils' responses is that older pupils can see a need for English, and this provides them with a reason for learning it. The seven to eight-year-old pupils may be too young to feel any need for English. Their attitude is mainly affected by whether they like the teacher *(It depends on the teacher)*, the way

English lessons are taught *(It is fun)*, their parents' views *(My mother likes it)* and what their friends feel about English *(I'm with my friends, it is cool to learn English)*.

There do seem to be differences in attitudes to English between age groups. Younger children tend to be more enthusiastic, while older children (11–12 upwards) often become less interested, embarrassed by having to learn a language or even hostile because they don't want to seem foolish in front of their friends. ■

« Conditions for language learning p10

Attitudes do not remain fixed and can be affected both positively or negatively by influences on pupils from outside school, for example their parents' views, their friends' views. They can be affected by influences from inside the school, for example how their teacher views English and what he/she does to stimulate their interest. Attitudes can also be influenced by the learning process itself and by its outcomes. So if pupils enjoy their English classes and are successful, this may in turn develop positive attitudes and increase motivation. If both you and your pupils have positive attitudes to learning English, this will help to create the kind of learning environment in which language learning will flourish.

The diagram below shows the different influences on the development of pupils' attitudes both outside and inside school. What other influences can you think of?

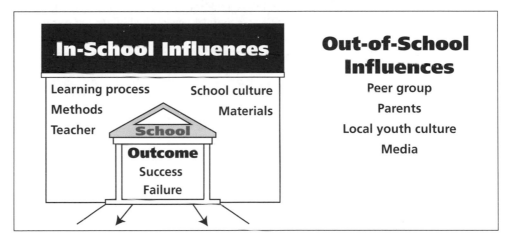

2 Finding out about pupils' attitudes

We have just looked at pupils' feelings and the factors that influence them. Now we will consider teachers' views about their pupils. A group of Spanish primary English teachers were asked to give their opinions on how their pupils felt about learning English. Some of their replies are given below.

Task 3 What do teachers think influences pupils' attitudes?

■ Compare the teachers' views of pupils' attitudes with what pupils said earlier. Do the views match?

Children like English (some of them) because they do different activities in the English class.
Children like English because it is the language of the Ninja turtles.
They're learning English because it is a subject included in the official curriculum.
They will feel English as a duty or as an alive language, a vehicle of communication, depending on the way you teach.
Young children like it a lot but they don't decide whether they have to (should) learn or not.

My children (Class 3 and 4) like English when it is a game. After this, when they must study or work, they don't like English, but they don't like any subjects anyway.
They like it less as time goes by or as an effort is demanded.
In general, children do not like English.

Commentary ■ ■ ■

Teachers and pupils both mention the teaching method and a focus on *games* and *communication* as being very important. They also both refer to the influence of youth culture. One child says it is *cool* to learn English. Teachers also point out that children have no real need for the language: they have to learn it because it is on the curriculum. The older pupils quoted earlier, however, all see a need for English. Two teachers indicate how attitudes change as pupils move up the school and more effort is demanded.

Think about why attitudes seem to change as pupils get older. Is it because teaching methods get less interesting, more formal and more exam-oriented? Or is it because pupils are changing emotionally, physically and cognitively and are becoming more influenced by youth culture and peer opinion, which are sometimes anti-school?

The last comment says 'Children do not like English.' Is this the teacher's attitude rather than the pupils' attitude? As teachers, do we really know what our pupils think? Have we asked them? If a teacher thinks that pupils don't like English maybe this reflects his/her own opinion about English not the pupils' opinion. Our attitudes to English can affect pupils' attitudes positively or negatively. ■

It is important to find out what our pupils' attitudes are from time to time. We can't assume that we know what they are. Children are every bit as complex emotionally as adults, and are equally affected by their experiences with regard to their language learning.

The results of teachers' investigations of their pupils' attitudes show that positive attitudes are closely linked to successful learning. We need to keep in touch with how pupils feel so that we can help to counteract negative attitudes and build on positive ones. Here is one way to start off.

Action plan

Aim: To find out what pupils feel about learning English.

Procedure

» p20

- Choose a class you feel comfortable with. You want to find out what they feel about learning English and the reasons for their views.
- Prepare some simple questions to ask them. If pupils are very young, you may want to discuss with them orally in the mother tongue. With older pupils, you could use a questionnaire or prepare a wall chart on which they could write their views.
- Record their answers, eg on a poster.
- Discuss results with pupils (if necessary in the mother tongue) and the reasons for their liking or disliking English. In the case of dislike, try to identify some specific reasons, eg the materials used, the methods, failure, lack of need.
- Take one problem and together try to identify ways to overcome the problem. For example, to overcome a perceived lack of need for English, see the Golden Diary Project[1], where a class corresponds with another class in England or an English-speaking country, creating a need to use English.

Here are some ideas used by teachers for investigating pupils' attitudes. Think about their suitability for your context. What changes would you need to make in order to use them?

Questionnaire

Ann Gregory[2] used the following questionnaire to find out how primary children felt about learning French as a foreign language. You could adapt it for English.

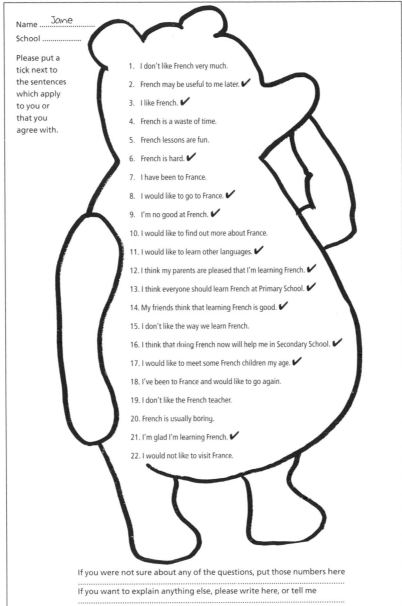

Name .... Jane ....

School ....

Please put a tick next to the sentences which apply to you or that you agree with.

1. I don't like French very much.
2. French may be useful to me later. ✔
3. I like French. ✔
4. French is a waste of time.
5. French lessons are fun.
6. French is hard. ✔
7. I have been to France.
8. I would like to go to France. ✔
9. I'm no good at French. ✔
10. I would like to find out more about France.
11. I would like to learn other languages. ✔
12. I think my parents are pleased that I'm learning French. ✔
13. I think everyone should learn French at Primary School. ✔
14. My friends think that learning French is good. ✔
15. I don't like the way we learn French.
16. I think that doing French now will help me in Secondary School. ✔
17. I would like to meet some French children my age. ✔
18. I've been to France and would like to go again.
19. I don't like the French teacher.
20. French is usually boring.
21. I'm glad I'm learning French. ✔
22. I would not like to visit France.

If you were not sure about any of the questions, put those numbers here
....
If you want to explain anything else, please write here, or tell me
....

Learning diaries

Ann Gregory also got pupils to keep diaries about their language learning which gave a lot of information about their feelings and attitudes. The children were learning French as a foreign language. They wrote their diaries in English, their first language.

Here is an example.

Tuesday 15th November

I think that learning french is nice. I enjoy it very much but I find it difficult to remember how to say things to people or ask them a question. When I first started it I thought ~~thout~~ it was going to be easy but it is not. I do not like making mistakes in front of people I feel very embarrassed.

19

Pupils' opinion chart

Here is another way of collecting pupils' opinions. Pupils write their views (in L1 if necessary) under the appropriate column, ie *like, dislike* or *not sure*. The teacher can then use this as a basis for discussion with the class later.

3 Ways of developing positive attitudes towards English

I asked a group of primary teachers in Hong Kong to tell me their main problems in teaching English. They mentioned pupils' negative or indifferent attitudes to English and lack of motivation. These problems are common, particularly in teaching situations where there is no obvious reason for learning English and where pupils have little exposure to English in the environment.

Task 4   Why don't they like learning English?

- What are your own worries or concerns about pupils' attitudes towards and motivation for English?
- Below are some worries or concerns that teachers have mentioned with regard to attitude and motivation. Tick those which best describe your situation or write down a sentence which describes your own situation.

a *My pupils only enjoy English lessons when I am doing games or songs.*
b *My pupils are interested in English just to pass their exams. So they do not want to do communicative activities.*
c *I have very limited resources or materials to teach English so it is hard to make lessons interesting for pupils.*
d *While my younger pupils are very free in using English, it is very hard to get my older pupils to say anything.*
e *Pupils rely on the teacher to motivate them: they don't know how to develop their own interest in the language.*
f *Some of my pupils start with positive attitudes to English but soon lose interest when they begin to fail.*

My pupils think ...

I feel ...

We know that successful learning is linked with positive attitudes, so when we have identified negative feelings, we can look for ways to counteract them.

Task 5   Finding solutions

■ Match the solutions or suggestions below to the problems identified in Task 4.

1   Encourage pupils to bring in materials they may have at home, eg postcards in English, labels in English, songs, stamps, etc. Use some of them to make a collage. Write to publishers, tourist offices, industries to find out if they have any free posters or materials in English. Share ideas and swop materials with teachers in other schools, eg tourist posters, songs.

2   Adapt activities to suit the level of your pupils so that you give each pupil a chance of being successful at his or her level. Pair pupils so that a stronger pupil works with a weaker pupil. Vary activities in each lesson so that you include some which all pupils can do successfully. For example, pupils could work through these three tasks based on following instructions to colour a picture of fish. They could begin with the easiest so that all pupils complete at least one task successfully. More difficult ones could be attempted in pairs.

A Colour the parts of the fish.
Children read the labels and then colour the different parts of the fish with appropriate colours.

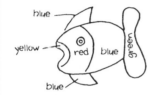

B Read and colour.
Children read the description and then colour the parts of the fish using the appropriate colours.

> **Read and colour.**
> The fish has a blue body. It has a green face and a red mouth. It has a yellow tail. Its fins are blue.

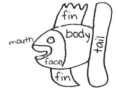

C Read and colour.
Children read the descriptions on their sheets and then colour the fish appropriately.

> The fish has a blue body with a green zigzag. Its face is red but it has a yellow mouth and a blue eye. Its top fin is black and its bottom fin is green. Its tail is the same colour as its body.

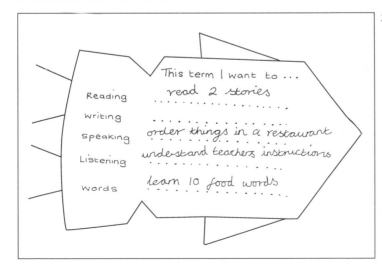

3   In the long term, you want pupils to be able to create their own reasons or goals for learning English, ie to self-motivate. Help them to create action plans for the term. Show some examples made by other pupils. Discuss with them some possible goals related to their needs and get them to make a learning plan, eg *This term, I am going to work on my reading. I will read one page a day.* Talk to them at the end of term to see how far they kept to the plan and if it helped them.

4 Maybe some pupils are only prepared to tolerate English as long as they can have a good time and not work too hard. But for many other pupils, it may be that they are unaware of why they do certain activities. If they could see the purpose for the activities you use with them, they might engage in them more actively.

>> Understand
task purposes
p169

Try to make sure that each activity has a clear and understandable purpose for the pupil, eg *Let's listen for the words of this song you like. Then you'll be able to sing it yourself.* Discuss at the end of the lesson which activities pupils have done and help them to understand the reasons for doing them. Get them to evaluate activities they have done which they did not like. Find out why. Maybe they did not realize it could help with English.

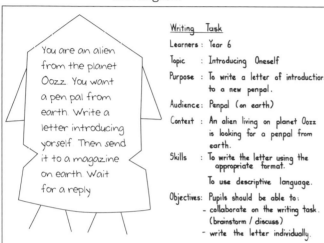

For example, many pupils do not like writing as it often seems like hard work. Create interesting reasons for writing and an audience to write to. For example, they could write poems, songs or jokes for their friends. In the example here, some Malaysian teachers designed a really imaginative writing activity for their 12-year-old pupils.

5 Younger pupils tend to have less fixed attitudes and to be more flexible. Older pupils (age 12 and over) are becoming more self-conscious, and some are becoming interested in sex. They are more sensitive to the opinions of others in the group and do not want to seem foolish. Try to find out what the older pupils' interests are through a questionnaire or through discussion. Find out how they like to work, eg in pairs or groups. Find teaching materials which are related to issues of interest to the age group.

Use real materials from English-speaking learners of the same age, eg tapes of them talking or videos or letters in English written by pupils from a school in another country. Here is part of a questionnaire used by teachers from La Coruña in Spain to find out about pupils' attitudes to some aspects of the teaching/learning situation for English.

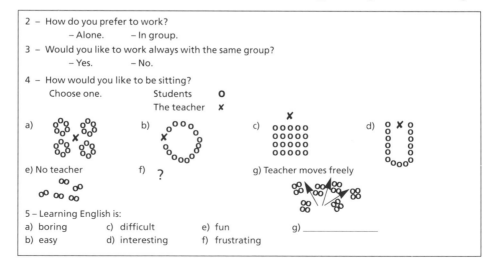

6 If you are in a situation where you have to prepare children for a formal examination which involves grammar, here are some ideas to make some of the exam-preparation material more pupil-centred and communicative.
– Pupils work on grammar exercises in pairs and check the answers of other pairs.
– Pupils develop their own exercises for other pupils in class.
– Pupils act as peer tutors and teach an activity to their group.
– Pupils practise grammar in the form of games, such as the one below, which uses grammar practice activities from workbooks.
Help pupils to see how communicative activities can develop skills which are needed in exams.

Collaborative grammar game

- Choose two pupils to act as your helpers, to check answers and keep a note of scores.
- Divide the rest of the class into groups of four or five. Each group chooses a runner to carry their answers to the teacher's table.
- Put up an exercise on the board or OHP and tell the groups that they must write only the answers to the exercise on pieces of paper given to each group.
- Groups have several minutes to write the answers to the exercise on a piece of paper. Their group name needs to be clearly written on their paper.
- Runners take the answer sheets to the teacher and helpers, who calculate the score and keep a total of the marks on a graph on the board.
- After each exercise, group scores are added to the graph so that pupils can watch the progress of their group, which adds to the excitement.

The work is done through collaboration and at the same time pupils are practising grammar for the exam.

Commentary ■ ■ ■

Here is a suggested match between solutions and problems: 1c, 2f, 3e, 4a, 5d, 6b. You may find alternative solutions to the problems. ■

4 Teachers' attitudes to their own English

In order to be able to develop positive attitudes to English in your pupils, you need to be aware of how *you* feel about English and teaching English. Do you feel worried about your own English? Do you feel enthusiastic about teaching English yourself or do you have some doubts?

Task 6 How do you feel about your own English?

■ Read the statements on the next page and decide whether you ... **SA** strongly agree, **A** agree, **NS** are not sure, **D** disagree or **SD** strongly disagree with them. Tick the appropriate column.

	SA	A	NS	D	SD
1 I feel quite confident about my own use of English when I am teaching.					
2 Teaching English to young learners in my country is a waste of time.					
3 I am not sure whether I am using the most appropriate methods for teaching young learners.					
4 I like meeting and making friends with people from English-speaking countries.					
5 I can't teach English effectively because of my heavy work load.					
6 I think English is an easy language to learn.					
7 I have a problem in teaching English because of a lack of appropriate materials.					
8 My young learners are interested in learning English.					
9 I worry about my own level of English.					

■ Compare your responses with those of Luz, a Colombian primary teacher:

1 **Not sure:** *I think I could do better if I would practise out of class.*
2 **Strongly disagree:** *By means of English, students have a wider vision of the world because they know about different cultures and compare with their own.*
3 **Not sure:** *I'm using effective strategies but I think they could be better.*
4 **Agree:** *The contact with native speakers would help me improve my English level.*
5 **Strongly disagree:** *I love my work and I love my children.*
6 **Strongly agree:** *It is easier when we are exposed to this foreign language.*
7 **Disagree:** *School provides materials to use in classes and students are creative to make what they need in special situations.*
8 **Strongly agree:** *They like English class because they think it's different. They are conscious that English is important for their development.*
9 **Agree:** *Yes, I am concerned that my English is not good enough to teach English, especially if I have to teach more advanced learners.*

Commentary ■ ■ ■

Generally Luz seems to have very positive attitudes to English, to teaching English and to her pupils. However, she seems to be less confident about her own English (Questions 1 and 9). Maybe for Luz, her own enthusiasm for teaching English and for her pupils will help to keep her motivation strong, despite her concerns about her own English. But for some teachers, this worry may eventually affect their attitude to English and to teaching it. This in turn may have an effect on their pupils and their attitudes. It is best to be honest with yourself about your worries and problems with your own English or teaching English. You can then seek help or look for solutions to your problems before they affect your attitudes to teaching. ■

Summary

In this chapter, you have considered:

● *pupils' attitudes to learning English.* Younger children tend to be more positive and enthusiastic, while older children are less interested, sometimes even hostile. The teacher, teaching methods and parents are a strong influence on younger children, while their peers and youth culture may have a stronger influence on adolescents. Nevertheless, in-school influences (teacher, methods, success, school culture) are clearly important for all age groups and you, as teacher, can play an important role in creating a learning environment which will help to develop positive attitudes to English.

- *ways in which you could investigate pupils' attitudes.* We can't assume that we know what pupils' attitudes are, as they are likely to vary according to each individual's experiences. If we find out about pupils' attitudes, we are in a better position to counteract negative feelings and build on positive feelings. You can monitor your pupils' attitudes through questionnaires, discussions, learning diaries and poster displays. The information collected and the discussion will help to raise your awareness about the variety of attitudes among your pupils.

- *suggestions for developing positive attitudes towards English.* Teachers are concerned about negative attitudes, which often relate to the pupils' lack of need for learning English, the effect of failure, changes related to age, eg increased embarrassment about using English in front of peers. There are ways to counteract this, which include making use of pupils' own materials, varying activities to suit ability, pupils setting realistic goals and plans for learning, helping pupils create their own reasons for learning English, enabling pupils to understand the learning purpose of activities, finding out about pupils' interests.

- *how your own attitudes to English or teaching English may affect your pupils' attitudes.* If, for example, you feel worried about your own English or about teaching English, this might affect your enthusiasm in class and so affect the learning environment and, in turn, pupils' feelings towards English.

You have no control over the attitudes and opinions children bring to class. But you can find out about them and take account of them in the way you plan your lessons and in the way you respond to children as individuals through your classroom interaction. You can also try and influence these attitudes through your own positive attitudes to teaching English, by creating a warm and friendly learning environment and by providing

>> Providing support pp79–80

support which enables all pupils to achieve some measure of success. For example, you would be able to help pupils like Andrea, a young Colombian girl. When the teacher asked her class if they liked English and the reasons for their like or dislike, all the children were positive in their response except Andrea, who drew a rather sad face on her paper. She said she didn't understand very well and also that she didn't pay attention in class. Perhaps she did not pay attention precisely because she had problems in understanding and needed extra support.

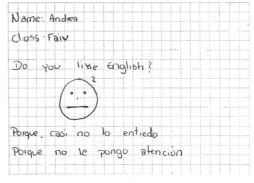

References

1 Treget, M. and Raymond-Barker, V. The Golden Diary Project. In Brumfit, C., Moon, J. and Tongue, R. (eds) 1991 *Teaching English to Children*. London: Collins ELT
This describes a project in which a teacher of French in England and a teacher of English in France exchanged teaching materials. Their pupils exchanged folders of materials, eg letters, timetables, leaflets of local events.

2 Gregory, A. 1996 *Primary Foreign Language Teaching – Influences, Attitudes and Effects.* (unpublished M.Ed. thesis. School of Education, University of Leeds)

Chapter 3 **Are they the same?**

Children come in all types

Nino, a primary teacher, is describing some of his pupils:

Mario can't sit still or concentrate. He enjoys action games.
Lucia is very quiet – does not say much. But she listens carefully and her written work is always good.
Emanuela has moods. Some days she takes part in everything. Other days she just sits silently and stares.
Carlo is very quick to answer and to finish his work.

Nino is describing differences among four of his pupils. Think how many more differences there would be if we were thinking of a class of 30 children. Some teachers say that they find teaching classes of mixed ability one of their main problems. But maybe the problem is in thinking of 'mixed ability' classes as a problem rather than as something natural in any group of individuals.

Mario Rinvolucri[1] says

… we do not teach a group but thirty separate people. Because of this, the problem of mixed abilities in the same room seems absolutely natural and it is the idea of teaching a unitary lesson that seems odd.

In this chapter we will consider:

1 **Teachers' experience of differences**
2 **Teachers' expectations of pupils**
3 **Strategies for responding to different needs**

The aim of this chapter is to consider in what ways you take account of pupils' differences, to reflect on the type of expectations you may have of your pupils and how this affects your response to them.

1 Teachers' experience of differences

Task 1 How different are children?

■ Describe four children in one of your classes in a similar way to Nino's descriptions above. What are the most important ways in which they differ?

Fong Say, a teacher from Malaysia, lists some of the differences she finds among her pupils:

My pupils differ in their …
… perception of the language
… relationship with the teacher
… family background
… types of intelligence
… interests
… gender
… attitude and motivation for learning English
… experience of the world

Commentary ■ ■ ■

There are many ways in which a class of pupils differ, quite apart from academic ability. Consider how some of these differences may affect your teaching and children's learning. For example, suppose there are more boys than girls in the class. This may affect girls' participation as they may be shy to answer in front of the boys. Some children come from poor homes where parents are too busy to support and take an interest in their children's education. This may affect children's attitudes to schooling in general and to language learning in particular. One child loves art and drama but does not like English. This may affect his/her participation in learning activities and may cause him/her to distract others.

An important question to consider is whether and how to respond to differences. Is it important to take account of children's differences in the way you plan your teaching and the way you teach? If you think it is important, how can you manage to do it in a class of 30 or more? ■

Managing classes of mixed ability children

As all classes contain children with different abilities and characteristics, you will have had experience of dealing with differences. Teachers find different ways to cope, depending on the resources available and the situation in which they teach. Fong Say and Nalaini, two primary teachers from Malaysia, made these suggestions for managing classes in which there are children of varying ability.

Fong Say says:

> *Use group teaching – group pupils according to their abilities.*
> *Give differentiated tasks, ie activities designed specially to suit particular levels/needs.*
> *Give attention to different groups at different times.*

Nalaini says:

> *Vary your teaching/learning methods to include activities like problem solving, games, story, etc.*
> *Have differentiated group activities.*

So the three strategies these teachers use are:

- Teach children in groups, according to ability.
- Prepare activities to suit the level of the groups.
- Vary teaching methods to cater for a range of different abilities and styles of learning.

How do you feel about dividing children into ability groups or designing special tasks for different abilities? Do you feel that this is helpful or do you consider it divisive? Later in the chapter, we will consider different strategies and their advantages and disadvantages.

Task 2   Challenges and ways of meeting these in mixed ability teaching

Many teachers find that catering for differences in learning needs is very challenging, particularly if the range of abilities in a class is very wide.

- What challenges have you faced in dealing with classes of varying abilities?
- How have you met these challenges?

Commentary ■ ■ ■

Here are some of the challenges mentioned by a group of Malaysian teachers. How far do you share their concerns?

> *a Time consuming to devise different activities to cater to different groups*
> *b Allocation of time/attention given to different groups*

c Insufficient time to cater for all the different needs
d Difficult to aim the lesson at the right level in the presentation stage
e Pupils' lack of interest or low ability in certain skills and certain types of activity.

Here are some possible ways of meeting the challenges:

a Planning differentiated activities

It does take time, but this has to be weighed against the satisfaction of seeing children make progress at their level. One way of reducing the problem is to collaborate with other teachers or to develop a materials bank which contains activities at different levels for particular lessons.

>> Chapter 11 pp159–61

b Giving enough time to different groups

>> Group teaching pp37–9

One way is to make pupils more independent so that they can work on activities without needing the constant attention of the teacher. This will then free you to spend time with individuals who need extra help or to work with particular groups. You could also plan your time so that every day you allocate a certain amount of time to work with particular groups.

c Catering for all the different needs

>> Chapter 10 p138
>> Peer tutoring pp35–7

Set work which children can start during class hours and finish off at home. Alternatively gradually prepare a bank of self-access materials in particular problem areas at a range of levels. You can cut up old workbooks and adapt activities. You could also get children to help in making practice activities if you provide them with a model to work from. Then once or twice a week children can work either independently or with a 'buddy' to practise a particular skill or to work on an identified problem area. This could also be a useful area for collaborative materials design or adaptation with other English or class teachers.

d Aiming your lesson at the right level

>> Group teaching pp37–9
>> Chapter 12

One possibility is to introduce an activity to the whole class and demonstrate what is required very clearly, involving pupils in the demonstration so as to give time for all to observe the procedures and work out what they have to do. Then pupils work in mixed ability pairs or groups to complete the task. If one pair or group has problems in doing the activity, another pair who has successfully completed it helps them to do it. The emphasis, however, needs to be on helping them to learn how to do things for themselves rather than doing things for them.

e Catering for pupils' lack of interest or ability

Lack of interest may, in fact, hide the fact that the child has a problem in a particular skill or aspect of language, eg speaking or writing. He/she may, therefore, come to dislike activities which, for example, involve speaking or writing. So the first step is to find out why a pupil is not interested. If the pupil has difficulty in using a skill, then it may help to adapt activities to his/her level or provide more support and try to create time to work with that pupil or other pupils with similar difficulties. ■

2 Teachers' expectations of pupils

As teachers we all have expectations of our pupils just as pupils have expectations of us as teachers. These expectations influence our behaviour.

Consider these questions as you think about the cartoon below:

- What is the message of this cartoon?
- How do your expectations of pupils affect them?
- How can you avoid labelling pupils?

The cartoon shows that children are very quick to know how they have been labelled or assessed by teachers. Although the teacher has carefully given each group a neutral label, eg animals, the children have worked out that the Monkey group are the slow learners. (*Thickie* is a colloquial term for someone who is slow or stupid.)

How do our expectations of pupils affect them?

We are likely to have views and prejudices about what children should be like as pupils. We may also have views about how individual children will perform in class because of what we know about their backgrounds or previous experience. For example, if I have heard other teachers say that Emanuela in Class 1 is very slow, this may influence my view of her when I teach her in Class 2, ie I respond to children according to my prejudices about them. If we think a child is clever, we will ask more challenging questions. If we think a child is weak, we will tend to give him/her more support in answering. Children then begin to behave as we expect them to, and so they end up becoming successful or failing according to our expectations. This in turn affects their self-image or concept, ie how they feel about themselves.

>> Self-esteem pp48–9

Here is part of an account from Barbara Shiel[2], a primary teacher in America, who ran an experiment with her class of 35 12-year-olds. It was a very difficult class to teach and contained many 'problem' children who were not interested in school, who were underachieving and came from difficult home backgrounds. She tried every possible technique with the class without making any progress, so she decided to try a more radical approach. She let children choose what they wanted to learn – to give them greater responsibility for their own learning. She helped children draw up their own work contracts for each day. Although some children found it hard to work without being directed, eventually most children in her class moved towards independent work. Here is part of her final progress report on the class:

> *I found that the children with the most difficulty learning also made great progress. Some who had been unable to retain the multiplication tables were able to multiply and divide fractions with a minimum number of errors by June. I cannot explain exactly what happened, but it seems to me that when **their self-concept changed**, when they discovered they could, they did! These slow learners became fast learners. Success built up on success.*

This quote suggests that success can change children's ideas about themselves. Barbara Shiel's pupils had built up low opinions of themselves through years of failing or perhaps being blamed for bad behaviour. In her programme, they got a new start – a chance to show they could be successful. This changed their self-image and, in turn, their behaviour.

>> Self-esteem pp48–9

How can we avoid labelling children?

If we take children's current level of achievement as a starting point, we can build on the skills and resources they bring to learning. We also need to find out pupils' views of themselves. This can help us to realize what worries or fears they may have which will hamper their progress. We may need to group children in order to facilitate management. However this grouping does not need to become permanent. Children need to have a chance to show that their skills and abilities vary according to situation, topic and activity.

We often use labels like *high ability, average, low ability, weak* when talking about pupils. What do these labels mean? Do these reflect our expectations of pupils rather than their actual ability?

Task 3 What do labels tell us?

■ Choose three different children from one of your classes, one from the top end, one from the middle and one from the bottom end. Describe them according to their personalities, typical behaviour and their abilities in listening, speaking, reading and writing. Put the information into a grid like the one below.

Name	Type of personality	Typical behaviour	Speaking and listening skills	Reading and writing skills

■ Which of your children was most difficult to describe and why?
■ Marta, a primary teacher on a summer school, was also asked to describe a child from the top end, middle and bottom end of her class of eight-year-olds. Her descriptions are given below. Rank the children into high, average and low ability, using her descriptions to help.

Gabor is very absent-minded. It is difficult for him to be attentive. He always wants to touch things during the lesson and play games. It is difficult for him to concentrate on the same activity for five minutes.

Katya is very able, always ready to answer, interested in everything. She listens carefully to all she is taught. She is highly creative, very imaginative and good at imitating.

Eva is very interested in the subject, ready to co-operate, sometimes a bit shy. She does not like to make mistakes and is eager to improve her faults. She is very good in writing but not so good in speaking.

■ What evidence did you use to rank them? What other information do you feel you need?

Commentary ■ ■ ■

You may find that your middle-range children are the hardest to describe. We tend to notice the extremes (the ones who always answer or the naughty ones) as they affect our teaching more. We may, therefore, neglect children in the middle range or quieter children.

Marta ranked the children as follows. I have identified some evidence from her descriptions which you might have used in trying to rank them.

Order of ability	Possible evidence
Katya: high	very able, listens carefully, creative, ready to answer, interested in everything
Eva: middle	interested and co-operative but sometimes a bit shy, not so good at speaking
Gabor: low	absent-minded, cannot concentrate, always wants to play

You may have had difficulty distinguishing between Eva and Katya. They seemed equally able. You may have wanted more evidence of why Katya was a more able child. When we label children as *high ability*, as *average* or *below average*, what are we basing our labels on? Children vary considerably in their performance on different sorts of activities. Do we really know what they can do unless we have evidence from a range of activities? Have we observed their work in a number of different situations on a range of activities, and in a range of different ways of working, eg individually, in pairs, in groups?

>> Assessing progress pp157–8

Marian Sainsbury[3] describes a boy called Kwame who rarely spoke in class discussions. During a visit to an arts centre, he took part in discussions with the adults there and answered a number of questions very thoughtfully. When asked why he participated so well, he said he was very interested in the sculptures he had seen. Kwame showed that he was able to take part in discussions quite effectively in situations where he was interested. This shows how easy it is to underestimate a child's ability and how careful we need to be in making judgements about their ability.

Did you notice how Gabor was described? Children at the bottom end of the ability range often seem to have behaviour problems. Is it the failure at school and lack of interest which leads to behaviour problems or is it behaviour problems which lead to underachievement? Perhaps, as you will see in Chapter 4, the problems all relate back to the child's poor self-image and low self-esteem ■

High expectations!

If we approach pupils with an open mind and expect the best from them, this will help to raise their expectations of themselves. These raised expectations may then encourage children to make more effort which in turn may lead to improved performance and increased positive regard from their teachers and other adults.

What would happen if you changed your expectations of the pupils you teach? Try out the following action plan.

Action plan

Aim: To find out how raised expectations affects pupils' behaviour and attitudes to learning English.

Procedure

- Choose a pupil who is slow or underachieving.
- Focus on this pupil for three to four weeks.
- Ask him/her more questions than usual.
- Be prepared to wait for the answers. Don't give up.
- Give plenty of encouraging smiles and show interest in what he/she says.
- Set tasks in which he/she can be successful.
- Get him/her to help you in class, eg hand out crayons.
- Keep a diary and write down the pupil's reactions.
- See if it makes a difference to his/her attitude and behaviour.

3 Strategies for responding to different needs

Most teachers agree about the need to have high expectations of each pupil and to try to treat each pupil as an individual. But they may feel doubtful about how to do this with a class of 30 or more children. There is no one simple solution, but in this section we consider some ways in which teachers can respond practically to pupils' individual needs in a class. We will look at three different teaching strategies: differentiating activities, peer tutoring, group teaching.

Differentiating

If you have the freedom to design your own curriculum, then it may be easier for you to respond and plan for individual needs. However if you are following a given curriculum, you need to keep in mind the goals that all pupils are supposed to achieve.

Anne Covery and Do Coyle[4] suggest that teachers can consider:

- core work for all pupils
- reinforcement work for more intensive practice
- extension work for helping to move pupils further on and to challenge them.

This will enable teachers to match work to pupils' needs, interests and abilities.

>> Chapter 6 for more on support

We can match activities to pupils' needs through differentiating in various ways. Here we will focus on differentiating according to type of support. This means that we expect all pupils to do the same activity, but we give more support to the slower learners. Support can be given in different ways, eg through giving more pictures or visuals to make the meaning clearer, giving clues, providing a framework (fill in the blanks) and so on. On the following pages there is an example of a writing activity from a Malaysian textbook[5]. A group of teachers considered it to be difficult for many pupils in Class 5 (11 to 12-year-olds). So they developed a range of other activities to suit different ability groups in their classes. The original activity in the textbook is given first.

Task 4   Differentiating by support

- Identify what types of support were provided in Activities B, C and D.
- Explain whether you think D is more difficult than B and C and why.
- In which situation do you think this type of differentiation would be most appropriate?
- What are the advantages and disadvantages of this strategy?

Activity A: Original

2. Pretend you are Hock Seng. Write instructions on how to keep pressed leaves and flowers. Use the sentences in the story and the pictures to help you. Begin in this way.

a. First, collect leaves and flowers.

b. Then put them between the pages of old newspapers.

c. Next...

Activity B: Matching sentences in column A and B

A. Match A to B to form correct instructions on how to make a scrap book of dried leaves.

A

1. First collect leaves
2. Then put them between
3. Next put heavy
4. When the pressed leaves are dried,
5. After that put the sheets together
6. Finally write the name of each plant,

B

● books on the newspaper
● and make a book
● pages of old newspapers
● the date collected and the place it was found
● and flowers, while you are on a walk
● glue them to thin cardboard sheets

Activity C: Fill in gaps and then sequence pictures

Complete the instructions. Use the phrases to help you.

glue them	put them between the pages	collect leaves
put heavy books	write the name	make a book

Now arrange the pictures in the correct order.

Activity D: Write instructions from phrases

Look at the pictures. Make a sentence from each phrase to describe how to press flowers and make them into a book.

put a heavy book
glue them
arrange the sheets
write the names

a. First collect the flowers and leaves
b. Then put them between the pages of old newspapers
c. Next

Commentary ■ ■ ■

The original activity is to produce a set of written instructions. It is designed to practise writing skills.

Activity **B** provides the most support. Pupils have to match the sentence parts in A to the appropriate sentence part in B to form the complete instruction. The sentence parts in Part

A and the pictures are in the right order and so will provide clues to help with matching. The labels on the pictures will also help to give further clues. Pupils do not have to produce any original writing in order to produce the instructions.

Activity **C** has less support than **B**. Pupils have to fill in the blanks using the phrases and pictures to help them complete the instructions. They also have to arrange the pictures in the right order, whereas in **B** the pictures were already in the right order. Being able to manipulate the pictures will help pupils to sequence them, as they can move them around and see whether they look right. They are not required to produce their own instructions.

In Activity **D** pupils have the pictures to give them clues; they also have a list of phrases from which they must build complete instructions; some instructions are completed to give them an example. So they are given some help with writing. However, a key difference between this and the other two activities is that pupils have to form their own sentences, ie they need to *produce* language rather than just understand it. So while the level of support for **D** is similar to **B**, the activity which pupils have to do in **D** has increased in difficulty. Activity **B** provides most support and is also the easiest activity.

This approach could be used particularly in situations where pupils have to follow a central curriculum and use a textbook. It would allow the teacher to adapt the textbook to suit the needs of the students.

One advantage of this strategy is that it allows slower children a chance to complete activities which are similar to the rest of the class and be successful in doing so. One disadvantage of the writing activities above is that the slower children may not get a chance to tackle activities like **D** and produce their own sentences. There may be pressure to move on to another unit with the result that slower children never get a chance to progress to more challenging activities. The teacher can, of course, solve the problem by systematically planning children's progression across units. ■

Peer tutoring: 'buddies'

In this strategy children work together with a partner or buddy. Slower or weaker pupils can be paired with a stronger partner for some activities, particularly where we feel they may need extra support. The pairing will be based on our knowledge of the pupils. As the year proceeds, pupils may express preferences or we may need to make changes where children in the pair do not work well together. An example of how it works is given below.

1   The system is introduced at the beginning of the year and the class agrees on some rules, for example:

> **Buddies are friends.**
> **They are there to help you.**
> **They support you, not dominate.**
> **They help you when you get stuck.**
> **They help you to do things for yourself – they
> do not tell you the answers.**

2   Demonstrate for pupils how a good buddy works using a pupil helper. Here is an example based on an activity from **English Club Student's Book 1**[6]. Whisper to the pupil helping you to pretend that he/she is not sure how to do the activity and to make some mistakes.

2   Look at Cissie and Spike's school timetable

Ask and answer questions.
Example
A: What time is English on
   Monday?
B: It's at nine o'clock.

Now talk about your school
timetable.
Example
On Monday we've got Maths at
quarter past ten.

	MONDAY	TUESDAY	WEDNESDAY	THURSDAY	FRIDAY
9.00–9.45	English	Maths	Maths	Science	Maths
9.45–10.30	English	History	Maths	Science	Library
	B	R	E	A	K
11.00–11.45	Geography	Science	English	English	History
11.45–12.30	Maths	Science	Geography	Maths	P. E.
	L	U	N	C	H
2.00–2.45	Games	Art	History	Computer Studies	English
2.45–3.30	Games	Art	Music	Computer Studies	Music
4.00–5.00		Computer Club	Swimming	Drama Club	

T Emile, will you be my partner? Imagine I am your buddy. OK, we have to do Activity 2
with the timetable. What do we need to do?

E Answer questions.

T Yes, and look here … (*points to instructions*) we also have to ask questions. How shall we
work? Shall we take it in turns?

E OK. You start.

T What time is English on Wednesday?

E 9 o'clock.

T Are you sure? Check again. (*pauses to give Emile time to check*) Look along the top and
find Wednesday. … Found it?

E OK.

T Now look down under Wednesday till you find English. … Found it?

E Yes.

T Now look at the time. What time is English?

E 11.

T Yes, 11 o'clock. You got it right. Now let's try another one.

» p173 for
another example
of modelling

3 Ask children how you helped Emile, ie by giving your partner *ways of finding the answers*
rather than *telling your partner the answers*.

Task 5   Peer tutoring

■ When could you use this strategy?
■ What are the advantages and disadvantages of this strategy?
■ What changes would you need to make in order to use it in your context?

Commentary ■ ■ ■

You could use this strategy for activities when you wanted slower or weaker pupils to get
more help and support. It works best where the task is straightforward and the helping
buddies know clearly what to do. For example, getting one pupil to listen to another pupil
read a story book provides excellent practice for pupils who may be slow or lacking in
confidence in their reading, in the early stages.

Advantages	Disadvantages
It involves pupils in helping each other.	Some pairs may not work well together. It may be difficult to pair pupils appropriately.
Both weaker and stronger pupils gain from the system, ie the weaker pupil learns how to do the task and the stronger pupil learns to think more strategically in order to help his/her buddy.	Stronger pupils may be less challenged. Stronger pupils may not necessarily be very good at helping their peers to learn how to do activities. They may want to give the answers.
Pupils become more involved in the learning process.	Some pupils may try to dominate their buddies.
Pupils are learning to be more independent.	It takes time to train pupils how to work effectively as buddies. It may be possible to use this system only for straightforward or routine types of activity.
It is a flexible system which can be used according to need. It allows different pupils the opportunity to be 'buddies' for areas where they have particular strengths.	Without careful handling by the teacher, this procedure may reinforce a lower status for the weaker students in the class. Weaker pupils will also need opportunities to act as 'experts'.

Your pupils may not have enough English to carry on the discussion in English. So you may want to let them use their L1 for some parts, eg where they are explaining how to do something. You may also want to use simpler, more structured activities like reading a story together, practising recognition of certain key words or phrases. ■

Group teaching

Primary teachers in South Africa face the problems of handling large classes, sometimes classes of 50 or more. One result of this is that they find it difficult to cope with children at different ability levels. However teachers working with the Molteno Project have developed a way of organizing their teaching so that they can give proper attention to pupils at different levels. Here is how they organize group teaching.

At the beginning of the year, pupils are organized into social groups, according to friendship or familiarity. Once the teacher knows their academic ability, they are normally divided into ability groups. (What difference would it make if you kept them in friendship groups?) During a lesson, the teacher will work with each group for an equal amount of time. So if there are four groups and the lesson lasts an hour, she will work with each group for about 15 minutes. Other pupils, sitting in their groups, work on activities set by the teacher, either individually, in pairs or in groups. The groups rotate at the end of ten minutes with approximately five minutes for changeover, and they move on to a new activity. They can physically move or just change activities at the table where they are sitting, which is less time consuming. The teachers often use a child (monitor) from one group which has completed an activity to explain to another group how to do it. They also provide completed answer sheets, where appropriate, so children can check their own answers.

Here is an example of how it might work in practice based on part of Lesson 3 of *Big Red*

Bus 1[7]. At the beginning of the lesson, the teacher writes on the blackboard the activities each group will complete and the order in which they will do them. He/she tells monitors what materials are needed for the activities and may also give instructions for any new or more complicated activities. The teacher then reads the story to the pupils in the teaching group (Red group) and helps them to understand the story before giving them follow-up activities taken from the Activity Book (AB). The groups who have not yet heard the story (Blue, Green and Orange) are working on activities related to the previous lesson or reading a story book. Each group gets its turn with the teacher. Some groups will need to complete their follow-up activities in the next lesson. During the changeover, the teacher might quickly check the work of other groups or answer queries from children.

Here is a plan of what each group would be doing.

10.00-10.10	Whole Class - preparation for class, setting up of group activities, briefing for group monitors			
Group	**Red**	**Blue**	**Green**	**Orange**
10.10–10.20	Teaching group: Teacher tells story	Dictionary work: AB activity based on previous lesson	Individual or paired story reading	Crossword: AB activity
10.25–10.35	Draw and colour: AB activity	Teaching group: Teacher tells story	Dictionary work: AB activity based on previous lesson	Individual or paired story reading
10.40–10.50	Listen and write: AB activity	Draw and colour: AB activity	Teaching group: Teacher tells story	Dictionary work: AB activity based on previous lesson
10.55–11.05	Draw and write: AB activity	Listen and write: AB activity	Draw and colour: AB activity	Teaching group: Teacher tells story
11.05–11.10	Teacher checks on groups' progress. Monitors clear away reading books, etc.			

Task 6 Group teaching

- What would teacher and pupils need to do in order for the group-teaching strategy above to work successfully?
- What are the advantages and disadvantages of using this strategy?

Commentary ■ ■ ■

The teacher will need:

- to be very well organized and plan the lesson carefully, eg know what each group will do during the lesson and what materials are required
- to develop a proper system for monitoring and checking work done by pupils on their own, eg keep a record of what each group has done each day
- to train pupils to be able to work independently for a large part of the lesson, eg get pupils to check each others' answers, help each other.

Pupils will need:

- to learn how to work more independently and to feel confident doing this
- to collaborate with each other and help each other
- to learn to follow instructions
- to learn to work quietly so as not to disturb others.

Advantages	Disadvantages
It helps pupils to become more independent as learners.	It takes time to train pupils to be independent.
It enables teachers to spend focused time daily with different groups of learners.	Pupils who are not interested or lacking in confidence may disrupt other groups
It ensures that teachers of large classes, in particular, give regular attention to different ability groups.	It may be very difficult to implement with younger learners who cannot read and write, as many of the independent tasks rely on reading and writing skills.
It encourages pupils to collaborate more and help each other.	It needs a lot of careful planning and preparation by the teacher.
It allows pupils to work at their own pace and be successful at what they do.	There may be a tendency for pupils to be labelled permanently according to the group they belong to. It may be difficult for them to progress to another ability group.

Think about the different needs of your pupils and how you can best respond to them. Why not experiment with some new ways? Try to put the following action plan into practice.

Action plan

Aim: To try out one of the strategies described with one of your own classes.

Procedure

- Choose one of the three strategies described above.
- Try it out with a group of pupils over a period of two to three weeks or longer.
- Note down aspects which worked well and aspects that did not work well.
- Decide what you would do differently next time in order to make it more effective.
- Try it out together with another teacher so you can share experiences.

Summary

In this chapter, you have considered:

- *some of the differences between pupils in the same class* and the strategies teachers use to manage classes of mixed ability. These include: group teaching by ability, designing activities to suit different levels, and using a variety of teaching methods. You have also considered how to overcome difficulties associated with these strategies: how to give sufficient time for each individual, how to aim lessons at the right level and to cater for pupils' lack of ability or interest in particular skills.
- *how teachers' beliefs and expectations about their pupils affect the way they respond to them.* This can lead to those expectations becoming self-fulfilling, ie a child begins to respond as the teacher expects him/her to respond rather than as he/she is capable. Labels used for pupils are often based on teachers' expectations rather than on pupils' actual abilities. Children's skills and abilities vary widely across different situations, on different activities and topics and can change over time. So there is a need to be cautious about labelling them as *low ability* or *high ability* as these labels tend to stick forever. If you have high expectations of all of your pupils, they are likely to respond positively to this.
- *three different teaching strategies for responding to pupils' individual needs:* differentiating activities by support, peer tutoring and group teaching. There is no ideal solution to managing the needs of a class of individuals but each strategy has particular advantages

and disadvantages for particular situations. Differentiation enables academically weaker children to work successfully on similar types of activities to their peers through support, but it doesn't help them to develop the skills they lack in the first place. Peer tutoring involves pupils in helping each other, which benefits both academically weaker and stronger pupils. However, it may reinforce a lower status for weaker pupils and it is difficult to pair children. Group teaching enables teachers to give regular attention to different groups, and children learn to work more independently. The disadvantages are that it takes very careful planning and management, and it may be difficult for pupils to progress out of lower ability groups. All three strategies involve children more fully in the learning process and develop their independence as learners, but they involve careful planning and take time to implement.

There are two implications in what has been discussed in this chapter. First, you will need to decide what works for your own situation by observing children, by trying things out and being open to change. It may be best to use a combination of strategies so that you provide varied opportunities which cater for different personality types and learning styles in your class.

>> Self-esteem
pp48–9

Secondly, differences are natural. You need to build on what children bring to the classroom and to expect the best from every child. Having high expectations of children raises their own expectations which may prompt them to increase effort and so lead to improved performance. This in turn may assist children in developing more positive self-images and levels of self-esteem.

References

1   Rinvolucri, M. 1986 'Strategies for a mixed-ability group.' In *Practical English Teaching* vol. 7, no.1, 1986

2   The story about Barbara Shiel comes from Rogers, C. and Freiberg, J. 1994 *Freedom to Learn.* New York: Merrill Oxford: Macmillan College Publishing Co. (3rd edition), pp79–80

3   Sainsbury, M. 1996 *Tracking Significant Achievement in Primary English.* London: Hodder & Stoughton
    This book is about monitoring children's progress. It gives examples of how you might recognize significant achievements for children in their learning and how to use this information.

4   Covery, A. and Coyle, D. 1993 *Differentiation – taking the initiative.* Pathfinder 18. London: Centre for Information on Language Teaching and Research
    This is a very practical book with many ideas on how to use differentiated tasks. The examples are taken from French, Spanish and German but are easily adaptable for English.

5   Ibrahim, F.J. and Thiyaga, R. 1986 *Moving On With English KBSR Year 5.* Kuala Lumpur: Penerbitan Kerajaan Malaysia

6   Read, C. and Salaberri, S. 1992 *English Club Student's Book 1.* Oxford: Heinemann, Lesson 11, p45

7   Lobo, M.J. and Subira, P. 1993 *Big Red Bus 1.* Oxford: Heinemann

Chapter 4   We've found our partners, Miss

Managing pupils' language learning

One of the main ways in which children learn languages in the classroom is through taking part in activities. But this does not happen automatically. As we saw in Chapter 1, we need to set up the conditions which will enable children to learn. We have an important role in creating these conditions and then managing what goes on in order to maintain those conditions. These conditions are supported by:

>> Chapter 5
>> Chapter 6
>> Chapters 7 and 10

- positive teacher–pupil relationships and learning environment
- effective organization of pupils and resources
- effective communication between teacher and pupils
- appropriate support for children's language learning
- interesting and stimulating learning materials and resources

The last three points are dealt with in subsequent chapters. In this chapter, we will focus on aspects of the first two and consider:

1 **What kind of classroom manager do you want to be?**
2 **What kind of teacher do pupils think you should be?**
3 **Ways of developing a positive classroom atmosphere through:**
   - **creating a sense of security**
   - **developing pupils' self-esteem**
   - **developing teachers' self-esteem**
4 **Organizing pupils for language learning in pairs and groups**

The aims of this chapter are to raise your awareness of the conditions which support pupils' language learning, in particular the creation of positive teacher–pupil relationships and the effective organization of groups; to explore how these conditions can be set up and maintained; and to examine how the decisions and choices you make as a manager can affect pupils' learning.

For many teachers, when we talk about classroom management, discipline or classroom organization spring to mind. But an important part of managing classrooms is the development of effective teacher–pupil relations. This is the focus of the next three sections.

1 What kind of classroom manager do you want to be?

What are the qualities needed to manage a class effectively? Here is an activity adapted from a book on classroom management[1]. It will help you to identify the qualities you think are most important and to decide what changes you may need to make so that your behaviour reflects these qualities.

Task 1   What kind of classroom manager are you?

- Think back to your teachers in school or to recent tutors who taught you on a course. Remember one teacher you liked and one you disliked. What did you like about the first one? What did you dislike about the second?

Here is an example based on my own school days:

> *Mrs Evans was strict but kind. She had a nice sense of humour and was patient when I did not understand. I remember Miss Bevan, the art teacher with less affection. She wasn't interested in me because I was very poor at drawing. She ignored me or was very rude about my drawings.*

- Identify the qualities of the teacher you liked (eg *strict, kind, sense of humour, patient*) and the teacher you disliked (eg *not interested in pupils, impatient, unfair*). You now have some positive qualities and some negative ones. Then make a grid like the one below and write the qualities in. Write the positive words under the smiling face and then write the opposite of these words under the sad face. If you have some more negative qualities, write these under the sad face and write their opposites under the smiling face. This is my example:

Positive ☺   **Negative** ☹

Strict	1	⊘2	3	4	5	Lets learners do what they like
Kind	①1	2	✗3	4	5	Cruel
Has a sense of humour	①1	2	✗3	4	5	No sense of humour
Interested in learners	①1	2	3	4	5	Not interested in learners
Patient	①1	2	3	✗4	5	Impatient

O : ideal   *X* : actual

- Think about your ideal teacher, someone who would be very good with children. Then complete your grid by circling a number for each pair of opposites as in the example above. For example, your ideal teacher may be fairly strict (2), be very kind (1), have a nice sense of humour (1), be interested in her pupils (1) and be very patient (1).
- Next rate yourself honestly for each of the pairs of opposites in the grid. Choose a number and cross it for each pair. Let's take an example. Suppose you feel that you are fairly strict (2), are quite kind (3), have some sense of humour (3) but are not very patient (4).
- When you have completed your self-assessment, you can compare with your ideal teacher to see how far or close you are to your ideal for each of the pairs of opposites, as in the example above. Use this assessment to identify aspects of yourself which you would like to change or qualities you would like to develop. For example, you may rate yourself only 4 for *patient* whereas you would like to be closer to your ideal teacher.
- Decide why you want to change and what changes you could make.

Commentary ■ ■ ■

The purpose of the task is to give you a way of thinking carefully about your own teaching. Comparing what you think your ideal teacher would do with what you actually do may help you to identify areas where you would like to change. Then you can work out what actions to take. ■

You may want to change but you need to be realistic. Here is an example of an action plan which you could adapt to your own needs once you have decided you want to make a change.

Action plan

Aim: To become more patient.

Before you begin thinking about action, first consider why you are impatient. Do you get angry with pupils when they do not finish or are slow? What is the reason for this? Perhaps you do not leave enough time to do the activities. Perhaps pupils do not understand the activity. Or perhaps pupils do not like an activity and so do it very slowly as a kind of protest. Perhaps you are under stress which makes you impatient.

Then think about why it is important to be patient. Perhaps you have noticed that pupils respond better if you are patient, eg they manage to say something in response, they give a longer answer or are willing to try. Here are some suggestions for being more patient. Maybe you can think of some more related to your own needs.

Possible actions

- Allow enough time for pupils to do activities.
- Tell pupils how long they have to do an activity.
- If some pupils have not finished, either give them more time or arrange another time for them to finish.
- If a pupil is slow in answering, smile encouragingly. Pause and count up to 20 slowly in your head before saying anything.
- If a pupil cannot understand something, explain again in a different way using actions or visuals and see if it makes a difference.
- If you think a pupil is deliberately being slow, find out why.
>> p52
- Consider your own level of stress and try to reduce it.

2   What kind of teacher do pupils think you should be?

If we ask pupils what they expect from teachers we may be surprised by what they say.

Task 2   What do pupils expect of their ideal teacher?

- Ask some of your pupils what they expect an ideal teacher to do in the classroom to help them learn English.
- Compare your pupils' views with those of the Spanish children quoted below. Are there any similarities?
- Is there anything you find surprising in what your pupils said?
- Did you find any difference between what you think an ideal teacher should do (Task 1) and what pupils think?

Magaly, a Spanish primary teacher, asked her seven-year-old pupils to draw and describe their ideal English teacher. Two of their replies are given here in translation.

> *A teacher that would do a lot of games and parties, that would not let us speak Spanish, that would never get angry, that would teach us in fun ways, that would bring surprises, that would love me a lot and would not be a bad person. Above all she would be 'cool'.*
> *(Paula)*

> *My ideal teacher is Consuela. Because when we play we learn English; she does not let us speak Spanish, pronounces very well; when she explains something, if we do not understand she helps us; when we do parties she does quite well; she never gets very angry; she never hits us; she is pleasant and draws well.*
> *(Sara)*

Commentary ■ ■ ■

I find it interesting and also surprising that Magaly's pupils want teachers to make them use English. I have often heard teachers argue that they use the L1 because their pupils insist on it. We need to ask our pupils what they want and not assume that we know.

Magaly's pupils are most concerned with classroom relationships and atmosphere. They clearly value a teacher who cares about them, is patient with them, does not get angry, and who helps them to learn. They are also concerned about methods and like having to use English. ■

The information from Magaly's pupils suggests that one of the important conditions to promote learning is for teachers to build good relationships with pupils and a happy and secure learning environment. This is what we will consider next.

3 Ways of developing a positive classroom atmosphere

In our own lives, we are affected by the atmosphere in which we work and the way people behave towards us. If the atmosphere is tense or unfriendly, or if people are angry with us, rude or ignore us, this makes us feel insecure or unhappy. If the atmosphere is warm and relaxed, people around us are friendly and supportive and we sense that they value us, we feel more confident and secure. This can affect our desire to participate in events. It is the same with classrooms. If there is a friendly atmosphere in the classroom and teacher and pupils get on well together, then they will both feel more secure and learning is more likely to be encouraged. In order to develop a positive classroom atmosphere, two things are very important:

● a sense of security
● a sense of self-esteem and confidence

This is true for teachers as well as for children.

Sense of security

Classrooms usually contain an adult and a number of pupils who have to spend large amounts of time together. The potential for chaos and breakdown is very great, and yet in most classrooms, pupils and teachers find a way of managing their relationships. How do they do this?

Task 3 Classroom rules

■ What has happened in the classroom scene above?
■ What effect does this kind of situation have on the teacher and pupils?
■ Think about your own classroom. Do you have any formal or informal classroom rules? If you do, write down the ones you think are most important. Why are they important?

Commentary ■ ■ ■

It looks as if the teacher has lost control. Perhaps the teacher was doing a group activity which involved a great deal of movement, and children became noisy and got out of hand. This can easily happen. Sometimes when you are new to teaching, children deliberately try to test you. I vividly remember the anxious feeling I had every time I entered one particular class and the sleepless nights I experienced wondering how to control the class.

If this situation continues, it can create an uncertainty both for teacher and pupils. The teacher does not know how the pupils are going to react or respond to things he/she does; similarly the pupils cannot predict how the teacher will respond to them and what they do. This uncertainty is stressful and creates feelings of insecurity which are not supportive of teaching and learning. Uncertainty also makes it difficult for both teacher and pupils to develop confidence in themselves, because this needs a settled and secure classroom situation where teacher and pupils feel able to take risks.

The classroom rules which are most important for you will depend partly on your situation and the type of learners you teach, and partly on your own beliefs about what is important. For example, if you teach younger learners, you will need rules to manage the way they work, move around in the classroom and relate to each other. Perhaps you think the most important aspect of teaching is the relationship between pupils and yourself. So your rules may relate to how to behave to each other. Or perhaps you think rules are unnecessary and that you can manage without them. However, even if you do not have formal rules, it is likely that you have hidden rules, hidden until a pupil breaks one. For example, how would you feel about a pupil looking inside your bag or bullying another child? ■

Do you introduce pupils to the class rules in the first few days of class or do you allow them to emerge gradually as they are needed? Think of the advantages of each approach. If we introduce rules right at the beginning, then pupils know what to expect. If we do not state them openly, then pupils only know about the rules when they break them. This can cause unpleasant surprises and some uncertainty. Having rules does not mean becoming a harsh and uncaring teacher who likes to run their class like an army camp. It means being open about the way we want to work with pupils and helping them to understand the rules before they begin, rather than when they accidentally break one.

Task 4   Short-term or long-term solution?

How are you going to manage relationships with your pupils? How can you set up a system which will work for you?

■ Read the following description of an actual class management situation in a trainee teacher's lesson. What would your response be to this situation?

It is an English lesson with 30 eight-year-old pupils. Robin, a trainee teacher, is revising some words he taught the day before. He writes up some sentences on the blackboard, leaving gaps. Children have to suggest the missing word. They begin to shout out the answers, so Robin tells them to put up their hands if they want to respond. The shouting out gets steadily worse. Robin occasionally reminds them to put up their hands. By the time the activity finishes, the children are paying no attention to Robin.

■ Read the three different teachers' responses below. How do they differ?
■ What effect would each response have on the situation?
■ Which one do you agree with most strongly and why?

A I would change to a new activity as they are probably quite restless and difficult to control after shouting out a lot.

B *I would sit down with children at the end of the lesson and discuss what happened. I would ask them why shouting out answers is a problem and ask them to suggest what to do about the problem. I would agree with them on a rule we could use for this situation. I would also discuss what action should be taken if someone breaks the rule.*

C *I would act immediately, would speak very firmly to the whole class and punish the children who were shouting out as a warning to the others not to do it.*

Commentary ■ ■ ■

The following table summarizes the differences in the teachers' responses and the effects they would have.

Responses	Differences	Effects
A Hope it will go away.	**A** ignores the problem while the other two responses involve some type of intervention.	The problem would probably get worse, as children quickly realize that the teacher is not serious about his rule of not shouting out.
B Work it out together.	In response **B**, rules are jointly agreed on by teacher and class. The children are involved in the process of solving the problem together and deciding on class rules. **A** and **C** assume that only the teacher is in charge of the rules.	If the children understand why shouting out causes a problem and they agree on a way of solving the problem, they may be more willing to keep the rule, making it is easier to enforce. Involving children in the management of classroom learning helps to make them more responsible for their actions. They are not just blindly obeying a rule. They have to judge whether their behaviour meets their agreed standards.
C Show them who is the boss.	**C** involves immediate punishment without any apparent warning or statement of a rule beforehand. It is a temporary solution.	Unless the rule has been clearly stated at the beginning of the lesson or activity, children may think it very unfair to be punished without any warning. This could cause resentment against the teacher.

Maybe you found it difficult to decide which response you agreed with most strongly. You could probably think of advantages and disadvantages for all these responses as there might be occasions when each one would be appropriate. For example, with response C, if pupils have broken a rule deliberately and they have already been given a warning, it would be important to follow up the warning with some kind of appropriate punishment. However, consider whether some responses are like sticking plaster on a cut or wound – an immediate solution to a medical problem but not a cure, whereas other responses may be a kind of guide to good health, ie how to avoid getting sick. For example, response B is concerned with setting up systems to manage classroom behaviour and relations. The teacher tries to ensure that pupils and teachers have a way of working together in which everyone knows what the rules are. If a rule is broken deliberately there are sanctions (punishments) but these are not threatening. There is a security for both teacher and pupils; they know what is expected of them. ■

Task 5   Negotiating rules

■ What kind of rules could you negotiate with children and how would you do it?
■ Consider the suggestion below. What would be the benefits and the problems?
■ If you wanted to try out this idea with your pupils, what would you need to change or modify in the suggested procedures?

Negotiating rules

● Explain to children that you want to work out some basic class rules together.

● Give them some typical classroom management problems using pictures and ask them what the problem is, eg shouting out the answers together, running out of the classroom.

● As a class, suggest an appropriate procedure/action for each one.

● Start with just a few. Don't be too ambitious.

● Get younger pupils to make illustrations to go with the procedures and stick them on the wall as below. Older children could write them as a poster to put on the classroom walls.

● If children break a rule, gently remind them of the agreed behaviour.

● Stick to the rules and take action if a child keeps breaking them.

● Start it at the beginning of year or school term rather than in the middle of a term.

● Try this scheme out with children for a term and see how it works.

● Talk to your head teacher and see whether he/she will agree to do this as a whole school exercise at the beginning of the year.

When	What to do	
The teacher asks a question and you want to answer.	Raise your hand.	
One pupil is answering a question.	Listen quietly to him/her.	
The teacher asks you to move into groups.	Move quietly. Lift up your chair quietly.	
Someone starts a quarrel with you.	Cool off! Count to 20.	

Commentary ■ ■ ■

Benefits	Problems
It involves pupils more actively in the classroom management process.	Parents/other teachers may not understand what you are doing and protest to the school.
It encourages pupils to take responsibility for their own behaviour.	The school may already have agreed rules.
If pupils are involved in making the rules, they will be more likely to accept them and to ensure others keep them.	Pupils may take advantage of the unexpected freedom to misbehave.
Negotiating class rules can bring pupils and teacher closer together and build warm and friendly relationships.	Pupils may expect the teacher to be in charge of rules and not accept any attempt to change the situation.

It may be impossible to fully negotiate the rules in your situation. So you could compromise by deciding on the rules yourself but involving pupils in illustrating them or writing them out in English. Children really appreciate being involved or consulted. You could choose to focus on other aspects of classroom behaviour that are more relevant to your needs. If you work in a situation where you have considerable freedom, these suggestions may not go far enough and you may also want to negotiate the teaching/learning activities. ■

Developing pupils' self-esteem

Feeling secure is *important* for learning, but not sufficient, as this story is designed to show.

I'm no good at English.

My sister is better than me.

I feel left out when my friends are doing English.

I can't do it.

'Ana, what are you doing?' came the familiar question from the English teacher. Ana, as usual, was wandering around the classroom chatting to other children. She was not involved in the pairwork task set by the teacher. Ana was a friendly, lively nine-year-old child but she created a headache for her English teacher. Ana never did what she was supposed to do. If she was given an activity to do on her own, she would wander around the class disturbing others or spend most of the time sharpening her pencil. If she worked in a pair or group, she would soon distract the other children and they would end up doing something else. One day, the English teacher kept Ana back after class to talk to her. 'Do you like English, Ana?' 'Yes, I'm with my friends,' said Ana. 'But you never do any work in your English class. Why not?' 'Miss, I can't,' sobbed Ana. 'What do you mean?' said the English teacher. 'I'm no good. Miss Steiner (former teacher) told me I was no good at English, not like my sister.' said Ana.

The story illustrates the fact that Ana has developed *low self-esteem*[2] with regard to her ability in English. Self-esteem is based on the value we place on ourselves. Low self-esteem develops, as in Ana's case, when there is a gap between our *self-image*, ie our awareness of ourselves, our characteristics, etc and our *ideal self*, ie the self we would like to be. Children develop their self-image through the responses and reactions of other people to them. So Ana may have developed a negative self-image of her ability in English mainly through the response of her former teacher, Miss Steiner. With regard to her ideal self, Ana was compared by the teacher to her sister and so realized that there was some kind of standard to which she did not measure up. Children may often generalize from feelings of failure in one aspect of life, for example, school performance, to a feeling of failure as a person. So an overall low sense of self-esteem develops. We don't know if this is the case for Ana, but an incident like this can often have serious effects on children's self-esteem.

«Teachers' expectations p28–9

Children's sense of self-esteem is developed through their perception of how other people view them. If they receive positive feedback from others and are respected by them through praise, acceptance, being listened to and not laughed at, they will feel they have worth and value. It will give them more confidence to take risks in future. Children with low self-esteem often feel frightened of revealing their feelings in case they are laughed at or rejected. We can help to influence the way pupils respond to each other and show that respecting the opinion of others is valued behaviour in our classrooms.

How can we give pupils confidence in themselves and so help to develop their sense of self-esteem? Developing positive teacher-pupil relationships will help in building a sense of security and confidence. But it may also be necessary to focus more explicitly on building self-esteem. We will consider the use of a procedure called *Circle time*.

Circle time

This procedure, suggested by Murray White[3], is designed to help pupils to express and share their feelings with others in a supportive atmosphere. It also provides opportunity for language learning.

Organization

Everyone including the teacher sits around in a big circle. If you have a large class, you could do it outside or in a hall so everyone can sit on the floor. Alternatively, split the class into two halves and give one half some work to do. The smaller the group, the more intimate the atmosphere.

Procedure

Establish some basic rules first, eg

- *No laughing at each other.*

- *No speaking when someone else is talking.*

- *Everyone must listen to each other.*

- *Everyone has a turn.*

- *No-one is forced to speak, if he/she doesn't want to.*

Each person takes it in turn to say something, starting with the teacher. This is important so the teacher can model what to do and give children confidence to have a go themselves. You could do circle time regularly, maybe once a week either at the beginning or end of class. Vary the focus each time, choosing from the examples below. Let a child speak in L1 if he/she can't say it in English and then rephrase it for him/her in English.

Task 6 Using *Circle time* activities

Three *Circle time* activities are given below, each with a sentence stem.

- Suggest other sentences stems for each example.
- The activities are based entirely on talk, which may make it difficult for L2 children to understand what to do. Think of ways in which you could make them more concrete by providing more visual or physical support.
- How could these activities help pupils' language learning?

1 Sharing hopes and fears

Children take it in turns to say a sentence about how they feel or felt, eg after doing a project or drama work. This encourages them to express their feelings in a supportive atmosphere, without being rejected. They will learn that others may also share their feelings, which will give confidence, particularly to children with low self-esteem. They also learn to accept that others have feelings which may be different from theirs.

eg *I feel scared when I have to talk in front of the class.*

2 Special child of the week[3]

Children take it in turns to be the child of the week and sit in the happy chair. Children can be chosen by placing names in balloons and blowing them up. One is popped every week to choose the child of the week. To begin the week, the child goes out of the room while others think of nice things to say about him/her. The special child then sits in the happy chair and other children say some nice things about him/her. This may need some help and prompting initially.

eg *You are very good at …*

3 Feeling proud

Each child tells the group one achievement about which he/she feels proud.

eg *I know a lot about cats.*

Commentary ■ ■ ■

Other sentence stems might be …

1 Sharing hopes and fears

I feel sad/afraid/glad when …
I was happy when…

2 Special child of the week

You are wearing a nice dress/shirt/badge …
You always share your sweets …
You have a happy/smiling face …

This provides children with positive feedback about themselves and gives other children practice in thinking of positive things to say about each other.

3 Feeling proud

I can run very fast/play chess.

This encourages pupils to recognize that they do have achievements and to be aware of other pupils' achievements.

Here are some ideas for making the activities more concrete and supporting the language:

● The speaker holds a flower or a pretend microphone so when it is a child's turn to speak he/she has something to hold on to.

● Children do a drawing of their idea first, eg *I can play chess, I know a lot about cats* and then write their sentence with the teacher's or a friend's help. They then hold up their drawing or read out their sentence which provides them with language support when it is their turn to talk.

● Children follow each talk activity with a physical activity, eg *Circle hands*[3] (hold hands and give strength to each other), deep breathing, relaxing, swaying back and forth, clapping and so on.

Although the activities above were not specifically designed for language learning, they are very helpful because they are structured, repetitive and purposeful. The same sentence pattern is being repeated all around the class, but at the same time the content is controlled by the children. A child chooses what to say, and the information is new for the others so there is a real purpose for speaking and listening.

Some of the activities could easily be adapted to make them relevant for discussing aspects of language learning with the class. *Circle time* could provide a nice relaxed setting in which >> Chapter 12 « Finding out about pupils' attitudes pp17–20 to find out pupils' feelings about learning English, about different activities, about how to become a more successful learner. For example, you could do the following activity, which emphasizes sharing and helping each other to learn English. You could use *Circle time* to report the children's ideas, to celebrate what they have done to help each other and encourage them further. ■

Things people did to help me with English this week

Each child writes their ideas in a diary or displays their ideas on the leaves of a plant at the end of a week as shown here.

Things people did to help me.

Finally let's consider possible problems that might be encountered in using *Circle time* activities. Firstly, older children (12 onwards) might be extremely reluctant to reveal their feelings in front of their peers. Unless we feel quite confident in our knowledge of the children, we might also find it hard to prevent children from making fun of each other after the class with the intimate knowledge they have gained about each other. Secondly, there are practical problems like class size and time. Sharing feelings is an intimate process, and it is best to do it in small groups. Thirdly, it takes time to organize, particularly with a large class. However, though there are potential problems, these can be overcome by beginning very gradually and introducing one type of activity at a time. There will be many benefits if children gain more confidence.

Hester

Developing teachers' self-esteem

The way we feel about ourselves will affect the way we feel about others around us and the way they feel about us. So if we are confident and happy about ourselves, we are more likely to help children to develop positive images of themselves. However, teaching is a very demanding job, and there may be many sources of stress which lead to feelings of anxiety or inadequacy. These can affect our self-esteem. So it is important to learn how to cope with stress and problems at work and to retain confidence in ourselves.

Here is how one teacher coped with a problem:

> *Jamie was driving me mad in class. He was constantly trying to disrupt others and caused the class to become quite noisy. I found I couldn't sleep at nights because I was worrying. I began to hate teaching in that class. Finally I decided to do something about the situation. I talked to a friend. She advised me to talk to Jamie on his own and try to find out whether he had any problems at home. I found out through talking to him that he had an elder brother who was very ill. His parents gave all their attention to this brother and Jamie felt neglected. My friend also advised me to ask other teachers about him. I soon discovered that he was disruptive in other classes too. That immediately made me feel better. I began to chat to Jamie whenever I could and to give him small jobs to do for me. I used him frequently as a group leader. His behaviour got better and I felt I could cope more. In fact, I gained confidence in myself because I had solved the problem!*

Task 7   Coping with stress

- What aspects of your daily work can lead to stress?
- Which of the problems below[4] have you faced?
  - coping with difficult or disruptive children
  - coping with difficult parents
  - having to spend every evening and weekend preparing or marking
  - using new material you are not familiar with
  - having difficulties finishing the syllabus
  - feeling responsible for your pupils' failure in their exams
  - worrying about whether your pupils like you and your teaching
  - getting into an argument with a colleague
- Choose one of these problems or any other you have and think of ways you could solve it.

Commentary ■ ■ ■

Everyone's problems are slightly different, and teachers will have their own way of coping. The first five problems mentioned are common to many teachers – they are part of the job of teaching. However the last three are more personal and related to particular individuals, their circumstances, their personality and so on.

All problems can be potentially stressful. However, a lot depends on your own level of health, self-confidence and self-esteem. If these are all fairly high, you will cope with your problems much more easily. The difficulty arises if your health or self-confidence and/or self-esteem are low and you become overwhelmed by your problems. You may then start feeling depressed. It is very important to deal with problems before they overwhelm you and you lose confidence in yourself. For example, in the story above, the teacher took action before she lost confidence in herself; she went and talked to a friend. You can also find ideas to help you in books such as *Readings in Teacher Development* by Katie Head and Pauline Taylor[5], which has a section called 'Supporting yourself'. ■

4   Organizing pupils for language learning in pairs and groups

Warm and friendly teacher–pupil relationships and a happy, secure working atmosphere are very important to promote learning, but on their own they are not enough for young learners. I remember, when I first started teaching children, I developed a very exciting game which involved crawling around the floor to hunt the lion. I hadn't considered what would happen with 30 excited children all wanting to join in simultaneously. Chaos ensued! I quickly realized that children are less able than adults to regulate and organize themselves and are more easily distracted. We need to organize them in ways that will maximize opportunities for learning.

A key difference between working with adults and children is that adults are able to understand the point of group- and pairwork, even if they do not particularly like working in this way. They are usually willing to co-operate in order to carry out the activity in the belief that it may help their language learning. In other words they are able to be analytical about an activity and to regulate their behaviour in order to achieve their language learning goals. Children (particularly five to eight-year-olds) will find it much harder to understand the intellectual reason for working in a particular way. They may not be able to regulate their behaviour unless the activity makes sense to them in human or imaginative terms. So telling them to get into a group because you want them to practise English won't have much effect on their willingness to co-operate.

However, if we set it within a context which they can relate to on the basis of their previous experience of stories, they are likely to co-operate fully, eg

> *You are all living in a special country ruled by a nasty dragon. When the dragon comes, you have to hide in one of the magical circles. But there is a problem: only six children can go in a circle. Let's count together. So you have to count the number in the group each time.*

>> Teacher
language
pp63–5

It may also be more difficult for pupils to understand verbal instructions. So we need to keep these very simple, backed up by actual physical demonstration involving the pupils. Their concentration may be limited and so they need many short activities rather than one long one. The activities we choose also need to be quite carefully structured with definite outcomes and clear repeated procedures. This will help them to feel secure and to be successful in carrying them out.

Introducing children to pair- and groupwork activities

<< Chapter 1

Most modern primary English textbooks tell teachers to use pair- and groupwork because of the opportunity this offers for increased language input, pupil practice and greater involvement in language learning. Children are by nature very sociable, and so pair- and groupwork make use of this natural tendency. However, don't feel frustrated if it does not work the first time. Your pupils may be unfamiliar with working in these ways or may take advantage of the new freedom to misbehave. In order to work effectively in groups, children have to be able to co-operate and communicate with others. They may need to learn how to do this.

Task 8   Introducing children to pair- and groupwork

Children may have no idea what working in pairs or groups means initially. So they need to understand what it means and hopefully to develop positive associations with working in this way. We can use a number of different techniques for forming pairs and groups which may help to engage children's interest and make this form of working meaningful for them.

- Here are some ideas for forming pairs and groups. Which would you begin with to introduce this way of working?
- What problems might you find? How could you overcome them?

1 Find your partner

Choose a set of animals and create two pictures of each so that there is one picture for each child. Give each child a picture of an animal, eg pig, cow. Each child then has to find the child with the matching picture or badge and sit down beside him/her. They should ask and answer, eg *Have you got a cow? Yes, I have/No, I haven't.* For older pupils (ten upwards), you could choose the names of sports, pop groups or other topic areas of interest.

2 Musical circles

Draw a number of circles on the floor. Children walk around the room and when the music stops, they must stand in a circle. Only six children can stand in a circle. Each circle forms a group and you can do some simple action games in the groups (see below).

3 Get together

Get children sitting beside each other to work as pairs. This does not involve movement around the class and so may give more control. Give them some simple instructions to carry out together as a way of getting them used to working as pairs. It can be done for a few minutes every day. For example:

T Face your partner. Say hello.
Catch hands. Make an arch with your hands. Move back and forwards.
Draw the letter A on his/her back.
Be a mirror. *(Child A copies the actions of Child B.)*

At a later stage, children can give instructions to each other. You could also get two pairs to move together to form a group.

4 Find your group

Choose different types of food such as vegetables or fruit, eg peach, grape, apple, etc. Give each child a picture of one of the types of fruit. The child goes around searching for other members of his/her group:

P1 Have you got an apple?
P2 No, I haven't.
P1 Have you got an apple, Eva?
Eva Yes, I have. We're in the same group.

Place pictures of the fruit in different parts of the room and children have to find their group homes.

Commentary ■ ■ ■

Which activities you use will depend on your situation. Some are less likely than others given your classroom size and the age or the number of the pupils. You could begin with *Get together* because it does not involve any movement around the room. Pupils are likely to have chosen the person who they want to sit next to and feel comfortable talking to them. Pupils may be easier to control if they are not moving around. You could then later move on to an activity which involves movement, eg *Find your partner*. Once pupils are familiar with pairwork, you could then introduce them to the idea of working as a group, eg *Musical or Magical circles*. In *Find your group*, children have to search for several people rather than just one person. So you might leave it until later as it is a little more complex.

Pairwork activities tend to be more manageable initially than groupwork activities as both pupils in a pair are occupied. In groupwork, it may be easier for some pupils to do nothing or to misbehave.

There are several potential problems:

Problem	Solution
The desks may be fixed so pupils cannot move around.	Do activities in the playground, school hall or use the limited space you have at the sides of the desks.
Some pupils may dominate pair- or groupwork.	Plan the composition of groups more carefully. Put dominating pupils together or swop them around. Raise awareness of effective ways of working together.
The school may not allow pupils to make a lot of noise.	Discuss the purpose of the activities with the teachers next door to you and the head teacher. Agree on a suitable time. Train the pupils to keep their voices down.
Pupils may be unused to pair/group activities and use them as an excuse for misbehaving.	With older pupils (nine upwards) discuss why you want to do pair- or groupwork. Establish clear rules/procedure with them. With younger children, create a purpose for doing pair- or groupwork that makes sense to them.
Pupils may use L1.	Try to choose activities which ensure that all or at least some part of them has to be done in English, eg reporting back to the class. If pupils are old enough, discuss with them the reason for talking in English or develop imaginative reasons for groupwork, eg as part of a story or game.

Choosing suitable pair- or groupwork tasks

Not all tasks are suitable for pair- or groupwork. For example, children can be seated in groups reading books but working independently. In this case the task does not require them to work together. Activities may need planning quite carefully to provide a reason for pupils to work together.

Task 9 Choosing suitable pair- and groupwork activities

■ Which of these activities do you find most suitable for groupwork? Why?
■ Try to adapt the one which is less suitable so that it provides a clear purpose for collaborative groupwork.

1 Bring me

The teacher sits in the middle of the floor, at an equal distance from each group. Each group chooses a runner and only the runner can take things to the teacher. If anyone else tries to approach the teacher, they will lose points for their group. Children put their bags and other possessions on the table or floor. The rules need to be made clear at the start. The teacher then calls out a command, eg

T Bring me a black shoe.

Bring me a watch.
Bring me a Mickey Mouse pencil case.
Bring me the person with the longest hair.
Bring me something square in shape.

The group collaborates in trying to find the object and the runner then takes it to the teacher. The teacher accepts the first correct object given to her. The winning group is the one who has given most objects to the teacher.

2 Bingo

Children are seated in groups. Each group has a bingo board with pictures. As the teacher holds up cards with various words written on them, eg helicopter, train, etc, pupils have to cover the appropriate pictures on the board with counters. The first group to cover its pictures calls out *Bingo!*

Commentary ■ ■ ■

Both tasks involve children sitting in groups. However the *Bring me* task involves a reason for pupils to work together. They have to find the objects that the teacher asks for. They can only do this by co-operating and working together. In the *Bingo* task, there is no reason for the pupils to be working together. Each child does not have a specific part to play, and it is likely that the fastest child will dominate the game and give all the answers.

A simple way of making *Bingo* more collaborative is to number each child in the group. Then each child takes it in turn to put down a counter on the board when the teacher says or shows a word so that each has to contribute to the group outcome. ■

Grading activities for pair- and groupwork

Children seem to respond best if new practices or procedures are introduced gradually. So if we want to get them used to the idea of working independently in pairs and groups, we can grade the activities we use. If we take a game like *Simon says*, the teacher can start by giving all the instructions to the class, ie having total control. The teacher could then release some control by asking a pupil to take over giving instructions. Then children could move into groups and each group member in turn act as the instructor. In this way the teacher has released control and handed it over to the children. They are now running the game. This gives them more chance to practise; it also gives them a chance to take on the teacher's role and ask questions, something they do not normally get a chance to do.

Task 10   Who's in control?

■ Choose three or four pair or group activities you have already used with your learners. Show where they come on the scale below. How learner controlled or teacher controlled are they?

Teacher controlled   *Learner controlled*

■ Order the activities below according to how controlled they are by the teacher. Put the most controlled first.
■ How could you adapt the most controlled activity to make it freer?
■ How do children benefit from taking greater control?

1 Making a surprise picture

Children sit around in groups of four. Tell them they are going to create a mystery creature. Each child draws a head on a piece of paper, folds the paper over and passes it to the child on her/his right. Then each child draws a neck on the paper he/she receives, folds over the paper and passes it to the child on the right. The third time, each child draws a body on the paper, folds it over and passes it to the right. Finally he/she draws legs and feet and passes on the paper after folding. The children then open up their papers and will enjoy seeing the pictures they have made together. They then have to name each picture and create a group story which involves each of the characters they have drawn.

2 Describe and draw

The teacher gives each child a simple picture. Children work in pairs and take it in turns to describe their picture to their partner who has to try to draw a similar picture, eg

P It's a monster. Draw two heads on the monster…

They are not allowed to look at each other's drawing till they have finished. They then check to see if they have similar drawings.

3 Do what I say not what I do

The teacher tells the children to do what he/she says but to ignore his/her actions. The teacher will give various instructions, eg

T Jump up and down. *(The teacher sits down.)*
Fly like a bird. *(The teacher claps his/her hands.)*

Children who copy the teachers' actions rather than his/her words are out. The winners are those still left in after a given period of time, eg three minutes.

4 Serve your group

Form groups and choose, or get each group to choose, a monitor or helper. Monitors are responsible for one week (or more) for giving out crayons, paper, textbooks and other materials needed and for collecting in their group's materials and books at the end of lessons. Their group members have to co-operate with them to collect and clear away the materials at the end of the lesson. The monitors must use English in making requests for things from the group, eg *Please give me your crayons.* The teacher comments on each group's performance at the end of a week.

Commentary ■ ■ ■

Activity 3 is the most controlled as the teacher is telling pupils exactly what to do. Activity 4 is slightly less controlled as pupils have some choice, ie they can choose a group monitor. However, the activity does not really depend on working together and sharing. One person in each group has the main responsibility and could probably do the things he/she has been told to do even if the others did not co-operate. Activity 2 gives more freedom to pupils than Activity 3 or 4 as children have to work together to carry out the activity, ie produce pictures which are the same as their partners'. However the teacher still retains some control by giving the pictures. Activity 1 is the least controlled. It gives most responsibility to the pupils and involves the greatest need to co-operate. If each child does not co-operate fully, the pictures and the story will not be completed. There is, therefore, a much greater need for skills of co-operation in this activity. It would be more suitable for children with some experience of working in pairs and groups.

To make Activity 3 freer, it could be directed by the teacher initially, but once children are clear how to do it, different children could take turns to give instructions. Later children could be organized into groups and children take it in turns to give instructions. In this way, the teacher gradually releases control and hands over to children. Most activities are capable of being graded in this way so as to gradually hand over more control to the children. David Vale[6] has a number of ideas on this. He describes a series of lessons based around action games in which children are gradually given more control over the games.

Children benefit in several ways from being given greater control. If they are in control, they have more choice over what to say, which allows them to experiment with language. They play some of the roles the teacher would normally play, which involve giving instructions, asking questions, checking, etc. This provides opportunities for them to use a wider variety of language functions. They are also learning how to become more independent as learners. ■

« Conditions for language learning p10

Pair- and groupwork is valuable in providing more opportunities for children to get more language exposure and practice. But it needs careful and thoughtful management in order to be effective. Here is a checklist of important points to keep in mind. Perhaps you can add to the list or make your own checklist.

How to make pair- and groupwork POSSIBLE

Prepare children carefully for the activity.

Organize them in ways appropriate to the goal of the language-learning activity.

Structure the activity carefully so there are clear working procedures and outcomes.

Show them how to do the activity.

Involve them in your demonstrations.

Be positive about their efforts.

Loosen your control of the activity gradually.

Engage their interest through having a clear and meaningful purpose for the activity.

Summary

In this chapter, you have considered:

- *a technique for identifying the aspects of classroom management* you think are most important and using this information to decide how you might make changes to your teaching.
- *some pupils' expectations of their teachers.* It is helpful to discover pupils' expectations about your role as these may be rather different from what you predicted. Finding out more about your pupils' views helps you understand them better and helps you create a more harmonious working environment.
- *the importance of creating a positive classroom atmosphere.* Giving children a sense of security, confidence and self-esteem helps to create an environment in which children want to communicate and feel free to experiment and take risks.
- *how a sense of security can be built up* through negotiating a set of rules or procedures for classroom management with children so that you and your children know what is expected of each other. This reduces uncertainty and provides a set of guidelines for working together in an orderly way which allows learning to take place.
- *how children's self-esteem is developed* through their perceptions of the way others view

them. You can assist children to develop confidence in themselves and increase self-esteem by showing interest in them, accepting them as they are and valuing their achievements. You may also need to focus explicitly on building self-esteem through *Circle time* activities which build confidence and model positive ways for pupils to behave towards each other.

- *how teachers can control or overcome problems which create stress and may damage their self-esteem.* Your ability to help children develop positive self-esteem is linked to your own sense of confidence and self-esteem. If you are happy and self-confident yourself, you are more likely to be able to help them to develop positive self-images.

- *ways of introducing children to pair- and groupwork,* choosing suitable activities for pair- and groupwork and ways of gradually giving pupils more control in pair- and groupwork. These three aspects contribute to ensuring that children learn to work effectively in pairs and groups and can therefore benefit from the opportunities for language input and practice which these types of organization provide.

Two implications which arise from the chapter are these. Firstly, what is good for children's learning is also likely to be beneficial for you. If you have created a happy and secure learning environment with good teacher–pupil relationships, you will also feel more confident and fulfilled.

Secondly, in managing your classroom, there are a range of options available to you and different consequences which result from choosing particular options for children's language learning. For example, every activity can be adapted to make it more or less teacher controlled. If you always choose to control language-learning activities, this will affect children's opportunities to experiment with the language system. If you develop this awareness of possibilities, it will give you greater flexibility and more control over your decision-making in the classroom.

References

1 Wragg, T. 1991 *Class Management.* London: Routledge
   This book is designed to help teachers to develop their classroom management skills. It contains a number of practical tasks.
2 If you would like to learn more about self-esteem, this would be a useful book:
   Lawrence, D. 1987 *Enhancing Self-esteem in the Classroom.* London: Paul Chapman
3 White, M. 1991 *Self-esteem. The Meaning and Value in Schools. Set A & B.* Cambridge: Daniels Publishing
   A book full of lovely ideas for developing self-esteem with children.
4 Kyriacou, C. 'High Anxiety.' In *Times Educational Supplement* 6 June 1980
5 Head, K. and Taylor, P. 1997 *Readings in Teacher Development.* Oxford: Heinemann
6 Vale, D. and Feunteun, A. 1995 *Teaching Children English.* Cambridge: Cambridge Educational Press.
   A book for teacher trainers, containing many examples of teaching and learning activities.

Chapter 5 **Who has some good news for today?**

Effective teacher – pupil interaction

Teachers do a lot of talking in classrooms. They often get criticized for this because they are not giving pupils enough opportunity to talk. But we need to consider first the purposes for which teachers use talk in the language classroom. It is through our talk that the teaching gets done. We manage the classroom through talk: we instruct pupils what to do; we control them; we motivate them; we provide feedback. We also provide language input for learning. But it is not just *what* we say that is important, it is also *how we say it* which may be important in terms of what pupils learn and how they learn. It is through our tone of voice, use of pausing, use of facial expression that we convey our attitudes to our pupils and our interest in them or lack of it. In this chapter, we will consider:

1 **The purposes of teacher talk in the language classroom**
2 **Some advantages and disadvantages of using English to teach English**
3 **Developing classroom interaction strategies which create an environment supportive of risk-taking**
4 **Teachers' concerns about communicating with pupils through English**

The aim of this chapter is to raise your awareness about the importance of teacher talk in supporting pupils' language learning and to develop your ability to monitor and improve your own ways of communicating with your pupils.

1   The purposes of teacher talk in the language classroom

Teachers tend to use some types of talk a lot more frequently than others, eg for managing, checking answers and controlling, while other types of talk are neglected, eg asking for real information about the children, praising, getting children to think.

Task 1   Talking for what reason?

- Below are some reasons why teachers talk in classrooms. Add other reasons you can think of.
- Put a number in the *Frequency* column to show how often you talk for that reason
  (1: very frequently; 2: frequently; 3: sometimes; 4: never)
- In the end column indicate which language you use: English (L1) or your own language (L2) or both sometimes.

Reasons for talking in the classroom

Functions of talk	Frequency	Which language(s)
to give instructions		
to control/discipline		
to give feedback		
to praise		
to ask for information		
to give information		
to provide examples of the target language		
to give models of procedures or strategies		
to check or test pupils' understanding		
to joke		
to maintain a good atmosphere		
other ...		

Commentary ■ ■ ■

It is important to consider which types of talk you use in the classroom because this affects the kind of learning environment you create. If you mainly use talk for controlling, giving information, providing examples, and testing, then you are doing most of the talking and your relationship with children will probably be quite formal. Consider what would happen if you used talk for other kinds of purpose as well. For example, what would the pupils' response be if you asked for real information about them more often or joked more often or asked thinking questions? Delwar, a Bangladeshi teacher trainer, worked with a group of primary teachers to improve the way in which they responded to pupils' answers by encouraging them, and showing more interest in what pupils said. He found that later when he visited those teachers' classrooms, pupils were much more willing to speak than they had been on previous visits. So one of the effects was to increase the amount of talking children did. They were also more enthusiastic about their lessons.

Teachers vary widely in how much English they use in their classrooms. It may depend on how comfortable they feel using English, the level of their pupils' language or the purpose of the talk. For example, a teacher may want to use the L1 if a child is upset or very angry in order to reduce any barrier to communication. A teacher may also sometimes use the L1 and sometimes use the L2 for a particular purpose. For example, when introducing a new activity, some teachers have told me they use the L1 initially if the instructions are rather complicated, but then use the L2 on subsequent occasions when children are familiar with the activity.

One of the points to keep in mind here is that the teacher's talk provides the main or only form of language input for children in a foreign language situation. So if we restricted our input in English to only giving them examples of the language and we didn't use English for the other purposes listed above, eg joke with them, give instructions, etc, we would be providing them with a very limited range of input. This is an issue which we will discuss more in the next section. ■

2 Some advantages and disadvantages of using English to teach English

Teachers vary considerably in their views on whether they should use their own language while teaching English. There is often a gap between what they would ideally like to do, ie use English to teach English, and the reality, which is that it is often difficult to make children understand or that children demand the use of the L1. However as an English teacher, it is important for you to understand both the advantages and disadvantages of using English to teach English so that you can make up your own mind what to do in your situation.

Task 2   Why use English to teach English?

■ What do you think are the advantages and disadvantages of using English to teach English? Write them in the grid below.

Advantages	Disadvantages

■ Compare your views with those of a group of Indonesian teachers who discussed this issue at a training workshop on teaching English to children. Do you agree with their views? Did you think of other advantages or disadvantages?

Using English to teach English

Advantages	Disadvantages
It increases the amount of exposure pupils get to English.	It can take a long time to explain things, even using gesture, etc. Pupils who are anxious to do the activity may lose interest or lose concentration.
It develops pupils' confidence in the language.	Weaker or slower pupils may lack the confidence to believe they can learn through English; they may be frightened or put off English.
It provides real reasons for using English to communicate, eg in giving instructions, getting information from pupils.	Teachers may have limited English or insufficient fluency in the language. They may give pupils incorrect models.
Much classroom language, eg instructions, has a simple and repetitive pattern which can be picked up by pupils (as chunks, see Chapter 1) without them being aware that they are learning.	It may be very difficult to do any reflection on learning or discuss pupils' opinions about their learning in English because pupils have limited English.
It can motivate pupils to want to learn.	For pupils who are not highly motivated, it may involve too much effort to try to understand.
It develops greater fluency, as pupils are encouraged to think in English from the early stages.	It may take longer to cover the syllabus.

Commentary ■ ■ ■

« Conditions for language learning p10

If we look at the debate simply in terms of learning English, then it does seem best to use English for teaching English because it gives pupils more exposure. However, there are many other things to consider; for example, your own confidence in using English, pupils' age, their motivation and previous experience with the language, which may make it unrealistic or difficult to use English all the time. If you think that it is useful to teach through English, set yourself a goal to gradually increase the amount of English you use. Let us consider a strategy which could help you to do this. ■

Task 3   The teacher's language

Here is a way of introducing a memory game (Pelmanism) to a group of children who have limited English and who are just beginning to read in English.

- What do you notice about the teacher's language? Consider how she adjusts her language to the pupils' level.
- What do you notice about the actions? How do these link to the teacher's words?
- Would the technique that she demonstrates for introducing pupils to a memory game work with your pupils? Why or why not?
- What would you need to do differently for your pupils?

Teacher's talk	Teacher's actions
Today we are going to play a game called *Remember*. (Say the word *game* in L1 if necessary.)	Holds up a large size set of matching picture and word cards and emphasizes the word *Remember*.
Look.	Places 6 large cards face down on a flannel board on the wall.
I need a partner. Who will help me?	Gestures to class and picks a child who has volunteered.
Thank you, Anna. Now it's my turn. I take two cards. I turn over the cards.	Points to herself as she says *It's my turn*. Takes two cards from the flannel board and turns them over slowly and shows them to pupils.
What is this picture? And what is this word?	Points to one card which shows the picture of an ice cream and then to the other which shows the word *cake*. Looks at Anna and other pupils encouragingly to see if they can answer.
It is an ice cream. This word is *cake*.	Points to each card again as she speaks.
Do they match? No, they don't match.	Looks at pupils inquiringly. Points to the picture and to the word card and shakes her head as she says *They don't match*.
Now I put the cards back in the same place.	Places cards back on flannel board in same place.
Now it is your turn, Anna. Take two cards. Turn them over. What is this picture? Anna: Cake. What is this word? Anna: Cake.	Gestures to the pupil what to do; gets the pupil to show the cards to the class, points to a picture of a cake and then points to the word card *a cake*.
Do they match? Anna: Match. Yes, they match. You have one set.	Points to the two cards and asks Anna if they match and then gives Anna the two cards.
Now it's my turn. I take two cards. I turn them over.	Takes two cards and turns them over.
This is an ice cream. This word is *ice cream*.	Points to the cards as she says the words and encourages pupils to say the words with her.
Do they match? Yes, they match. Pupils: Match. Now I have one set.	Looks at pupils inquiringly for an answer.
Now who wants to play?	Gestures to class and picks two pupils who repeat the activity in front of the class.

Commentary ■ ■ ■

The strategy is to use very simple language and support what you say with actions and gestures so as to give plenty of clues to pupils.

Language

- The teacher uses simple instructions which require a non-verbal response, eg *Look* or simple questions, eg *What is this?* which require a single word answer.
- Sentences are short, eg *They match.*
- They have a repetitive pattern, which makes it easier for pupils to follow, eg *I take two cards. I turn them over. What is this? Do they match?*, etc.
- The vocabulary is simple, familiar and repeated several times.

Actions

- The actions link to the words, so that pupils can understand and interpret the situation from observing the action and knowing what the teacher is trying to do (teach them a game), eg *Now I put the cards back in the same place* and as she says this, the teacher puts the cards back in the same place.
- The teacher uses objects, eg cards, to manipulate, which helps to make the situation more concrete.
- Children are involved in the action through acting as partners and through helping the teacher with answers.

Susan Halliwell[1] gives many examples of how to give simple instructions in her book *Teaching English in the Primary Classroom.*

Some pupils may resist the teacher's attempts to use English initially. You can motivate them by making the process into a challenge or a game. For example, tell the pupils in the L1:

> *Today we are going to play a game. I will explain in English. See who can work out what to do in the game. I will ask you afterwards in (children's L1).*

If you set it as a challenge, you may stimulate their determination to prove to you that they can understand. ■

If you really want to teach in English but feel doubtful whether children will understand, do it first with an activity they already know. This will help to give you confidence and children will not have a problem with understanding as they will be familiar with the activity. However, you need to gradually move to unfamiliar activities if you want children to learn to follow your message in English and not just rely on their memory of how to do the activity.

Use of the mother tongue (L1)

You have considered how you might increase the amount of English you use in the classroom. But how do you feel about the use of L1 in the English lesson? Are there some situations where it is appropriate for you or your pupils to use the L1? Let's consider what these may be and the reasons for using L1 in those situations. As you read through the list below, compare with your own situation. Do you use the L1 in the same way? If not, think about when and how you use the L1 and the reasons for it.

Here are some situations where the L1 could be used in an English lesson and the reasons for its use.

Situation	Reason for use of L1
Child is upset.	To soothe the child and demonstrate sympathy/closeness.
Child knows the answer to a question that the teacher has asked but does not know how to say it in English.	To show knowledge of the answer. To communicate the answer to the teacher.
Child wants to share an experience/real information with teacher/pupils in an English lesson but has limited English.	To communicate a message to friends/the teacher.
Teacher or pupil wants to joke.	To develop rapport/closeness with teacher/pupils.
Teacher wants to introduce a new game which has complicated rules.	To save time. To assist communication of a message.
Teacher does not know if children have understood.	Wants to check if children have really understood.
Teacher wants to get children to think about the reasons for learning English or to be aware of strategies to help learning.	To assist language learning when children do not have sufficient levels of language to discuss through the L2.

Task 4   Use of L1 as a resource

Study the two examples below in which children are using their L1.

- Why do you think the pupils are using L1?
- In each situation, what is the attitude of the teacher to the children's use of L1? How might this affect pupils' views about their L1 and English?
- If you were the teacher in each situation, what would you do differently?

Example A: In this example Marianne Nikolov[2], a Hungarian primary teacher, tells her eight-year-old pupils the story of the three little goats.

T   This is the story of the three little goats. Here you can see them, the three little goats. *(holds up a story book)* One is

P1   A feher a lany. [The white one is the girl.]

T   These are all boys, there is no girl in this book. These are three billy goats. Three boys, like Balint, Tamas and Feri.

P2   De nincsen szarva! [But it has no horns.]

T   That's right, because the white goat is a baby goat. OK? This white billy goat is a little goat, a baby. *(gestures)*

P3   Kicsi meg, de kar hogy fiu. [It is still small, what a pity it is a boy.]

T   I'm sorry. In this story there are three billy goats. Is that a problem?

Example B: In this lesson, Tuti, an Indonesian teacher, is holding up pictures of different flowers and asking children to name them.

T   Children, what is this? *(shows a picture of a rose)*

P1   Bunga mawar.

T   No, don't say it in Indonesian. I want to know the word in English.

Commentary ■ ■ ■

In example A, children seem to be using the L1 as a strategy for checking their understanding and for reacting to the story. As the teacher tells the story, pupils respond by commenting in the L1. This helps them to share their understanding and their views with their peers and with the teacher. They would not have enough language to be able to do this in English. In example B, the pupil knows the answer in his own language but not in English. By using the L1 word, he demonstrates that he has understood the question and knows the name of the flower, though not in English. So he is using L1 to communicate with the teacher. The alternative would be to remain silent but most children are keen to respond if they know the answer.

Marianne seems to accept children's use of L1 as a natural means of communication at this early stage in their learning of English. This enables children to participate more fully in the story telling and to check out their understanding. She responds to the meaning of children's comments rather than their form and an interesting dialogue develops about the story that she is telling. Tuti's response to the child's answer suggests that she does not accept the use of L1 in an English class. *(Don't say it in Indonesian.)* She responds to the form of the answer (given in L1) rather than to the meaning or content, which is correct.

If you tell children they are wrong for using their own language, you may be giving negative messages about the use of the L1. This may confuse them and possibly turn children against English or their L1. Both languages are a resource. It may be most helpful to view pupils' use of L1 as a useful strategy for communicating at a stage when they do not have enough English to express their own ideas. As we could see in the examples, the use of the L1 was helpful for language learning. It enabled pupils to check their understanding and communicate with the teacher at a stage when they have very limited knowledge of English. So you could view the use of the L1 as a strategy to be used when it will assist pupils' learning or assist communication, ie it is a means to the goal of learning English not an end in itself. However, it is important to keep this main goal in mind as you are likely to be the main source of English input. If a large part of every lesson is conducted in the L1, children will get limited exposure to English.

Would you do anything differently? In example A, you might be tempted to use more L1 than Marianne. She does not, at any point, use Hungarian though she accepts it from the children. This is because she wants children to associate her and her lessons with the use of English. If you had a group of learners who had more English than the children in Marianne's class, you might want to encourage them to say more in English. So you could accept their answers in the L1, but rephrase in English things which they might be capable of saying, to give them confidence to respond. In example B, you could respond more positively to the child's answer by acknowledging first that it is correct. Then you might rephrase it in English so that the child knows the word next time he needs it, eg *Yes, that's right. In English we call it a rose.* ■

3 Developing classroom interaction strategies

Young pupils are still developing: their bodies are still growing; their minds are still developing; some aspects of their first language are still developing. As teachers we play an important role in that development and we achieve it through our way of interacting (communicating) with children. One way in which we can do this is by creating a classroom environment in which children can explore their understanding and experiment with language without fear of being wrong. For example, in Chapter 1, we saw how the Bhutanese girl used the phrase *flower's stick*. She wanted to say *flower's stem* but did not know how to express this. The example shows that the child was experimenting with language, ie with how to express the concept *stem*. The classroom situation allowed her to do this because the teacher was warm and supportive and allowed opportunities for children to use language freely through the discussion. This enabled the child to take risks and so try out her guesses about the language. She was not worried about making mistakes. Children need to have opportunities to experiment and be creative in order to develop their internal language system.

Task 5 Let children take risks in language learning

- Recall an experience where you were learning something new. What risks did you take? How did this help you to learn?
- As a teacher, how can you give pupils the confidence to take risks and feel free to make mistakes?

Commentary ■ ■ ■

Perhaps you can remember learning to ride a bicycle. Maybe you can remember someone helping to hold the bicycle in the beginning while you pedalled, so you could practise the movements. Later perhaps, your friend persuaded you to try cycling a little by yourself and encouraged your attempts when you fell off. This may have inspired you to try again until eventually you succeeded in cycling some distance without support. If however, you had been laughed at when you fell off, you may have had less confidence in yourself to try again.

If your style is open, friendly and sympathetic to pupils, they will feel more confident and free to make mistakes, which is important for their learning and language learning. ■

Consider the ideas below for encouraging risk taking. These are small ways in which you could begin. How effective would they be for your pupils?

- Create special times when pupils know they will not be corrected, eg during activities which are designed for communication.
- Make mistakes yourself and share this with pupils. Be open about it, eg *I have forgotten how to spell 'astronaut'. Can you help me?*
- Develop some activities which encourage risk taking and where you can make it clear that there are no wrong answers, eg making guesses about what is going to happen in a story.

  T What animal do you think will come next? Guess.
  P1 Cat.
  P2 Dog.
  P3 Horse.
  T Any others? OK, shall we turn over the page and find out which animal comes next?

- Praise 'having a go' or 'trying' by pupils. Show you value it.
- Become a more sympathetic listener by:
  - making eye contact while a child is speaking
  - nodding or make an *uhuh* noise to show that you are following
  - giving your full attention to the child
  - turning to face the child or leaning forward to show you are listening carefully.

If pupils are used to more formal styles of teaching, they may take advantage of the greater freedom. You would need to introduce your ideas gradually and also discuss with pupils what you are trying to do and why.

Let's now look at some examples of how teachers interact with pupils in the classroom. We will identify which strategies are the most effective for supporting pupils' learning and language learning and creating an open and sympathetic environment for risk taking.

Task 6   Strategies for interacting with children

Read the two lesson transcripts below, taken from real classrooms. Think about these questions as you read:

- What is the teacher's main purpose in the lesson?
- How does he/she achieve it?
- Does each teacher create an atmosphere in which pupils can take risks and which is supportive to pupils' language learning? If yes, give evidence. If not, explain why not.

Example A

In this classroom, Lena, a primary teacher, is teaching children in their second year of learning English. The main aim of her lesson is to get pupils to practise a dialogue which contains new language. She has put up the dialogue on the blackboard.

May I borrow your pencil, please?
Here you are.
Thank you.
You're welcome.

There are no pictures. Pupils are seated at tables in groups. The teacher has a loud, clear voice. She looks very serious, is business-like in her approach and does not smile.

T	Stand up, Adam. Stand up, Evi. OK, Adam will ask and Evi will answer. *(points to dialogue on blackboard)* Um, yes, read this one.
A	May I borrow your pencil, please? *(reads from blackboard)*
E	Here you are.
T	Now come on, Evi, look at Adam. *(Evi is looking fixedly at board)*
A	Thank you.
E	You are welcome. *(turns round and looks shyly at Adam)*
T	Oh, er, Shona *(pause)* and *(pause)* Brenda. *(pause)* Come on, Shona, ask ... *(pause)*
S	May I borrow your pencil, please?
T	Brenda, look at Shona.
B	You are welcome.
T	welcome *(teacher is not satisfied with pupil's pronunciation)*
B	welcome *(pupil repeats)*
T	May I borrow your pencil, please? Brenda, a bit louder. Look at each other when you ask questions.

Example B

Yenti is working with a class of (eight to ten-year-old) pupils in their third and fourth year of learning English. The pupils are all sitting on the floor gathered close to the teacher who has a large sheet of paper and a pen and is sitting on a low chair. He is about to start the daily news session, when children report on their news or an event of interest. At the end of the session the teacher chooses one person's news to write down and display.

T	Who has some good news for today? Very good news. I am going to write with a smart new pen. *(teacher looks around and smiles)*
Pps	Yes, sir, sir *(several pupils eagerly bid to be allowed to describe their news)*
T	Yes, Dema? *(pause)*
D	Yesterday I ... *(pause)* Aulham and Chenco Dem is buying chick peas and noodles to my shop.
T	Sorry? *(teacher queries)*
D	Yesterday Aulham and Chenco Dem is
T	is? *(teacher queries the use of 'is')*
D	was

Pps	*(several pupils offer help to Dema)*	
D	coming in my shop.	
T	Ah. What did they do there?	
D	They buy	
T	They …?	
D	bought some chickpeas and noodles.	
T	Ah, right. *(smiles and looks interested)*	
D	I was eating food.	
T	Eating food. Good. Let's see from Ugyen?	
U	On Sunday Gyeltshen's mother beat Gyeltshen.	
T	Oh, Gyeltshen! *(smiles at Gyeltshen and sounds sympathetic)*	
	OK, let's see from Kesang.	
K	Yesterday I saw a Dorji …	
Pps	*(many pupils compete to correct the child's use of 'a')*	
P2	Not yesterday, sir. On Saturday. *(pupil 2 is anxious to correct Kesang)*	
T	On Saturday, yes …? *(prompts child)*	
K	On Tuesday … *(speaks quietly)*	
T	*(again gently prompts)* Yes?	
K	On Tuesday I saw a Dorji.	
Pps	Not 'a'. I saw Dorji.	
K	I saw Dorji and Karma were stealing apples.	
T	They were stealing. Oh! *(teacher looks and sounds surprised)*	
Pps	They were stealing plums. *(pupils talk excitedly together adding details)*	

Commentary ■ ■ ■

	Lesson A	Lesson B
Teacher's purpose	To get pupils to reproduce a dialogue accurately and appropriately.	To get pupils to report on their news appropriately and accurately.
Achievement of purpose	Through giving feedback on pronunciation problems and presentation.	Through showing interest and so motivating other pupils to want to try and give their news.
	Through getting pupils to practise the dialogue several times.	Through supporting pupils in trying to tell their messages by prompting and giving cues.
		By giving indirect feedback about error through request for repetition of message.
Talk which is supportive	Provides feedback to pupils.	Motivates and involves the pupils initially.
	Instructions are clear and simple.	Provides a meaningful purpose for pupils in using language, ie they want to talk about their news.
	Knows pupils' names.	Establishes a meaningful context in which to talk, ie pupils' own recent experiences.
		Shows interest in what pupils say (smiles/nods/listens patiently).
		Accepts pupils' answers positively.
		Prompts pupils to give more information.
		Encourages rephrasing if their sentences are inaccurate in tense.
		Teacher leans towards pupils as he listens to

	Lesson A	Lesson B
Talk which is not supportive	The purpose for doing the dialogue is not shared, ie it is teacher directed and not meaningful to pupils.	Teacher's concern for tense accuracy may be confusing for pupils while they are actually trying to communicate their news. It might be better to do this at the point of writing down the message. However it does not seem to inhibit the pupils who seem eager to contribute their ideas and to correct each other.
	Teacher does not show interest in pupils' answers.	
	Teacher does not respond positively to pupils' efforts either verbally or non verbally.	
	No attempt to create a meaningful context related to pupils' own experience.	
	Reason for giving feedback was not shared with pupils, ie why it was important for them to look at each other.	

Both teachers have thought carefully about their teaching objectives and seem equally concerned to achieve them. However, it is the second teacher who has managed to create a classroom in which pupils are willing to take risks and make mistakes. His style of interaction supports pupils in their attempts to express their messages. Both pupils and the teacher appear to be working jointly to construct meaningful messages, ie they are working in partnership. ■

The strategies which seem supportive are:

- showing genuine interest in and responding positively to pupils' answers so as to motivate them to want to speak, eg *Yes?* with an encouraging smile
- encouraging attention to language accuracy but in a constructive way
- using English at a level pupils can understand so that pupils are getting more input
- helping pupils to express their messages by prompting or cueing pupils to say more (so they are 'pushed' to use the language to communicate)
- relating talk to familiar contexts which are meaningful for pupils and so encourage them to want to talk, eg pupils' own news
- working in partnership with pupils to achieve a common goal, eg in example B, both teacher and pupils want to produce a piece of news.

You may be interested to try out some of the supportive strategies which the teachers were using in their lesson and see what effect they have on your pupils' responses and the classroom atmosphere. It may be best to try out one or two strategies first. If they work, then you can try others.

In the action plan below, the focus is on preparing children to listen to a dialogue. You want to activate their own background knowledge of the situation in the dialogue so that they can anticipate what will happen and can draw meaning from the words they hear more easily. This may encourage them to respond and want to talk.

Action plan

Aim: To encourage pupils to want to talk and to take risks in using the language.

Procedure

Choose a dialogue from your own textbook or use the one on the following page from *Stepping Stones*[3]. Just focus on the preparation stage.

- Write down what you will say to your pupils, eg the instructions you will give and the questions you will ask.
- In planning your teacher talk:
  – use simple language
  – build up a meaningful context for the dialogue, eg where and why is the conversation taking place, who is involved, etc?
  – draw on pupils' own experience of such situations, eg what happens when they get dressed at home?
  – show interest in pupils' answers (through smiles and nods and helping them to answer if they have difficulty)
  – accept pupils' answers in a positive way (not rejecting them if incorrect, but helping them to rephrase or accepting them in L1 and rephrasing in English)
  – create a shared purpose for listening to and practising the dialogue which is meaningful to the pupils, eg *Let's find out what Susy says to Bill.*
- Try it out with a class who you know well. Tape record it if you can or get a friend to observe.
- Notice what happened when you responded positively to children's answers.
- Identify what worked well and what did not work well. Think why. Identify one or two steps which you would do differently next time.

4   Teachers' concerns about communicating with pupils through English

Good interaction skills are essential for working with any learners, but are particularly important when working with children. With young children who have not yet learned to read and write in English, talk is our main means of communication. However, even with children who are literate, it is likely that talk will be the most immediate means of communicating in the classroom. It is also the main source of language input. In order to communicate effectively, we need not only to take account of children's limited levels of English but also of their conceptual level. So we have two concerns: keeping our language simple, but also ensuring that our messages are framed in a way which make sense to children. This may seem very challenging.

Task 7   Overcoming problems in using English to teach English

■ Write down some of your concerns about communicating with pupils in English and possible ways to deal with those concerns. Here is an example.

My concerns	How to overcome them
My English is very limited. How can I use it to teach?	Maybe I can try and do part of a lesson in English every day to give myself more practice. I can take an English course locally or go on a course in the vacation.

Commentary ■ ■ ■

Here are some other concerns commonly mentioned by teachers together with suggested solutions.

If children do not understand clearly what I want to say they lose interest immediately.

● Try to make using English into a game for them, ie guessing what the teacher is saying in English.

Pupils want me to teach in L1.

● Talk to them about the reason for using English. Get agreement to try using English for some activities.
● Invite English speakers to visit the class and so give pupils a reason for wanting to speak.

It's difficult to make children understand me.

● Write down what you want to say so that you can focus on keeping things simple.
● Tape record yourself and then analyse your talk so you can identify language which is too complex.
● Listen to your friends talking to their children. Notice the language they use.

An open and supportive style leads to discipline problems.

<< Chapter 4 on management

● Introduce it gradually, small steps at a time.
● Be firm and agree on rules together.

I don't feel comfortable using an informal approach.

● Be yourself. In the end if you genuinely care about students, they will respond to this underlying feeling.

The first four concerns above do have solutions, but the fifth worry is of a different kind. Our style of teaching is closely related to our personality – the way we are. It would be very difficult to expect someone to change their personality. Consider this story.

I remember working with two trainers, Bina and Lisa. Bina was lively and vivacious and was very popular with trainee teachers; Lisa was serious and formal in her style of teaching. She was very unhappy because she felt that trainee teachers did not like her classes as much as Bina's. However, Lisa received positive feedback from trainees at the end of the course. She came to realize that personality is not as important in the end to learners as their perception that we are genuinely concerned about them and interested in them. Learners are astute at distinguishing between teachers who really care about them and those whose friendliness is only superficial.

Summary

In this chapter, you have considered:

- *the kind and frequency of talk used in the classroom.* This is very important, as the type of talk may affect the kind of classroom relationship you build with children (relaxed or formal and distant) and in turn their willingness to respond and to take risks with language. Your talk is also their main source of exposure to English. So the amount and type of English you use will affect the quantity and quality of input they receive.
- *the advantages and disadvantages of teaching English through English.* While teaching through English is essential in providing input in a foreign language situation, there are also occasions when the L1 may be entirely appropriate. You considered strategies for using English in very simple ways so you could build up children's confidence with English, which is the ultimate aim of your teaching, but in ways which valued children's L1.
- *strategies for effective interaction* in order to create a relaxed and supportive environment in which pupils want to talk and are willing to experiment with the language. Some of the strategies included: showing interest in your pupils' responses; using language at a level they can understand; helping them to express what they want to say without initially worrying about their mistakes; choosing familiar and meaningful contexts; working in partnership with pupils to achieve the teaching/ learning goals.
- *teachers' concerns about using English* in the classroom which include their own level of English, the use of the L1, problems in using simple English, potential discipline problems in using a more open style, and the difficulty in changing their personal style of teaching to create a more informal relaxed classroom environment. Most of these problems can be overcome, though with the latter you may need to accept that your personality won't change. Changing the way you use talk in order to create a friendly classroom environment does not mean having to change your personality. It means being more aware of your talk and its effect on pupils.

One implication which emerges from the chapter is that in order to develop your own ways of communicating with pupils, you need to become more conscious of the ways you use language in the classroom and the effect on pupils. You also need to consider your own beliefs about the way you use talk. Do you normally translate all instructions into the L1? If so, why? If you examine the way you communicate with pupils in the light of your beliefs, you may uncover mismatches between your actions and your beliefs. This will help you to re-examine and to make changes in the way you use talk in the classroom.

References

1 Halliwell, S. 1992 *Teaching English in the Primary Classroom*. Harlow: Longman
2 Marianne Nikolov has written about her experiences in teaching children English in an article entitled 'Negotiated classroom work with Hungarian children.' In Breen, M. and Littlejohn, A. (eds.) (forthcoming) *Classroom Decision-Making: Negotiation and process syllabuses in practice*. Cambridge: Cambridge University Press
3 Clarke, J. and Ashworth, J. 1989 *Stepping Stones Book 1*. London: Collins ELT

Chapter 6 Do you need a hand?

Supporting children's language learning

The right help now ... assists independence later.

The illustration shows a woman helping a child to walk. Through her support, he is learning to stand upright, to walk and gain strength in his legs. Eventually as the child gains strength in his muscles and develops confidence, he will not need any support. In the same way, children need support for language learning, ie assistance to carry out learning activities that they would not yet be able to do unaided. Providing support helps children to gain the knowledge, ability and confidence to eventually function more independently. It is also one of the ways in which we maintain the conditions which aid language learning. In this chapter, we will consider:

1 **Support and how to provide it**
2 **Ways of supporting children's language learning**
3 **How to assess the support needed**
4 **How to adjust and reduce support gradually**
5 **Teachers' questions about providing appropriate support for young learners**

The aim of this chapter is to raise your awareness about the importance of providing suitable types of support for language learning and to encourage you to examine the nature of the support you provide and consider whether it is helpful for learners.

1 Support and how to provide it

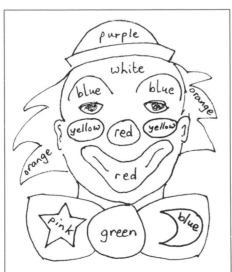

Consider the *Read and colour* activity opposite (used by a Colombian teacher with her six to seven-year-old pupils in their first year of learning English). How would you help children to carry out this activity successfully? They need help (support) to enable them to do the activity. Without help, some children might not be able to do the activity. The support you provide would depend on the children's current level of English and their familiarity with the language and with the activity. There are some suggestions on the next page. Which of these would be relevant for your learners?

Suggested procedure

- Find out what pupils know about clowns in order to activate their knowledge about the topic, eg *Have you seen clowns? Where? What did they look like?*
- Relate the topic to their own experience, eg *Have you been to a circus?*
- Discuss the picture and check if pupils are familiar with the different parts of the face. Revise the colour words, eg *pink, orange.*
- Give a purpose for doing the activity, eg *Let's make nice pictures for our circus display.*
- Check if pupils can read and understand the colour labels on the drawing.
- Demonstrate how to do the activity with their help, eg *Look at the picture. What colour shall I put on the nose?*
- Put up a colour chart with word labels on the wall for children to consult in case they can't read a particular word label.

If children are familiar with the colour labels, there might be no need to provide a colour chart on the wall. If this type of colouring activity is familiar, it might not need a demonstration, just verbal instructions and a check that children know what to do. So the support we give is linked to what we know children can and can't do. Support is a kind of graded help which enables pupils to carry out an activity successfully by themselves. In the process they learn the procedures and skills they need to gain greater control over and awareness of their underlying language system. They may also gradually develop their capacity to regulate their own learning.

2 Ways of supporting children's language learning

Here is an actual example of a teacher providing support for her learners in the classroom. Let's consider how it assists language learning.

Aishah, a Malaysian teacher, is teaching a class in their second year of learning English (eight to nine-year-olds). Her unit of teaching is based on the topic of wild animals. Her overall aim in the lesson is to get children to understand and practise a dialogue about animals. This contains some of the key structures and vocabulary to be practised in her teaching unit.

The dialogue which she wants the pupils to practise is:

Yani	What animal is that?
Yapin	Oh, it's an elephant.
Yani	An elephant. Wow it's so big! Is an elephant a wild animal?
Yapin	Yes, it is.
Yani	Where does it live?
Yapin	In the jungle.
Yani	How about its food?
Yapin	It eats leaves and bark and fruit and vegetables.

Task 1 Support for language learning

Read the lesson transcript and, as you read, do the following:

- Notice each piece of support which the teacher offers pupils.
- Mark on the transcript whether the degree or quantity of support was just right, too much or insufficient.

1	**T**	Where can you find animals?
	Pps	Zoo.
	T	OK. Have you been to the zoo before?
	Pps	Yes.
5	**T**	What kinds of animals can you find in a zoo? Yes, Hazidah?
	P	Tiger.
	T	Tiger – good.
	P	Monkey.
	T	Monkey. Yes, Rudi?
10	**P**	Elephant.
	T	Elephant.
	P	Crocodile.
	T	OK, crocodile. That's good. You've been to the zoo. Last week your friend Yapin *(T holds up picture of a boy)* and … this is Yani. *(holds up picture of a girl)* They
15		went to the …?
	Pps	… zoo.
	T	Yani never been to the zoo before … uh she's never been there, *(makes shaking gestures with hands to indicate 'never before')* so Yapin took her along the … around and round the … *(shows action of walking around holding pictures in her*
20		*hand)*
	Pps	… zoo. *(pupils complete the sentence)*
	T	While they were walking, suddenly Yani saw a big … *(makes gesture with two hands to show how large)*
	P	… elephant.
25	**T**	Yes, a big elephant. I think she didn't know what is … was the animal *(points to Yani's picture)* animal.
	Pps	Animal. *(repeating teacher's last word)*
	T	Animal … so big. OK. *(holds up a picture of a large elephant)*
	P	Wow! *(expresses wonder at the picture)*
30	**T**	*(places pictures of Yapin and Yani on board. Then a few minutes later …)*
	T	So when Yani saw the elephant she was so surprised. *(makes a gesture of surprise)* What is she so surprised at? What do you think Yani would ask Yapin?
	P	What is the animal, Yapin?
	T	What animal is that, Yapin? *(holds up a sentence card)* Can you read the
35		sentence?
	Pps	What animal is that Yapin? *(pupils chorus after teacher)*
	T	What animal is that? *(sticks sentence on the blackboard)*
	P	that Yapin *(inaudible)*
	T	OK, so Yapin said … *(holds up a sentence card)*
40	**Pps**	Oh, it is an elephant. *(pupils read in chorus)*
	T	Yes, it is an elephant. *(sticks up the sentence on the board)*
	P	It is a big elephant.
	T	Then Yani wants to know more and more about the …?
	Pps	… elephant.
45	**T**	… elephant.
	P	What …? *(pupil begins to make up a question)*
	T	So she asked Yapin, her brother … *(shows sentence card)*
	Pps	Where does it live? *(pupils read aloud)*
	T	Where does it live?
50	**P**	It lives from … in jungle.
	T	Where do you think the elephant lives?
	Pps	Elephant live in jungle.
	T	Yes, in the …?
	Pps	… jungle.

Commentary ■ ■ ■

The teacher provides support for the pupils in the *language* she uses. She adjusts her language to suit the level of the pupils, as parents do. She ...

- repeats pupils' answers, (line 25 *Yes, a big elephant.*) which confirms the answer and provides reinforcement.
- rephrases answers, (line 53 *Yes, in the ...?* where she adds the article which pupils have omitted).
- prompts through a rise in her intonation (line 43 *Then Yani wants to know more about the ...?*).
- frames sentences (line 22, *While they were walking, suddenly Yani saw a big ...*) and encourages pupils to finish them. This keeps pupils involved and provides support for less able pupils who may not be able to frame complete sentences.
- uses gestures and actions to support and show meanings (lines 22–23 *makes gesture with two hands to show how large*).

She also provides support through the *techniques and resources* she uses. She ...

- uses pictures of the characters involved to help to make the meaning clear.
- activates background knowledge about the topic so that pupils can link new knowledge to what they already know. The knowledge they already have about zoos and animals enables them to anticipate what is to come. Therefore they are ready to receive the new information.
- responds positively to pupils' contributions (line 13 *OK, crocodile. That's good.*).
- creates a meaningful purpose for using language. (She draws on a familiar context of a visit to a zoo and creates a situation where a young sister has not seen an elephant before.) The reason for asking the questions, therefore, makes sense to the pupils.
- encourages pupils to predict (line 32 *What do you think Yani would ask Yapin?*). This allows them to draw on their background knowledge. It gets them more actively involved in thinking about the topic and brings in some of the vocabulary needed.
- confirms answers so pupils know if they were right or wrong (line 25 *Yes, a big elephant.*) which provides feedback to them.
- provides the written forms of the questions and answers as a visual reinforcement of what has been said. In some cases, it rephrases pupils' attempts. (line 33 *What is the animal, Yapin?* is rephrased as line 34 *What animal is that, Yapin?*)

The teacher gives further support by choosing contexts which:

- are familiar to the pupils, eg a visit to a zoo
- provide clues to the meaning of the language
- begin from the concrete, physical, 'here and now' and move to the more abstract, eg from a dialogue acted out orally with visuals to a written dialogue on the board.

On the whole, the support seems to be quite well matched to the level of the class. For example, as pupils are already familiar with zoos and the names of a large number of wild animals, the teacher does not need to bring in pictures of a zoo and all the animals. However the picture of the two children and the elephant are helpful as they create a specific context for the discussion and building up of the dialogue. The teacher's gestures help to make the meaning clear and also arouse interest in the pupils. The pupils seem to be in touch with what is going on and eager to respond. So the lesson seems pitched at the right level.

There are just a few points where the support seems too much for pupils. Pupils seem eager to guess the questions which Yani asked Yapin and readily volunteer information. This suggests that they are already familiar with some of the material and capable of contributing more than they are allowed to. Perhaps the teacher could allow more opportunity for pupils to predict or suggest the questions and answers. She does not always respond to and build on pupils' suggestions. For example, one pupil volunteers a question in line 33, *What is the animal, Yapin?* but the teacher for some reason ignores this suggestion. Instead she provides her own question, which is almost identical to the pupil's, without acknowledging and praising his attempt. In line 50, a pupil volunteers the answer. *It lives from ... in jungle.* This is almost identical to what the teacher has on her card, but she fails to acknowledge the pupil's answer. She could build on answers like this and in so doing also provide feedback on any language errors the children make, so enabling them to revise hypotheses about the language. ■

We can summarize the different types of support which teachers can use to help their pupils as three main types:

Language

This refers to all the things the teacher does through speech or gesture which provide support for children in carrying out a learning activity:

- using language at children's level, eg choosing words and structures they will be able to understand, such as *put the book on the table* rather than *place the book on the table*
- adjusting one's language to help children understand, eg repeating, rephrasing, extending what a child says
- adjusting one's speed and volume; using pausing to give children time to think
- using gestures, actions, eg spreading your arms wide to show that something is big, a nod of the head for 'yes', facial expressions, making noises, eg noise of a hen 'cluck cluck', noise of a bus 'brm, brm', to help understanding.

Techniques/Resources

This refers to all the techniques and resources the teacher uses to help pupils to do the activities:

- moving from known to new, from concrete to abstract, eg showing a toy bus and later talking about *a bus* using only words
- focusing on things, actions, events which children can see, eg *Look at these puppets you made. What colour are they? Do they have sad or happy faces?*
- using practical 'hands-on' activities in which language is supported by action, eg action games, making paper animals
- giving children a clear and understandable purpose for doing activities, eg *Let's find out what happens at the end of the story*
- revising vocabulary or language needed for activities, eg colour words for the clown activity
- providing language prompts or models to help pupils carry out the activity, eg a 'fill in the gap' activity with words or phrases to choose from, flash cards, wall charts containing the words needed
- giving clear feedback on pupils' responses and on learning activities
- using visual support to help pupils understand a story or dialogue, eg pictures, objects
- providing a clear situation or context for language activities, which is familiar to children, eg a story, a visit to a park
- providing opportunities to learn through a variety of senses, eg hearing, seeing, touching, feeling, smelling, moving
- demonstrating and modelling for children how to do an activity
- creating activities which are interesting to children, eg games, drama, making things and personalizing activities so they relate to children's own experiences.

Children themselves

The support that children provide for each other is so obvious that we often forget to acknowledge it. Children can get support by working with other children:

- learning by watching other children (as models)
- learning by listening to and getting help from other children (as tutors)
- learning by practising with other children (as partners).

3 How to assess the support needed

When selecting learning activities, we need to decide what type of support is needed by pupils to carry out an activity. Some initial whole-class preparation may be sufficient for most pupils, but not for all. Others may need support in actually doing the activity.

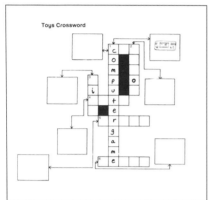

Toys Crossword

Look at the *Toys* crossword below taken from *Stepping Stones Book 1*[1]. This activity revises some of the vocabulary introduced earlier in the unit. Some pupils might find it very difficult and need more support than is provided within the activity.

Task 2 How much support to give?

- How would you prepare the whole class for doing the activity?
- What support is already provided by the activity?
- What support would you provide for weaker pupils while they were doing the activity?
- After doing the activity, identify how you assessed the support needed.

Commentary ■ ■ ■

Here are some suggestions on how to prepare the whole class. They will not be appropriate for all situations because the actual decisions teachers take will depend on the needs of their own learners. Pupils using *Stepping Stones* will already have done some crosswords earlier in the book. This one is slightly more challenging because it does not provide many contextual clues. They have to rely on their memory of the toys they have learned.

- Give pupils a clear purpose for doing the activity, eg *Let's see if we can do this puzzle. We have to guess what the mystery words are.*
- Put an example of this type of crossword on the blackboard, making sure it is not identical to the one in the book.
- Ask pupils if they know what they have to do.
- Fill in one or two examples with their help on the board. Show how they need to make sure the number of letters fits the spaces provided.
- Encourage them to think about where they can get help with spelling the names of toys. (In *Stepping Stones* the complete survey form on the adjoining page of the activity book gives a list of all toys needed to fill the crossword.)

The activity itself provides support by giving at least one letter for each word. The blank boxes for drawing pictures of the words gives pupils a way of checking that they have found the right words. An example is provided for them.

Weaker pupils can be given picture cues to go with the crossword puzzle. The visual support will help to remind them of the toys. You could also show them the completed

« Peer tutoring
pp35–7 survey list so they can find the spelling for the names of the toys. In addition, you could get pupils to work in pairs so that they get support from a partner.

To assess what support is required, the following checklist may be helpful, though you will always need to be able to respond flexibly in each case.

- Has the child done a similar activity before?
- How personalized is the activity, ie does it involve children's own ideas or material?
- Which skills/language does the child already possess relevant for doing the activity?
- Which new skills/language/procedures are required for doing this activity?
- How much contextual support is built into the activity itself?
- Can the child work independently?

The day-to-day aim of support is to enable children to achieve some success at their own level so that they make visible progress and are, therefore, motivated to continue learning. As we saw in Chapters 2 and 4, if children feel some sense of achievement, this helps to build self-esteem and promotes positive attitudes to language learning.

4 How to adjust and reduce support gradually

It is important to gradually reduce or adjust support as children become familiar with the procedures and skills required for doing a task. For example, in using TPR (total physical response) activities involving familiar actions, we can gradually decrease the amount of gesture we use so that children have to rely more on following our words. If we provide support when it is not required, it reduces the level of challenge and children may not make progress. Once they have developed the skills, the language or the concepts required to do an activity, we can give them opportunities to try out and transfer their new-found skill or knowledge to similar but more challenging tasks in slightly different contexts.

Task 3 Gradually reducing support

Let's imagine that a primary school teacher wants to teach this song to her class.

1 The wheels on the bus
Go round and round
Round and round
Round and round
The wheels on the bus
Go round and round
All day long.

2 The driver on the bus
Turns right and left
Right and left
Right and left
The driver of the bus
Turns right and left
All day long.

3 The children on the bus
Jump up and down
etc.

■ These are the steps she follows, but they are jumbled. Put the steps in the right order.

a She narrates the song using the model bus to demonstrate the actions, eg the wheels of the bus going round.

b With some prompting from the teacher, pupils sing the song together by themselves, making appropriate hand gestures.

c She sings the song, using hand gestures to indicate the wheels of the bus going round and round. She gets pupils to make the gestures and to begin to join in.

d She introduces pupils to the key vocabulary in the song by pointing out of the window to a real bus, or showing them a model of a bus or a photo of a bus. She shows them how the wheels go round and round all day and discusses with them where the bus goes, ie along the roads, and how it turns left and right (demonstrating with the model bus) and who travels on it. She demonstrates with model people or pictures how people get onto the bus, etc.

e Pupils think of new verses for the song, eg *The people on the bus go ...*, *The driver on the bus goes ....* They illustrate their new verses and put them up on the wall to join the rest of the song.

f She gets pupils to recall the song by using hand gestures as cues to remind them of the words and to sing along with her. This is done on several occasions (maybe over several days).

g Pupils discuss, select and sing their favourite songs of the term and discuss why they liked a particular song.

h She asks individual pupils to come out and turn the wheels of the bus round while she sings the song.

i She divides pupils into groups and each group sings a different verse without gestures. Individuals begin verses and groups finish the verse. (This may be done on several occasions.)

Commentary ■ ■ ■

The suggested order is: 1 d, 2 a, 3 h, 4 c, 5 b, 6 f, 7 i, 8 e, 9 g. This procedure provides a great deal of support, but the nature of the support changes as children become more familiar with the activity. The context moves from the concrete to the abstract.

The idea on which this activity is based is taken from an article by D. Scott Enright[2].

Task 4   Matching support to pupils' understanding and experience

■ How does the teacher, in the example above, adjust support to match her pupils' level of understanding and experience of the task?

■ If you were teaching this song to your class, what would you do differently?

Commentary ■ ■ ■

She adjusts the support in several ways. She moves from a concrete 'here and now' situation, where meaning is conveyed through visual and physical contextual clues, to a more abstract context where the focus is more on the language itself. At the beginning, she shows the model bus and pupils get a chance to turn the wheels. She shows the meaning of the words through physical gestures and actions in relation to the object. She then gets pupils to represent or symbolize the wheel movements and other concepts, eg *all day long*, *left and right*, through hand gestures.

Later, when the pupils are familiar with the song, they sing it without gestures or real objects. Then they create new verses based on the original pattern. Finally pupils have to compare different songs and give reasons for liking their favourite. By adjusting the contexts, the teacher helps to provide the pupils with the right level of support each time. She builds on what is familiar, but moving the pupils another step forward towards a greater degree of control and awareness of language.

What would you do differently? No two teaching situations are alike and so it is very likely that you would need to make different adjustments for your pupils. You might omit some of the steps or move more quickly through them. For example, you might not need to bring in physical objects if children are very familiar with the vocabulary and concepts. On the other hand, you might find you have to move more slowly. You might not be able to get to the final step because your pupils have insufficient English or are too young to discuss the songs in this way. ■

Support is not a fixed thing. It is closely linked to the specific needs of the pupils at specific points in time. We need to gradually adjust or remove it as pupils acquire the skills and language to do activities independently.

Summary of support

concrete

d   use of real objects, models, gestures or actions to show meaning of words and expressions

a

h

c   use of gestures (to symbolize ideas/words) to accompany words

b

f

i   words alone (without gestures)
    focus on singing it well/fluently

e   manipulating the words/creating new verses based on understanding the pattern of the song

g   talking about the song – comparing it with other songs, ie generalizing from the experience of *The Wheels of the Bus* song. Categorizing it as a song in memory, to be stored with other songs.

abstract

Try to observe the effect of adjusting the amount of support you give, using the following action plan.

Action plan

Aim: To investigate the effects on pupils' performance of gradually reducing levels of support.

Procedure

- Find a learning activity you want to use with your pupils, eg a song or game.
- Plan how you will introduce it to the pupils and what type of support you will provide.
- Plan how you will recycle the activity and the language used over three lessons in slightly different contexts, moving from the concrete to the more abstract. Use the teacher's procedures as an example to help you.
- Decide how you will adjust the support provided each time.
- Make a note of how many pupils were able to carry out the activity successfully on each occasion. Did some pupils need additional support?
- Reflect on what you learned about support from carrying out this plan.

5   Teachers' questions about providing appropriate support

Here are some questions that teachers often ask about the support young language learners need.

1   How will I know when I need to reduce support?
2   How can you give the right support to each child when you have a class of 30?
3   Isn't it spoon feeding if I give support?
4   Even if my support helps a child do an activity today, will she be able to do it herself tomorrow?

Task 5   Questions and answers about support

■ Answer the teachers' questions above and compare your answers with those given below.

■ What other questions do you and your colleagues have about support? What answers can you suggest?

Commentary ■ ■ ■

1   *How will I know when I need to reduce support?*

There is no right answer: it is a matter of trial and error to begin with. We have to learn to judge when children are ready by observing them closely when they are doing activities. If they are doing them confidently and they are successful, then it is probably time to reduce support. If we find they are having difficulty, then they may need more support.

2   *How can you give the right support to each child when you have a class of 30?*

>> Chapter 12

<< Group teaching pp37–8

It is unrealistic to expect teachers to be able to get it right for each individual. It is probably more effective in the long term to train children to become better learners so they know how to get the help they need. But we can also gain more freedom to help individuals if we put children in mixed ability groups for some activities. Stronger pupils in the group can help to support weaker pupils, leaving the teacher free to monitor and work with individuals within groups who need extra support.

3   *Isn't it spoon feeding if I give support?*

If you throw someone in the deep end of the swimming pool before they can swim, there is a risk that they will drown. Even if they do not drown, they may be so frightened that they are put off swimming for ever. It is the same with language learning. By providing support, we are helping pupils to learn in a more humane and enjoyable way – more like the way they learned their first language. However we need to be sure that a child is developing the necessary skills and knowledge to be able to carry out such activities independently in the end. We must be clear why we are providing the support and how we are helping the child to become able to do the activity him or herself. In other words, is he/she making progress?

4   *Even if my support helps a child do an activity today, will she be able to do it herself tomorrow?*

>> Chapter 12

Not necessarily. To improve the chance of transfer, we need to make explicit to children, ie model and state very clearly to them, the procedures and strategies necessary for doing activities. We also need to remind them when to apply these strategies. They need help in learning to make decisions about the best way of carrying out their learning activities; and in monitoring and identifying their own learning needs. This child, for example, seems to have worked out how to support himself: *If my teacher says a sentence in English and I don't understand, I think back to the last time she said it and what she said it meant.* ■

Summary

In this chapter you have considered:

- *the concept of support.* Support is a kind of help you provide for pupils to enable them to carry out language learning activities successfully by themselves. The level of support is adjustable, not fixed, and depends on children's current level of ability and the level you would like him/her to move towards next.
- *three main types of support: teachers' language,* ie all the things they do with language to help pupils' understand; *techniques and resources,* ie all the techniques, procedures, and resources teachers use to help children to do activities; *children themselves,* ie children provide support for each other as practice partners, by providing models, etc.
- *how to assess the amount of support needed* so that the level of support provided enables each child to gain some success in doing the activity. There are a number of factors to consider, including: the skills and knowledge which children already possess for doing the activity and the new skills which will be needed, the degree of contextual support provided by the activity itself, children's familiarity with the activity type and the degree of personalization.
- *the need to adjust support* in tune with the progress children are making. The level of support provided is not something fixed, but should be constantly changing so as to ensure children make progress. As children gain control over the skills and language required to do particular activities, support is reduced while other more complex or challenging activities are introduced for which they may require increased support initially. Adjustment involves: reducing or increasing the help provided in tune with the level of challenge; varying the contexts in which the activity is carried out by moving from concrete situations with plenty of visual support to more abstract situations which rely more heavily on language itself.
- *some teacher concerns about support* which raise important issues about the question of providing support, of adjusting support appropriately and of long term gain, ie does it help children to develop?

There are no easy answers to these questions though there are several implications that follow from this chapter. The overall or long-term aim of providing support is to enable children to eventually carry out activities successfully by themselves through helping them to acquire the skills and strategies needed and the ability to apply these flexibly in a range of contexts. This theme looks forward to 'learning to learn' in Chapter 12.

The challenge for you is to develop your ability to observe and monitor children's ways of working so you can plan and provide support more sensitively and flexibly based on children's constantly changing needs. The process will provide you with a deeper understanding of how children learn language and make progress.

References

1 Clarke, J. and Ashworth, J. 1989 *Stepping Stones 1 Activity Book.* London: Collins ELT, p56
2 Scott Enright, D. 1986 '"Use everything you have to teach English": Providing useful input to young language learners.' In Rigg, P. and Scott Enright, D. (eds.) *Children and ESL: Integrating Perspectives.* Washington: TESOL

Chapter 7 ## Can we do 'Poker face' again, Miss?

Creating, adapting and evaluating activities for language learning

Materials are an important resource for teachers in assisting pupils to learn English. In this book, I shall take a broad view of materials, meaning anything which is used specifically with the intention of increasing pupils' knowledge and experience of the language[1]. So materials could include textbooks, workbooks, story books, videos, cassettes, pictures, brochures, menus or other real-life artefacts. But it is not the materials in themselves which

>> Chapter 10 materials as part of resources

are important, but how they are used to help pupils' language learning. Take the example of a story book. A child might spend ten minutes happily looking at the attractive pictures, but this would not help him/her learn English. In order to use the story book for language learning, the child needs to engage in activities with the book which are intended, directly or indirectly, to provide experience of the language. And for that reason, I am going to focus on the activities which may be based on our materials, as for example the activities we find in textbooks, or which we need to create so that our materials will assist language learning.

In this chapter, we will consider:

1 **Teachers' views on creating their own materials**
2 **How to analyse and evaluate activities**
3 **How to select activities for language learning**
4 **The benefits of adapting activities and of creating your own**

The aims of this chapter are to provide you with the means of examining your teaching activities and to demonstrate some ways of creating, adapting, and evaluating activities. Developing your ability to do these things will give you more independence and greater control over what you do in the classroom.

1 Teachers' views on creating their own materials

In this section, I will start globally by considering the kind of situations which exist with regard to materials and some teachers' views about creating materials. This will help to establish a reason for encouraging teachers to get involved in materials design and analysis. In later sections we will then focus more specifically on activities.

Teachers' situations vary widely with regard to materials. Some have access to a range of textbooks and supplementary materials to choose from, some have to follow one prescribed textbook. Others do not use or do not have textbooks and produce their own materials. Most teachers, however, probably have access to at least one textbook. However, textbooks are designed for a general audience, and it may be that our textbook does not fully meet our pupils' specific needs. This prompts many teachers to adapt or create their own materials.

Task 1 Creating your own materials

■ Do you create your own materials? If so, why?
■ What difficulties are there in creating your own materials?
■ Can you suggest any solutions to your own difficulties or to those mentioned below by three primary school teachers from Malaysia?

Do you think teachers should create their own activities/materials? Why?

'*Yes, I definitely think teachers should learn to prepare their own materials. If we depend entirely on the textbook, it will not be suitable for the students, for they are of different levels and have different interests.*' *(Norimah)*

'*Yes, but only if the teacher has experience of how to create materials. Teachers don't do it because they have textbooks and the idea of making up their own does not come into their heads.*' *(Roseta)*

'*Yes, I think so. Every teacher has a different teaching situation and pupils' needs will differ, so we can't say that the one textbook will be enough for them.*' *(Nalaini)*

What do you feel are the problems in creating your own activities/materials?

– *Lack of ideas.*
– *Time – always rushing against time so no time to prepare. (Norimah)*

– *Knowing what kind of exercises to design. If I was given an example, I might do it. We have no materials to fall back on, no handbooks to look at, to give me examples of what to do. (Roseta)*

– *Insufficient guidelines or models to give insights how to go about it.*
– *Need time to make your own materials.*
– *Monetary – may need to buy your own materials if the school does not have things, but it is cost effective in the end because we can re-use them. (Nailaini)*

Commentary ▣ ▣ ▣

The reason why teachers create or do not create their own materials depends on many factors including the amount of freedom they have, the time available, their interest and experience. The teachers above, all support in principle the idea of creating their own materials, mainly because it allows them to meet their pupils' needs better. However, you need to be realistic and consider what is possible as well as what is best for your learners. There is nothing intrinsically virtuous about creating your own materials. It can be very time consuming and often needs resources like photocopying facilities. In some circumstances, it may be better to adapt activities from the textbook or use the material in the textbook more creatively, rather than spending hours creating your own.

The Malaysian teachers summed up the most common barriers to teachers producing their own materials, which are:

- lack of time to design materials/activities
- cost involved in making/photocopying
- lack of handbooks or reference books from which to get ideas
- lack of skills/expertise to design their own activities.

This chapter will provide some solutions to your problems with materials by showing you ways of analysing, adapting and creating your own activities. By developing or improving such skills you will be in a stronger position to work out your own solutions to the problems you face. Here are some suggestions for overcoming the difficulties mentioned above.

Lack of time

>> Pupil involvement pp136–8

Involve your pupils. Get them to help you in cutting, sticking, copying. They can also do the illustrations for you. You can gradually get pupils more involved in creating activities for each other. It gives them a real reason for using language and yet at the same time, it helps you to make more materials.

Cost involved in making/photocopying

Getting together with other language teachers in a school or district to make materials and then sharing them can help to overcome this problem. This works particularly well if there are several of you teaching in one school. Gavi Marcus from Sabah also suggested preparing a set of workcards based on class exercises which could be laminated in order to make them last. Each learner group uses one workcard and writes the answers to questions in their books. As the workcards can be re-used, it saves photocopying.

Lack of skills/expertise to design own activities

If you have taught for several years, you will have a great deal of expertise you can make use of. The main thing is to have confidence and a willingness to try. Pupils will appreciate your efforts. If you have not had much experience, then it may be best to start by trying out activities from textbooks and then later adapting them in small ways. There are several teachers' handbooks which can give you ideas how to do this[2]. You can learn from your experience, particularly if you get your pupils to help you by giving their opinions about the activities you have used with them.

Lack of handbooks or reference books from which to get ideas

Try to get together with other teachers in your school or locally in order to generate ideas. Or join a local teachers' group as a way of keeping in touch professionally and as a source of ideas. Take out a subscription to a magazine for teachers, eg *English Teaching Professional*[3], perhaps sharing the cost with another teacher.

2 How to analyse and evaluate activities

In this next section, I will move from considering materials in general to focusing on the kind of work or activities we give pupils to do in using materials. Individual learning activities are a very good starting place for teachers who are interested in adapting or designing their own materials as they are manageable in size. To adapt or design an activity would not take up too much of a teacher's time, but done on a regular basis could gradually develop his/her confidence. This could lead on to the design of several linked activities for a lesson, and later to the creation of a series of lessons to form larger units of teaching materials.

As we may not all share the same understanding of the term 'activity' I will begin by defining how I will use the term in this book.

A language-learning activity

- has a clear language-teaching goal
- has a clear and meaningful goal or purpose for learners
- has a clear outcome(s) for the learners
- involves learners in work or activity which requires the use of the L2
- facilitates language learning.

If we want to create our own activities, it is helpful first to have a way of analysing them. This enables us to consider how and why they are constructed in the way they are. Here is a system I have adapted from David Nunan[4].

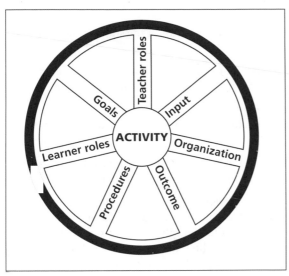

Goal The teacher's purpose or aim in using the activity, ie what he or she wants to achieve through the activity. The children's purpose in carrying out the activity.

Input The material that children will work on, eg text, oral instructions, etc.

Procedures What children actually do with the input, eg they read it or talk about it, etc.

Outcome What children produce as a result of the activity, eg a story book, an answer to a problem, a picture, etc. The outcome might vary from child to child or group to group. We can also distinguish between *product* outcomes, ie something tangible like a set of answers, a completed crossword, a drawing and *process* outcomes – skills, attitudes, etc which develop during the learning process, eg increased confidence, ability to work together.

Teacher roles The roles that the teacher will need to perform which are implied or suggested by the activity. For example, a drill will require the teacher to direct and control the children, whereas a communicative game will require the teacher to set up the task and then step back and monitor.

Learner roles The roles that the activity will require learners to perform. For example, some activities may require learners just to listen and respond as directed; others may require learners to make decisions or choices.

Organization The way the learners are organized for learning, eg as a whole class, in pairs, etc.

Task 2 Analysing a language-learning activity

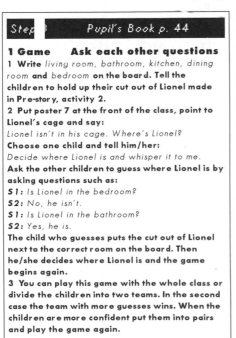

Here is an activity taken from *Big Red Bus*[5]. It includes the teacher's notes and the excerpt from the child's book. Analyse it into the components listed above.

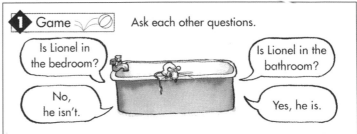

Commentary ■ ■ ■

Here is a suggested analysis of the activity which takes account of the stated aims of the textbook authors.

Goals The teacher's overall purpose is to encourage pupil–pupil oral interaction through a guessing game. The children's purpose could be to guess successfully where Lionel is.

Input Words written on the blackboard, eg *living room, bathroom,* etc; poster at the front of the room; teacher's initial questions and instructions, eg *Where is Lionel?*; question and answer examples in the Pupils' Book.

Procedures Pupils guess where Lionel is through asking *Yes/No* questions. They stick the picture of Lionel next to the appropriate room word on the poster if they guess correctly.

Outcome The product outcomes for children are correct guesses and the attachment of Lionel's picture in the appropriate room; for the teacher they are the children's recall and use of *Yes/No* questions and names of rooms. The outcome will vary each time the game is played, ie the name of the room will vary each time a different pupil guesses. If the outcome is varied, then the activity can be repeated many times without children getting bored. The language structure could also be varied so that children later ask questions like *What is Lionel doing?* once they are familiar with the basic routine of the game. Process outcomes could include the development of positive attitudes to English, improved ability to take turns, etc.

Teacher role The teacher directs and controls. But at a later stage it is suggested that children may play in pairs, at which point the teacher would monitor rather than direct.

Learner role Pupils act as conversational partners with the pupil at the front by asking questions. They have to volunteer questions and the pupil at the front has to respond to them. Later in pairs they will have more freedom in deciding who will guess and who will respond.

Organization Initially pupils are organized as a whole class. Later it is suggested that they could be organized as two groups and later still, in pairs. ■

It is quite revealing to analyse an activity in this manner. Among other things, it allows us to decide whether the activity is appropriate for our own pupils' needs, how teacher-controlled it is, how much pupil participation is involved and so on. It also enables us to identify aspects which could be adapted or modified. For example, if we wanted to make the activity above more challenging, we could change the procedure so that children have to guess where Lionel is and also what he is doing. This means pupils have to ask two types of question, eg *Is Lionel in the bedroom? Is he riding his bike?* However, it is important to remember that we are only considering the potential of the activity at this stage. Whether this potential is realized depends on the way we implement it in the classroom and the way children respond to it.

3   How to select activities for language learning

Before you select an activity for use with your class, you will probably have a number of questions or criteria in your mind which guide your decision whether to use the particular activity, to reject it or to adapt it. This activity helps you to make those criteria explicit.

Task 3 Identifying criteria for selecting activities

■ What are the questions you ask yourself when you want to select or design an activity to use with your pupils?
■ When you have finished, compare your questions with those prepared by a group of Spanish teachers below.

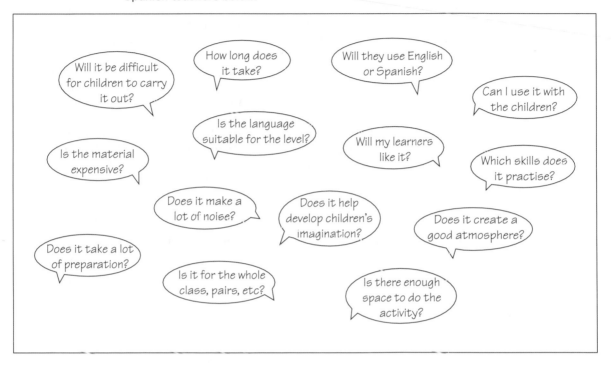

Commentary ■ ■ ■

You may not be aware of asking yourself questions or having questions in your mind when choosing activities. This is because you do not usually need to make them explicit. But it can be helpful to bring them into the open from time to time so that you can reconsider them. This and later tasks are designed to get you to think about your own criteria for selecting activities by comparing them with the ideas you will find expressed by other teachers and professionals.

The Spanish teachers' questions show that teachers are concerned with many different aspects of an activity: the purpose of using the activity, its suitability for the given pupils, its management and whether it reflects appropriate language-learning principles. ■

There are five points to highlight. These draw on some of the points made by the teachers, and on those which we discussed in Chapter 1 related to developing an environment
≪ p10 suitable for language learning. The five points we need to keep in mind are the need to:

● provide a clear and meaningful purpose for using language which capitalizes on young learners' desire to communicate, eg activities which involve a game, or puzzling something out or getting missing information from another person. All these make sense and are meaningful to young learners.

- challenge learners and make them think, so that they are more engaged and so process language more deeply. There is a danger that activities are just used because they work well or because learners enjoy them. We also have to think about what language-learning value an activity has.
- provide activities which are enjoyable and interesting and which make children want to continue doing the activity so they get more practice, eg creating monsters, guessing, games with a winner or prize, 'hands on' or 'doing' activities like making masks. However it is important that these all have a clear language-learning purpose so that children are practising language, and that they are not done just to keep pupils amused.
- provide activities which create a need or pressure for children to use English. One of the teachers above mentioned that pupils may use Spanish or the L1 when the activity is very exciting. Because of the natural urge to win, they may 'cheat' or speak in their first language. We need, therefore, to design the activity so that it requires children to use English at some stage, eg by making them record their answers in writing or getting them to report back to the class in English. This increases exposure to and use of the language.
- provide activities which allow children to be creative with language, experiment and notice language. This will help them to test out their hypotheses about language and assist the development of their internal language system.

« Conditions for
language learning
p10
« Use of English
p63
« Chapter 1
Task 3 p4

The following checklist provides a summary of the main points to remember.

Checklist for selecting or creating language-learning activities

	Activity A	Activity B
Learning purpose		
relevance to language learning/learning all language skills included? (receptive and productive?)		
Learners		
difficulty level language level enjoyment/interest		
Management		
organization amount of noise type of material needed length of activity amount of preparation needed space needed pressure to use English suitability for age group		

	Activity A	Activity B
Learning principles: **Does it develop ...**		
... a positive atmosphere? ... language creativity, opportunities to experiment and notice language? ... imagination? ... purposeful and varied language use? ... thinking skills?		

You may find the checklist above particularly useful:

- when you want to choose an activity from a book
- when you want to decide whether to buy a particular textbook
- when you want to decide whether to use some activities you have found in a magazine or been given by another teacher
- when you want to design your own activity.

When choosing or designing activities, we usually have a specific purpose in mind. For example, we want an activity to revise some vocabulary or to get pupils to use the language they have learned for communicative purposes or to practise independent reading skills. In the following task you will have an opportunity to apply the checklist as a way of deciding whether some activities are suitable for your teaching purposes.

Task 4 Deciding on the suitability of an activity

Think of a group of learners you are familiar with. You are trying to choose suitable games to revise language you have already taught.

■ Look at these two games which teachers have devised for their (six to nine-year-old) pupils who have already studied English for at least six months. Complete the checklist above for Activity A (*Who will finish first?*) and Activity B (*The Bottle Game*). Use these three symbols:

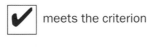 meets the criterion

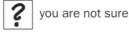 you are not sure

 does not meet the criterion

You may find that not all the criteria are relevant for your purpose.

The bottle game

Number of players: The whole class or a smaller group.
Materials: An empty bottle.
Organisation: Children sit in a circle.
Level: Elementary
Language needed: Commands
e.g. Sing a song.
Walk like an elephant.
Skills: Speaking
Listening
Understanding and acting out the commands
Procedure: ① All the children sit in a circle.
② The teacher gives the bottle "a spin" while it's on the floor. When the bottle stops, the child who faces the top of the bottle gives a command to the child who is sitting opposite.
③ If the child who is acting out the command fails to do it or doesn't understand, then both children are out.
Preparation:
* Give them instructions for the game.
* Teach them some commands.

Georgia Skondu

(created on an International Summer School in Leeds)

Who will finish first?

NO. OF PLAYERS: 3 – 30
MATERIALS REQUIRED: Blackboard ; Dice
ORGANISATION: Class divided in three equal groups.
LEVEL: Elementary
LANGUAGE NEEDED: Numbers
Parts of the head
Simple instructions: Come here !
Throw the dice !
SKILLS: Counting
Reading
Speaking
Elementary drawing

PROCEDURE:
1. Class is divided in three equal groups.
2. The first child from the first group throws the dice. He gets eg no. 2 and he draws a mouth on the group one face.
3. The first child from the second group throws the dice. He gets eg no. 5 and he is allowed to draw the hair on the second face and so on.
4. If a child gets the same number as another member of his group got earlier (eg no. 2 in the first group) he has to miss a turn.
5. The winner is the group who first finishes its face.
PREPARATION:
– Check they can read and understand words written on the blackboard.
– Check they understand the procedure.
VARIATION:
– We could change the words according to the topic we want children
to practise, eg   1. a flower in the vase   4. a table on the floor
2. a book on the table   5. a vase on the book
3. a chair under the table   6. a butterfly on the flower
N.B. Children should draw the picture in logical order eg first the table then everything else.

(created by a teacher on an International Summer School in Leeds)

Commentary ■ ■ ■

Deciding whether the activities satisfy your chosen criteria will depend on your teaching purpose, your pupils' needs and your teaching situation. As there is no right or wrong answer to the question of suitability, the commentary below will highlight certain points that might influence your decision.

Criteria	Commentary
Learning purpose	The relevance of the games will depend on your purpose, but both seem suitable for revision or practice of instructions. Activity **A** involves counting and receptive language skills, ie reading and listening. It could also involve speaking if the teacher got children to comment on what they are going to do, eg *Five. I am going to draw hair.* Activity **B** involves listening and speaking, eg giving and following instructions.
Learners	Both activities seem suitable for younger learners as they are simple to understand and carry out. Activity **A** requires children to be able to count up to six so it may not be suitable for very young learners (five and under). Activity **B** is more demanding in terms of language production as learners have to make up their own instructions. **B** could be adapted for use with any age of learners and any level. Activity **A** is less demanding linguistically and only requires pupils to read simple words and understand oral instructions. Activity **A** involves a winner and so is likely to appeal to learners' competitive instincts. Activity **B** is more collaborative as it is in the interest of one player to help his/her partner to carry out the instruction; otherwise they are both out. Both games involve physical movement, which is likely to appeal to younger pupils.
Management	Both activities are organized for the whole class, so in larger classes not all pupils will get a turn. So chances for practice are somewhat limited. However on the plus side, the whole-class organization means that you could keep tighter control if you feel this is desirable and so keep noise levels down more easily. Both activities could be done in groups once children were familiar with what to do. The whole-class organization also means that there is pressure to use English as all communication is done publicly. There is no preparation needed for either game. The only materials required are a dice and a bottle. Activity **A** can be done even in classrooms where desks are fixed to the floor. However Activity **B** requires an open space so children can sit on the floor. Both activities can be continued for as long as the pupils are interested.

Criteria	Commentary
Learning principles	Both activities are likely to create a sense of enjoyment and therefore contribute to a pleasant atmosphere. Activity **B** allows children to experiment with language and make use of their imagination, eg they can make up their own unusual instructions for their partners and in the process test out their hypotheses about language. Activity **A** creates a purpose for language use through the need to complete the face, though it is possible pupils will get frustrated if no group can finish the face, so the rules may need to be adapted so a group can win each time. Activity **B** creates the need to use language through the requirements of the game, ie the person to whom the bottle points has to give an instruction. Both games are likely to be motivating for younger learners. Both activities offer some element of mental challenge but in different ways. Activity **A** involves number recognition and memory skills, ie learners have to remember numbers which have already come up. Activity **B** is more challenging from a language point of view as children have to think up their own instructions and say them without support.

No activity can fulfil all the criteria simultaneously. You will need to decide what your priorities are. If you want an activity which allows pupils more freedom to use their own language, then *The Bottle Game* may be more appropriate. However you would need to consider carefully how to manage a lively class of younger children. When I watched a primary teacher use this game for the first time, the children were all so excited to 'have a go' that they became very noisy and boisterous. Activity **A** could be adapted so that children have to actually produce language, ie tell the class what number they have got on the dice and what they are going to do.

4 The benefits of adapting activities and of creating your own

You may be in a situation where you have to create your own activities or are encouraged to do so. If this is the case, the criteria on pp92–3 may provide you with a way of looking at your own activities from a different perspective. However if you have had no experience of creating your materials, a good way of beginning is to adapt those you find in textbooks or in magazines for teachers. This helps to give you confidence to get started. But whether you create your own activities or adapt them, the process of adapting or creating an activity to meet a need, the process of trying them out in the classroom and reflecting on how they work is a helpful way of gaining fresh perspectives on your teaching.

He has a pink body. He has blue teeth and blue hair.	He has a purple body. He has white teeth and red hair.	He has a blue body. He has yellow teeth and green hair. He has pink nails.	He has a green body. He has red teeth.

Here is an example of an activity which was adapted by a Spanish primary teacher from one I designed based on some monster pictures given in the magazine JET[6]. The original activity was designed to focus mainly on reading skills.

The teacher wrote the following instructions on the board for the (ten-year-old) pupils.

> Draw a monster with ...
>
> one head   four legs
> four eyes   four feet
> four mouths   four arms
> four noses   four hands
>
> Colour ...
>
> his/her head — pink
> his/her mouth — red
> his/her eyes — blue
> his/her feet — brown

Here is an example of the work of one of the pupils.

After her lesson, the teacher considered how effective the activity had been, using the following questions as a guide.

Objectives

To review parts of the body and get pupils to recognize them.

How many of the children could do the activity successfully?
All of them.
Could the slower children do the activity successfully?
Yes, they could with the teacher's help.
Did the activity work well? Why?
Yes, it did because children liked the monsters and it was quite easy for them. It was also a new kind of game.
Were there any problems? Why?
Some children did not remember some parts of the body.
What was the children's response?
Good.

Task 5 Reflecting on teaching/learning activities

- How did the teacher's activity differ from the original? Why do you think she adapted it?
- What do you think the teacher may have learned from the experience?
- Could she have thought more carefully about her use of the activity in the classroom?
- What are the benefits of trying out and then reflecting on your teaching activities?

Commentary ■ ■ ■

The teacher simplified the language of the descriptions to suit the level of her pupils, who were ten-year-old beginners. She did not use the pictures, but instead got pupils to draw their own pictures as part of the activity, which created more interest. So she adapted the activity to suit her own learners and teaching situation. She may have learned that it is important to prepare children before doing an activity, in this case revising the vocabulary they would need.

She wrote that all of the children could do the activity successfully. This seems unlikely, especially since she mentioned that some pupils did not know all the vocabulary. It is hard sometimes to detach yourself from your own teaching and look at it like a stranger. I find it often helps to get a friend to observe and give you a different perspective. It also helps to get pupils' opinions as this acts as a check on your own perceptions.

The process helps you to stand back from your teaching, think about the activity in a detached way – about what worked and what did not work. You can then improve it for next time. If you do this regularly, it can help to keep you thinking about your teaching in a fresh way.

Summary

In this chapter you have considered:

- *the reasons for creating your own activities and materials.* The main argument for designing your own materials is to ensure a better fit between your teaching and the needs of your pupils. However there are problems to overcome such as lack of time, lack of expertise in designing materials, lack of resource or reference material and the cost.
- *how to analyse an activity* into different components including: teacher and learner goals, outcomes, input, procedures, teacher and learner roles, organization. Analysing activities into their components gives you a way of deciding on their usefulness and a way of adapting them to suit your purposes better.
- *the kinds of criteria which you can use for selecting, creating or adapting and evaluating activities* for young learners. No one activity could satisfy all criteria simultaneously and you would need to decide on your priorities, depending on your goals and the needs of your learners on any particular occasion.
- *the value of creating or adapting activities,* trying them out in the classroom and assessing their effectiveness as a way of reflecting on your teaching. This process enables you to stand back from the routine of your daily teaching and consider it from a different perspective, which may give you new insights into your teaching.

One of the main implications which comes out of this chapter concerns your role in materials development. The difficulty with any published learning materials is that they are designed for a global audience, not specifically for your pupils. So you have a very important role in selecting and adapting published materials or creating activities specifically for your own pupils. But in order to develop your ability, you need to be able to step back from your materials and analyse them in different ways: to consider how they work, how pupils respond to them and your reasons for using them. If you can make explicit to yourself the basis for selecting, creating or adapting activities for pupils, by drawing on your understanding of the conditions which create a positive language-learning environment, you are in a better position to assess whether and why the activities helped you to achieve your objectives. You can then adapt or improve them. This increased awareness will enable you to gain greater control over your own teaching environment. You will be able to make decisions about using activities, based not just on a vague feeling or hunch but on clearly articulated criteria which are supported by your experience in the classroom.

References

1 This definition comes from Tomlinson, B. (ed.) (1998) *Materials Development in Language Teaching.* Cambridge: Cambridge University Press
2 Both of these books provide useful ideas on using and adapting materials: Deller, S. 1990 *Lessons from the Learner: Student generated activities for the language classroom.* Harlow: Longman (out of print)
   Grant, N. 1987 *Making the most of your textbook.* Harlow: Longman (out of print)
3 *English Teaching Professional* is published four times a year by First Person Publishing Ltd. It is obtainable from The Swan Business Centre, Fishers Lane, Chiswick, London W4 5EZ.
4 Nunan, D. 1989 *Designing Tasks for the Communicative Classroom.* Oxford: Oxford University Press
5 Lobo, M.J. and Subira, P. 1993 *Big Red Bus 1.* Oxford: Heinemann, *Teacher's Book* p95, *Pupil's Book* p44
6 Theme Pack on Monsters *JET*, vol.1, no. 3. This issue contained a whole pack of pictures and teaching ideas based on monsters. This magazine is no longer published, but collections of the articles and materials are published in *JET Primary Teachers' Resource Books 1 and 2*, Delta Publishing.

Chapter 8   Why did I do it like this?

Planning for children's language learning

Planning is something we do all the time in teaching though we may not always be aware of it. The four situations below show the different kinds of planning which teachers do frequently.

Planning the term's English work with a group of teachers

Before term begins

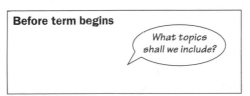

What topics shall we include?

Before class

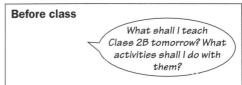

What shall I teach Class 2B tomorrow? What activities shall I do with them?

During class

A thought in your head as you observe an activity in class, eg three children have problems recognizing the colour words *purple* and *pink*.

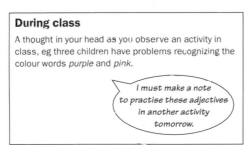

I must make a note to practise these adjectives in another activity tomorrow.

Reflecting after class

They really enjoyed the activity of colouring and produced beautiful clowns but they had quite a problem with the new colour words purple and pink. I did not spend enough time practising them first. Next time I need to do more preparatory work on colour recognition.

In Chapter 1 and following chapters, we discussed the importance of the teacher's role in creating a suitable language-learning environment in which children are exposed to meaningful language input and given plenty of opportunities for practice. Whereas in natural situations, opportunities arise haphazardly, the advantage of the classroom is that we can plan to create such opportunities in a more systematic way.

Although you may be involved in many different types of planning, this chapter will focus on daily lesson planning because most teachers do this regularly in one form or another, and it is a good basis for other kinds of planning. We will consider:

1 **Teachers' views on planning**
2 **Decisions involved in planning lessons**
3 **The content and organization of a lesson plan**
4 **A closer look at some of the steps in planning a lesson**

The aim of this chapter is to raise your awareness about the important role that lesson planning plays in your teaching and in your on-going development as a teacher. It encourages you to reflect on your own approach to lesson planning and to think more deeply about the relationship between your teaching and pupils' learning.

1   Teachers' views on planning

As teachers, we have had a lot of experience of planning. But sometimes when we have been doing something for many years, it becomes rather automatic. We often stop thinking about the way we do something and why we are doing it. So it may be helpful to re-examine the reasons for lesson planning.

Task 1   Why plan lessons?

- What are your reasons for planning a lesson?
- Compare your list of reasons with the list below, given by a group of Malaysian teachers. Which of them do you think are most important and why?

Teachers' reasons for planning

Lesson planning:

a) helps the teacher to be more confident in teaching
b) provides a useful systematic outline/guide/reference for smooth efficient teaching
c) helps the teacher to prepare for the lesson
d) helps to provide a useful basis for future planning
e) helps the teacher to be more organized
f) helps the teacher to plan practically lessons which cater for different pupils
g) helps the teacher to know whether he/she has achieved his/her teaching objectives
h) enables the teacher to judge his/her performance
i) is proof that the teacher has taken a considerable amount of effort in his/her teaching
j) gives a sense of direction in relation to the syllabus
k) helps the teacher to identify which areas/parts did not go well in his/her teaching
l) is an administrative requirement.

Commentary ■ ■ ■

There are many reasons for planning as the answers above show. The Malaysian teachers' reasons belong to the following categories in order of frequency:

- practical (guide/support for teaching): b, c, d, e, f, j
- professional development (self-assessment/improving teaching): g, h, k
- public accountability, ie proof of competence for authorities, parents: i, l
- confidence boosting: a

Practical

The most frequent reason which teachers gave was the practical one of planning as a guide or support. They found that it helped them to prepare for their lesson, to organize their time and to take account of different learners' needs. This concerns basic survival skills, ie what to do at what points in the lesson. This practical reason may be particularly important for less experienced teachers, for those who are changing teaching level or those who are teaching new materials or curricula. But if we look beyond basic survival, the effective management and organization of our time and resources helps us to set up and maintain those conditions which help children to learn language.

Personal development

The second most frequent reason which teachers gave concerns professional development, ie that having a plan enables them to monitor, assess, and improve their teaching. If we have a plan, then we have a set of intentions – what we expect learners to achieve. We can then check to see whether our intended outcomes match the actual outcomes. A mismatch tells us something is wrong and needs investigating. This aspect of planning is particularly important for the long term as it indicates a way for us to manage our own development. This reason tends to gain importance once a teacher has developed basic classroom routines and doesn't have to worry about survival in the classroom but has the confidence to stand back and look at his/her lessons in a thoughtful way.

>> Assessment pp152–5

Public proof/accountability

The third reason is concerned with public accountability, ie so that we can provide a public record or proof of what has been done which demonstrates to school authorities, inspectors, other teachers, and parents our ability to do the job. Another more positive way of looking at this is to say that a plan means we can show others what we are trying to do; we are being explicit or open about our teaching.

Confidence

The fourth reason concerns the affective side of teaching. It suggests that planning can give us more confidence about our teaching and make us feel more secure about what we are doing. In that sense, it is closely linked to the other reasons. If planning helps us to sort out how to run the class, then this will allow us to feel more confident. Similarly, if we feel we are improving our teaching this may also encourage us to feel more confident and develop our sense of self-esteem.

Your decision about which reasons are most important will depend on your experience of teaching and the type of situation you work in. Many teachers' views will probably change with experience. At the early stages of teaching or in a new job, teachers are most concerned with the practicalities of running the lesson. In this situation, the plan acts as a useful guide. (b, c, e, f and j above). More experienced teachers may use the plan more as a way of clarifying their thinking, monitoring how their lessons are going and becoming more responsive to children's needs. ■

2   Decisions involved in planning lessons

When you sit down to start planning your lesson, what kinds of things are you concerned with? Do you think about your pupils and what they have achieved so far and where they need to move to next? Do you reach for your syllabus to check which skills or functions you are recommended to teach? Or do you turn to the teacher's book, check the next lesson in your textbook and decide which activities to teach? Here is one teacher's views about what goes on in her head when she starts planning:

> *In planning one gives careful thought to what has gone before the lesson, meaning the outcome of the previous lesson and also considers what the learners already know about the topic or subject matter, what should be emphasized in the lesson and how the lesson is going to be carried out (activities, student organization, teaching aids/materials, teaching objective, teaching/learning outcome).*

This quote shows that there are many decisions involved in planning a lesson though we may not always be aware of making them! The number of decisions we make will vary depending on whether we are planning our own course or working from a prescribed syllabus or textbook. If the latter is the case, the teacher's book will indicate the language structures, the vocabulary, and the activities to be taught in a particular lesson. However even if a lot of the teaching content is provided, as in textbooks, it is the teacher who has to decide what to include and how to organize the learning activities depending on what is best for the pupils. There is always a choice to be made.

Task 2 Decisions involved in lesson planning

Below and on the next page is a lesson taken from *Project English 1*[1], a coursebook which is aimed at slightly older learners (age 11–13). The lesson is the first one in a series of lessons based on the topic *Our House*.

- If you had to teach this lesson, what decisions would you need to make before you could teach it? What information would help you to make those decisions?
- What changes (if any) would you make to the lesson plan in the book?

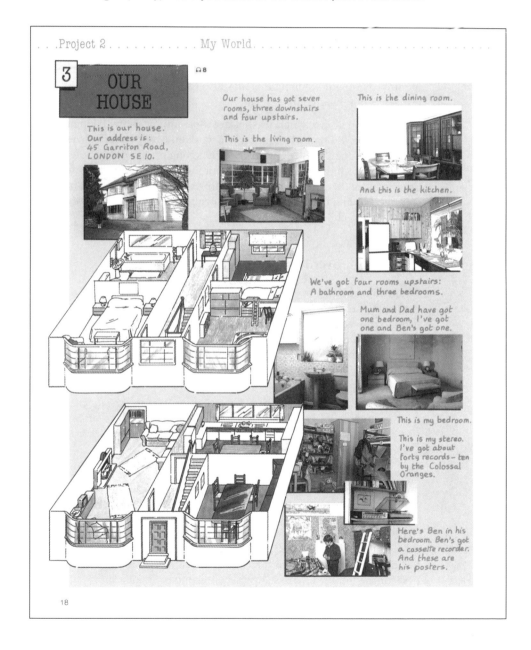

3 OUR HOUSE

Language focus
have/has got

Vocabulary
address, road, room, downstairs, upstairs, living room,
dining room, bathroom, bedroom, stereo, about, cassette
recorder, flat

Context
Mandy describes her house.

Lesson six

1   Briefly revise previous lesson.
   □ 'A spelling bee': Pupils ask each other to spell words.

2   Introduce the structures: *have got/has got*. Pick up a book.
   Say: *I have got a book*. Ask pupils: *Have you a book?*
   Repeat with *He/she has got*. (See Introduction, page ii:
   'Introducing a structure'.)

3   Pupils look at the pictures.

4   Ask pupils:
   Who are the people?
   What are the places?
   What things are in the rooms?

5   Introduce the expressions: *room, downstairs, upstairs,
   living room, dining room, bathroom, bedroom, stereo,
   cassette recorder.*

6   Play the cassette. **(Item 8)** Pupils follow in their books.

7   Ask pupils questions about each picture:
   – *Who is in the picture?*
   – *What has Mandy/Ben got?*
   – *Where is Mandy/Ben?*

8   Play the cassette again. Pupils listen.

9   Play the cassette again. Stop after each sentence. Pupils
   listen and repeat.

10   Divide the class into groups of 3. Each pupil takes it in turn
   to read one of the sections.

11   Pupils read the story in their groups. They change roles and
   read it again.

12   Get one or two groups to read the story in front of the class.

13   **Exercise 1** (page 19)
   □ Pupils look at the examples.
   □ Ask why it is *'have got'* in the first example and *'has got'*
      in the second example.
   □ Explain the activity.
   □ Play the cassette. **(Item 9)** Pupils listen and answer.
   □ The cassette gives the correct answer. Pupils listen and
      repeat.
   □ Repeat exercise, if you think the pupils need more
      practice.

14   **Exercise 2** (page 19)
   □ Divide the class into pairs.
   □ Pupils copy and complete the table.
   □ Copy the table onto the board.
   □ Get one pupil to come out and complete the table.

KEY

He She It	has 's		three rooms. two cats. a name.
I We You They	have 've	got	

   □ Pupils make as many sentences as possible using the
      table. (This can also be a homework task.)

15   **Homework**
   Pupils make two sentences from the table for each of these
   words: *have, 've, has, 's.*

   Workbook exercise 5

⌒ **9**

> Listen. Say what they have got.
>
> *Jane and Mandy* (. . .)
> Jane and Mandy have got records. (. . .)
>
> *Ben* (. . .)
> Ben has got cassettes. (. . .)
>
> *Cheryl* (. . .)
> Cheryl has got records. (. . .)
>
> *Ben and Jack* (. . .)
> Ben and Jack have got cassettes. (. . .)
>
> *Millie* (. . .)
> Millie has got records.
>
> *Mandy and Cheryl* (. . .)
> Mandy and Cheryl have got records. (. . .)

T18

Commentary

Here are some of the decisions you might want to make. These will vary depending on your learners and your teaching context.

Decisions	Information to help decision making
Which functions, language structures, skills, etc have pupils already learned? They may already know some words from outside school, eg *stereo*, *computer*.	– previous lesson plans in textbook – lists of vocabulary and structures at the back of the book and on the Contents page – pupils' exercise books
Which content to include as the new items for the lesson? eg understand questions with *have/has got*, produce answers with *has/have got* Include all the vocabulary items or only some?	– knowledge of pupils' language level – grammar reference book to check on use of *have/has got*
What are my objectives for the lesson? eg *Pupils will be able to listen to the tape and find out what Ben and Mandy have got.*	– knowledge of pupils' needs, levels, previous learning – activities in the textbook
Do I want to use the activities as they are or adapt or leave out some?	– knowledge of pupils' interests / how they seem to learn best – my own lesson objectives – time available for lesson
What resources do I need for the lesson? eg tape recorder, Pupil's Book, pictures of pupils' houses	– Check lesson plan in Teacher's Book. – Check activities.
How do I check their understanding? How do I check if I have achieved my objectives?	– Listen to their responses. Watch and note their participation. – Check actual against expected outcomes. – Previous experience of what worked well.
Other ...	

The changes you make will depend on your teaching situation, your learners' level, needs and interests, your own understanding of how learners learn best, and the time and resources available. No two teachers will do it in exactly the same way. Here are my suggestions, together with my reasons. Other changes are also possible.

Motivating pupils

Step 2: You could either get pupils to bring in photos of their houses or use the picture as a stimulus to begin the lesson. Use the picture to link the topic to their own experience, eg *What's your house like?*, *Is your house like this?* This would be to arouse interest and activate pupils' background knowledge about the topic, so relating it to their own experience. This would bring in a lot of the vocabulary needed quite naturally.

Contextualizing new language

Step 2: You could leave practice of the new structure until they have been exposed to it in context, ie after listening to Mandy's description on tape. The reason for this change is that it would be more meaningful if they were exposed to the new structure through Mandy's description, which together with the pictures would give more support for understanding.

Establishing a purpose for activities

Step 6: You could give pupils a purpose for listening, eg *Write down what things you have in your bedroom. Now let's find out what Mandy and Ben have got in their bedrooms. We'll see if you have the same or different.* Pupils need a clear purpose for listening to the tape which makes sense to them. Having a purpose helps pupils to listen in a more focused way. Having a meaningful purpose involves them more because they can relate to the intention behind it (in this case comparing their things with those of other children).

Cultural sensitivity

If you teach children who come from poorer homes or from very different homes to the ones in the coursebook picture, you might want to prepare your own illustrations of a house and family more familiar to your pupils. The reason for this change would be to ensure that there is no implied negative comparison with children's own homes, or to take account of children's own cultural contexts.

There are many decisions you need to make in planning a lesson and no one right way of making those decisions. But if you are actively aware of the kinds of decisions which need to be made, then you are less likely to take them for granted. You are more likely to keep questioning your own decisions in a continual process of self-monitoring. In the next section, we will consider an actual plan based on the results of the kind of decision making we have discussed above.

3   The content and organization of a lesson plan

There is no standard way of writing a lesson plan. We need to develop our own format which will suit our needs. As we gain experience of teaching, our plans tend to get much briefer. Some teachers may only make a simple list of activities to remind themselves of the order in which to do things. However, when beginning to teach a new group of learners or to use new materials, I find it can be helpful to plan a few lessons in some detail as a way of thinking through and clarifying my ideas. So in this next section I am going to analyse an example of a detailed lesson plan. This may be useful, particularly for those primary teachers who are new to teaching English, as it makes explicit the teacher's objectives and the language and/or skills focus for the lesson, which may not be obvious from looking just at teaching procedures and activities.

The first part of the plan below contains information about *what* the teacher is going to teach. The second part is a description of *how* the teacher is going to teach – the procedures she/he will use in teaching. The lesson is designed for children in their third year of learning English.

Task 3   What's in a lesson plan?

■ The box below contains background information about what to teach. However most of the sections are incomplete. Match the numbered information in the bubbles at the bottom of the page to the headings given in the lesson plan outline, eg objectives, language skills, etc. One example, Part F, is already completed for you.

Lesson Plan Part 1: Content – What to teach

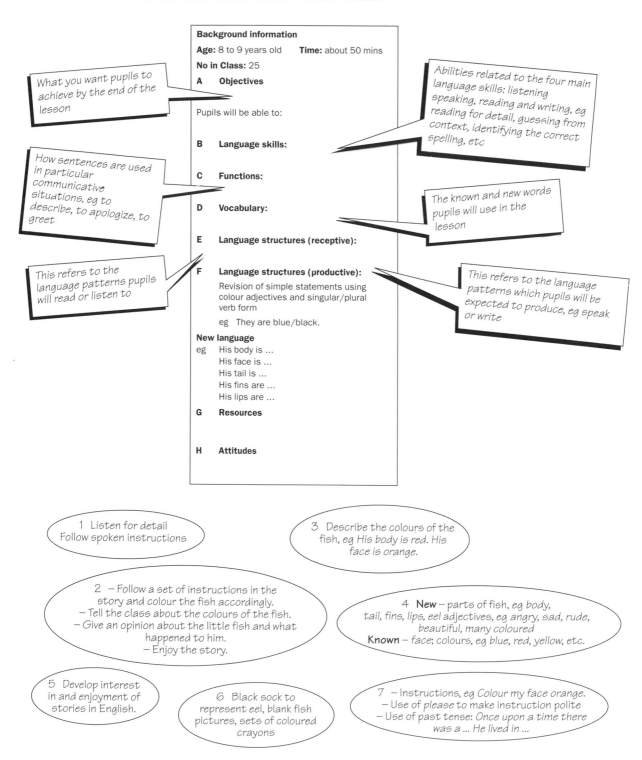

Background information

Age: 8 to 9 years old   **Time:** about 50 mins

No in Class: 25

A   Objectives

What you want pupils to achieve by the end of the lesson

Pupils will be able to:

B   Language skills:

Abilities related to the four main language skills: listening speaking, reading and writing, eg reading for detail, guessing from context, identifying the correct spelling, etc

C   Functions:

How sentences are used in particular communicative situations, eg to describe, to apologize, to greet

D   Vocabulary:

The known and new words pupils will use in the lesson

E   Language structures (receptive):

F   Language structures (productive):

This refers to the language patterns pupils will read or listen to

Revision of simple statements using colour adjectives and singular/plural verb form

   eg   They are blue/black.

This refers to the language patterns which pupils will be expected to produce, eg speak or write

New language

eg   His body is …
     His face is …
     His tail is …
     His fins are …
     His lips are …

G   Resources

H   Attitudes

1   Listen for detail
Follow spoken instructions

3   Describe the colours of the fish, eg *His body is red. His face is orange.*

2   – Follow a set of instructions in the story and colour the fish accordingly.
– Tell the class about the colours of the fish.
– Give an opinion about the little fish and what happened to him.
– Enjoy the story.

4   **New** – parts of fish, eg *body, tail, fins, lips,* eel adjectives, eg *angry, sad, rude, beautiful, many coloured*
Known – *face;* colours, eg *blue, red, yellow,* etc.

5   Develop interest in and enjoyment of stories in English.

6   Black sock to represent eel, blank fish pictures, sets of coloured crayons

7   – Instructions, eg *Colour my face orange.*
– Use of *please* to make instruction polite
– Use of past tense: *Once upon a time there was a … He lived in …*

106

Commentary ■ ■ ■

The answer to the matching task is: A–2, B–1, C–3, D–4, E–7, G–6, H–5

It is helpful in your planning to be aware of what language (structures, functions, vocabulary, etc) or skills will be new for pupils in a lesson and what they already know, so that you can build on this in your lesson, eg

Known language	New language
Colours, eg *red, blue*	Adjectives *sad, happy, angry, rude*
Instructions, eg *Colour the...*	Parts of the fish *body, tail, fins, lips*
Sentence pattern, eg *It is blue.*	Sentence pattern *His face is blue.*

The background information tells you *what* is going to be focused on in the lesson (the *content* you are going to teach). There are many different kinds of content, as you will see if you open any textbook, eg functions, structures (grammar), pronunciation (sounds), skills, topics, attitudes, vocabulary, learning strategies, text types, cultural information and so on. Though you may identify the language/skills involved in carrying out various activities in the lesson, you will probably choose to focus on only a few aspects.

Although language structures are listed as part of the content, this does not mean that you need to teach them formally as grammar rules. In fact, we know from Chapter 1 that younger children (up to about eight or nine) learn primarily through purposeful interaction with others. They do not naturally pay attention to the form (words) of the language. However, awareness of the underlying language system and of the natural pattern in language can help them to achieve higher levels of language ability eventually.

>> Task 5
p110

If we are to build on what we know about young learners, we can first focus on using the language to do interesting activities which emphasize the meaning, eg listening to a story to find out what happens, and then draw children's attention to aspects of the language system used to express that meaning. ■

Task 4   Lesson procedures: why do it in this way?

The second part of the lesson plan contains information about procedure – *how* you are going to teach. It has a section for teacher's and pupils' activity. These two sections ensure that pupils' activity is not neglected as there is a tendency in planning for teachers to focus mainly on what they are going to do rather than what the pupils will do.

■ The main input for children in this lesson is a story. Can you think of reasons for beginning in this way?

■ What is the main activity which pupils carry out in the lesson? Why choose this one? Think of a possible alternative.

■ How does the teacher prepare pupils to carry out the main activity? Why does she need to do this?

■ What is the purpose of the *Notes* section of the plan? What other information would you include in the *Notes* section if you were teaching this lesson?

Lesson Plan Part 2: Lesson procedures

Time	Teacher's activity	Pupils' activity	Notes
5–10 mins	**1** Warm-up Brief revision of colours, using a team game	Pupils stand in lines behind flags of different colours. As teacher says a colour, pupils behind the flag of that colour crouch down.	
10 mins	**2** Bring in goldfish or picture of fish to introduce topic to pupils. Discuss fish – what it looks like, its colour, its parts. Check who has a fish at home.	Pupils gather round tank and contribute what they know about fish. They tell about their own fish.	NB Remember to bring in fish and arrange classroom.
	3 Tell pupils you are going to tell them a story. Get them to predict what will be in the story.	Pupils try to guess what will be in story.	Arrange pupils on mat for story. NB remember picture of eel or black sock.
	4 Explain the activity, ie pupils have to colour their fish as the little fish in the story requests. Give out colours and blanks of fish drawing.	Group leaders/monitors give out crayons and blank sheets.	Get pupils to share if not enough. If warm-up revealed problems with colours, spend a few minutes revising as crayons are given out.
10 mins	**5** Tell first part of story with actions and pictures. Continue story with instructions for colouring.	Pupils colour in fish following instructions.	Check that pupils know what to do.
5 mins	**6** Get pupils to compare drawings.	Pupils compare to see if they have the same.	Go round and see if drawings are the same.
5 mins	**7** Go around class getting different pupils to describe the colours of the little fish. Use sentence prompts, eg *His face is ...*	Some pupils say the colours of the fish, eg *His face is ...*	
5 mins	**8** Ask pupils what they thought about the story in L1, if necessary. Ask whether the big black eel was right not to give the little fish colour for his lips.	Pupils give their opinions.	
	9 Display pupils' coloured fish on the wall.	Pupils write their names and help teacher to display.	

The little fish who wanted to be beautiful

Once upon a time there was a little fish. He lived in a big river with many other fish. But he was not happy. All the other fish were very beautiful. Their bodies were of many different colours, red, blue, green and so on. His body was white. He felt very sad. 'I want to have a beautiful body like those other fish,' he said.

So one day he went to see the king of the river, a big black eel who lived in a big black hole at the bottom of the river. He swam down and down and down to the bottom.

'Who's there?' said a loud voice.

'It's me, little fish,' said the little fish.

'What do you want, little fish?' said the big black eel.

'Please, sir,' said the little fish, 'make me beautiful like the other fish.'

'Hmm, hmm,' said the big black eel. 'Alright. What colours do you want?'

'Please make my body red,' said the little fish.

And his body became red.

'Please make my tail yellow,' said the little fish.

And his tail became yellow.

'Please make my fins green,' said the little fish.

And his fins became green.

'Please make my face orange,' said the little fish.

And his face became orange.

'And make my lips red,' said the little fish.

'You rude little fish. You did not say please,' said the big black eel. 'I won't give you any more colours.'

And so the little fish had white lips. But he was very happy because his body had many colours.
He was very beautiful.

Commentary ■ ■ ■

Stories like the little fish story provide meaningful contexts in which to expose children to language input. Through this story, they will encounter new vocabulary and language, eg *sad, happy, tail, fins, His face is blue*, but in a situation which they can relate to. They enjoy stories and are keen to find out what happens, which gives them a meaningful reason for listening. Their previous experience of stories, the teacher's preparation for the story and the visuals and actions used in telling the story will help children to work out the meaning conveyed by the words.

The main activity for pupils is to follow a set of instructions and colour in the parts of the fish, and all the other activities are linked to this. An alternative would be for pupils to point to or hold up the appropriate pictures as the teacher told the story or to sequence a set of pictures in groups or individually. However I prefer the *Listen and colour* activity as it involves children physically and mentally while the story is being told and leads to a definite outcome (coloured pictures) which can be used later.

The main reason for preparing pupils to do the activity is to provide them with support (as we saw in Chapter 6) so that they can carry out the activity successfully themselves. The teacher does this by:

● activating pupils' background knowledge about the topic by bringing in a real fish to discuss or using a picture

- introducing the key vocabulary needed in the story, ie body parts and also revision of colours through discussion of the fish
- getting pupils to predict what will be in the story
- revising colour vocabulary through the warm-up game at the beginning and also as crayons are given out.

The purpose of the *Notes* section is to provide a checklist to prompt your memory during the lesson. It represents the kind of things you need to do in order to ensure the lesson goes smoothly. For example, it contains reminders about materials needed, about organization of pupils, about possible problems which might arise and alternative actions if necessary, about ways of monitoring. I find such a section useful as a reminder, particularly for young learner lessons, which normally involve the use of a range of activities and resources. I have tried to make explicit the kind of things experienced teachers think about in their heads. When teachers are less experienced, it may be helpful for them to write reminder notes.

If I was going to teach this lesson, I might include notes on: how to seat children during the story; a reminder to provide a model for the description in Step 7; an additional revision activity for colours if children have problems remembering; some ideas for additional follow-up activities if I finish early, eg a song.

When this story was tried out with children, they were very interested in the little fish and keen to colour in his picture. They were able to draw on clues in the context to work out the meaning and to predict what colours the little fish would ask for. They could also join in the story at certain points when the teacher told it a second time. However they did not pay much attention to the language as they were too absorbed in the meaning of the story. So by establishing meaning first, we are building on children's strengths in interpreting situations. But if children are to develop their internal language systems, they need to become more aware of the words they are using. ■

Task 5   Helping children to notice language

- Why do you think children could join in the second time the story was told? Which bits of the story do you think they joined in?
- We discussed in Chapter 1 how children pick up chunks of language. Are there any phrases which they might pick up as a chunk from this story?
- If you wanted to help children notice some of the language in the story, what would you draw their attention to?

Commentary ■ ■ ■

The story has a pattern which recurs many times. This makes the language more predictable and so enables children to be able to join in. It also helps them to be able to guess what will happen in the story. Children tend to join in the patterned or repeated parts of the story, eg

Please make my body red. And his body became red.
Please make my tail yellow. And his tail became yellow.
Please make my fins green. And his fins became green.

Children might possibly pick up chunks of language such as *You rude little fish*. This may appeal to children as it is a short phrase and they usually enjoy language which they can use with their peers to joke or be rude. They may also pick up the polite requests, as these have a distinct pattern, are short, easy to understand and can be easily extended for use in other stories and games, eg *Please make his hair long.*

Once children spot the pattern, they can generate other examples themselves with your prompting and through feedback on their attempts. You can give them opportunities to do this through making up and dramatizing slightly altered versions of the story, etc. Noticing pattern in language helps children to generalize, which is a very helpful skill in language learning and for learning in general.

4 A closer look at some of the steps in planning a lesson

Lesson planning is something teachers do so regularly that it can become very routine. They are no longer aware of the steps in the process or the reasons which underpin the choices they make. In this section, I want to examine some of the steps involved in lesson planning in more detail and to articulate some of the reasons for making particular decisions or choices. I am not suggesting that we normally need to think about planning in such detail, but from time to time it is helpful to become aware of what we do when we plan and why we make certain decisions. When you read my thoughts on planning, this may cause you to think about your own planning processes. It is through such an awareness that you may question or reconsider aspects of your own planning, so leading to a deeper understanding of what you are trying to achieve through your plans.

Choosing learning activities

Let us assume that the lesson above is the first one in a unit of teaching based on and growing out of the little fish story. We want to plan for the next lesson which is 30 minutes in length. The first activity in the lesson is the following:

Fishy names

Pupils use the picture they coloured in for the first lesson. They each have to think of a name and an age for their fish. They write this information on the back of the drawing. In pairs, they then ask each other questions to find out the information, eg *What's the name of your fish? (Charlie.) How old is he? (50.)* They must also decide on the fish's favourite colour (or food/drink) and their partners have to guess within three tries, eg *Does he like blue?* The information could be collated on a large chart.

This activity makes use of the fish that children coloured in the previous lesson and so creates a link with the previous session, providing a shared context to relate to.

Task 6 Sequencing activities

Below are a number of possible activities, all related to the little fish story.

■ Which of these activities would you choose to follow *Fishy names*? Why?

1 Whose fish? Complete a worksheet

Pupils complete a worksheet which has pictures of four children. Each child has caught a fish but the lines are entangled. Pupils have to work out which fish (of different colours) has been caught by each particular child by following the fishing lines.

2 Dramatize

Pupils dramatize the little fish story. Two pupils take the parts of the big eel and the little fish. Other pupils act as other fish in the river. Some pupils act as a chorus to tell the story, using actions and key phrases with the teacher's support. They prepare a frieze of the river as a backcloth. As the little fish gets its different colours, some of the pupils stick different colours onto the pupil who acts as the little fish.

3 Read and colour

Pupils are divided into five groups. Each group receives a simple written description of a fish, eg

> *The fish has a blue body.*
>
> *It has a green face and a red mouth.*
>
> *It has a yellow tail. Its fins are blue.*

Each group's description is different. Pupils read and colour in their pictures.

4 Read and spot the difference

The teacher builds up on the board a written description of the little fish from the story with pupils' help. Children give it a name. She gets their help to draw and colour in a picture which matches the description, eg

> *The name of the fish is Goggle Eyes.*
>
> *He has a red body and a purple face.*
>
> *He has an orange tail and green fins. His lips are white.*

Then she reads the description aloud while children listen and she makes deliberate mistakes, eg *The name of the fish is Charlie. He has a yellow body and a purple face.* Pupils have to raise their hands when they spot a mistake. Individual pupils then take turns to come out and do the same.

Commentary ■ ■ ■

There is no one right answer to which activities to select for the next lesson. It will depend on your teaching objectives and the needs of your learners. One possibility is to follow the activity *Fishy names* with Activity 4, *Read and spot the difference.* This introduces pupils to a written description of the little fish. They are exposed to the language they have already heard orally, which acts as a support, but now they meet the language again in the form of a written description which increases the challenge. So Activity 4 builds on *Fishy names*, but also provides new learning opportunities. The checking for mismatches between the written text and the teacher's reading gives them a meaningful reason for reading. The activity is flexible in timing and can be extended by allowing more pupils the opportunity to act as teacher. *Fishy names* and Activity 4 together involve all four skills and combine a balance between stirring oral work and a more settling whole class reading activity (See Susan Halliwell's criteria for planning activities[2].)

Activity 3 *Read and colour* provides a good follow-on to Activity 4 for the next or a later lesson. It would not really be suitable before Activity 4 as it assumes that children can read the written description whereas Activity 4 introduces them to the written description of the fish.

Activity 1 would probably be quite appealing to children, but it has no obvious language-learning purpose and does not seem sufficiently challenging for the pupils' level.

Activity 2 would also be a good follow-up to the first lesson, but this would take up the whole lesson. You would probably need longer than one lesson if you wanted to do the drama with visuals and other aids. ■

Thinking about how and why you sequence learning activities encourages you to clarify the basis on which you are making decisions about children's learning. If you also monitor children's response, you will have a good basis on which to decide whether your decisions are justified or need modifying.

>> Chapter 9

Task 2 pp122–4

Checking the content

In choosing activities, you may find it helpful to identify:

- what language (functions, language structures, vocabulary) and skills (listening, speaking, etc) pupils will need in order to do the activity
- what language they have already acquired which they can make use of in doing the activity
- what attitudes or values you wish to develop through the activities, eg enjoyment and positive attitudes towards stories, politeness to others.

If you are working from a syllabus or coursebook, you could check whether the activities will enable pupils to develop the appropriate language content, skills, attitudes, etc that are required by your programme.

The chart below shows you a way of analysing the language and skills for an activity (*Fishy names*) which pupils will need to understand and use. This type of chart shows:

- the language/skills pupils already know (revision) which will be recycled
- the language/skills which will be new for pupils
- which language (if any) pupils will only need to understand (receptive)
- which language they will need to produce either orally or in writing (productive).

Activity: Fishy names

Language structures	Functions	Skills/ attitudes	Vocabulary	Pronunciation
Productive Revision *Wh*–questions, eg *What ...?* *How old ...?* *Yes/No* questions, eg *Does he like blue?*	**Productive Revision** Asking for and giving information about name/ age/likes, eg *What's his/her name?* *How old is he/she?* *Does he/she like red? Yes, he/she does.* **New** *No, he/she doesn't.*	**Speaking, Listening** Exchange information Turn-taking with partner Become aware of the purpose of communication. **Writing** Write notes of name/age/ favourite colour.	**Revision** Colours, eg *red, blue, yellow, orange*	**New** /z/ consonant in *does/doesn't*

Fishy names is mainly a revision activity so that it recycles language children already know from earlier lessons but in a new context. The new language item is the negative form of *does*, ie *he/she doesn't*. This might also cause some problems with pronunciation, eg the sound /z/.

Task 7 Analysing the language and skills in an activity

- Make a chart similar to the above and do the same for Activity 4, *Read and spot the difference*. You can compare your answers with the completed chart at the end of the chapter.

Writing objectives

Once you know what activities you want to do and are clear what language and skills the activity is practising, then it is easier to write your objectives. Some teachers, however, prefer to write the objectives first and then find or design activities to carry out their objectives. Work in the way you find most helpful. Objectives help you to be explicit about what you want pupils to achieve in the lesson. There are different ways of writing them. Here is an example based on *Fishy names*.

a Pupils will be able ask and answer questions about their fish in pairs, eg *What is its name? How old is it? Does it like blue?*

b To get pupils to practise *Wh–* and *Yes/No* questions and answers.

The difference between these objectives is that objective **a** is written from the pupils' point of view. Objective **b** is written from the teacher's point of view. Objective **a** makes it much clearer what activities pupils will actually do in the lesson. This way of writing objectives ensures that you take the pupil as your main focus and that you provide them with meaningful things to do. When writing from the teacher's point of view, there is a danger of forgetting the learning needs of young pupils, ie the need for active involvement and a meaningful purpose. However both types of objective can be included in your lesson plan.

Task 8 Writing objectives

Here are three objectives for Activities 1, 3 and 4 on pp111–2.

Whose fish?	Pupils will be able to fill in the worksheet.
Read and colour	Pupils will be able to develop their reading skills.
Read and spot the difference	Pupils will be able to spot the differences between what the teacher says and what is written in the passage.

- Which of the objectives provides the clearest information about what pupils will do?
- Rewrite the other two objectives to make them clearer so that even another teacher would understand what pupils have to do.

Commentary ■ ■ ■

The objective for *Read and spot the difference* is the clearest as it tells us precisely what pupils are expected to do in the activity. The objective for *Read and colour* is very vague as it does not indicate what pupils will actually do. The objective for *Whose fish?* is a little more informative, but it still does not tell us what type of activity the pupils will need to do in completing the worksheet. After all worksheets can vary from the simple to the very complex.

One way of improving the objectives is to rewrite them as follows:

- *Whose fish?*
  Pupils will be able to complete the worksheet by finding and labelling the fish belonging to each child.
- *Read and colour*
  Pupils will be able to colour a fish correctly using information from a written description.

You may have some other important objectives relating to the learning process or attitudes, eg to encourage children to value each other's contributions in class, to develop an interest in reading English stories, etc, which cannot be specified so exactly in terms of performance or outcome. This does not mean you should abandon them, but you may need to take a more long-term view of achieving them. Objectives are merely a tool to assist you in achieving your teaching intentions, and not something fixed and rigid. They are only helpful if they are based on and sensitive to children's changing learning needs and to the actual teaching–learning situation. They need to be applied flexibly.

Feedback on learning

Feedback for the teacher

>> Assessing
learning/teaching
pp157–8

While planning, you need to consider how you will know whether you have achieved your objectives, ie were pupils able to do the activity? You need to think about what counts as successful performance. For example, in *Fishy names*, you might go around and check to see how many pupils have successfully written down the information they got from their partners. You might also watch their interaction to see how successful they are at communicating verbally, eg can they ask questions? The information you collect will help you in planning for your next lessons. This process is a kind of self-assessment.

Feedback for the pupils

As well as feedback to you, however, it is also important to give pupils feedback on how they performed. This will help them to know their strengths and weaknesses so that they can make progress. For the *Fishy names* activity, you might have discovered that pupils were making mistakes with *Does he/she like red? Yes, he/she does./ No he/she doesn't*. You could write up some examples of their questions and answers on the blackboard and see if pupils can correct them. You might discover that pupils were just reading from each other's papers rather than asking for the information. You could discuss with them in the mother tongue (if needed) the purpose of such activities and why it is important to ask each other orally in English rather than just read the information.

Task 9   Feedback on learning and teaching

For the *Read and spot the difference* activity above, in the lesson we have been planning:

- How would you assess pupils' performance?
- How would you provide pupils with feedback on their performance?

Commentary ■ ■ ■

Here are some ways of collecting information on performance which would provide you with feedback about the achievement of objectives for the activity.

- Count how many hands go up when you say the wrong word.
- Get pupils to write down words which you changed.
- Check how many words they noticed.

- Check whether pupils carry out the activity correctly when they take over as teacher.
- Identify what words they have problems in recognizing or pronouncing when reading aloud.
- Note how they react to the activity.

Feedback for pupils

- At the end of each reading of the passage, get pupils to tell you which words you changed. This will help slower pupils to realize what they have to do.
- Repeat the activity several times, changing different words, and ask the slower ones to report back. Repeat what you read aloud if necessary, so they can check.
- At the end of the activity, go back over the passage, checking on/revising words which pupils had problems with reading aloud.

Action plan

Aim: To plan a lesson in more detail and reflect on the outcomes.

Procedure

- When you have some new material or a new class to teach, try planning one or two lessons in more detail. Identify your objectives and the language and/or skills you wish to focus on (see page 106 for one way of doing it).
- Plan your lesson procedures (see page 108 for a sample format).
- Alternatively jointly plan a lesson with a friend so you can explain your decisions to each other.
- Try out the lesson and then reflect on how it went. Here are some questions to ask yourself, or you could discuss them with your friend:
  – What worked well? Why?
  – What did not work well? Why?
  – What will I change next time?
- Did you need to make any changes to your plan while teaching? What difference did these make to the lesson?

Consider what effect planning in more detail had on your teaching. Did it give you more or less confidence? Did it enable you to adapt or make changes more easily? ∎

Summary

In this chapter, you have considered:

- *teacher's views on planning.* Teachers identified four main reasons for planning: practical, personal development, public accountability and confidence building. The reasons for planning may change as you gain more experience. The use of planning for survival initially may be replaced by the use of planning as a kind of reflection to develop your teaching at later stages.
- *lesson planning as an active process of decision making* which involves: using knowledge of pupils' previous learning and current needs and of the teaching/learning context to decide on learning objectives; choosing content and activities; organizing and sequencing these for learning; deciding how to assess learning. There are choices to be made, whether you are free to select your own content and materials or are required to work from a given textbook. If you monitor the consequences of these choices, you have a way of getting feedback on your teaching.
- *the type of content which can be included in a lesson plan (the 'what') and the procedures and activities the teacher uses to realize his/her objectives (the 'how').* We discussed the reasons

why certain content, procedures and activities were included in the lesson plan and highlighted the need to draw children's attention to the language they were using at a point when they were already familiar with the meaning.

- *the steps involved in planning a lesson* – how the decisions made are then translated into a teaching plan which contains information about what to teach and procedures for teaching. Planning a lesson includes: selecting and sequencing learning activities, selecting and checking the content, setting objectives, deciding how to assess your lesson. There is no fixed way of organizing a lesson plan: the way you approach it and the level of detail you include will vary depending on your experience and your purpose for planning.

There are two main implications I would like to draw from this chapter. Planning enables you to think about your teaching in a deliberate and systematic way that is not possible in the classroom, where your responses have to be fairly immediate. Provided it does not become a routine, it can be a useful way of supporting your development.

Plans only express your intentions. They need to be implemented in a real classroom with real children. Many things can happen which you had not anticipated or planned for, eg children don't understand the activity, new needs arise. In the end, you need to be able to respond flexibly and adapt your plans if necessary so that you respond to your pupils' actual needs during the lesson. This way you ensure that you are teaching the children not the syllabus.

Sample answer for Task 7

Activity: Read and spot the difference

Main language	Functions	Skills	Vocabulary	Pronunciation
New Receptive Pronoun *its*, eg *Its body is blue.*	**New Oral productive** Identify and state differences, eg *It's yellow not red.*	**Listening** Match spoken to written word. Identify differences between what is said and what is written. Follow teacher's instructions. **New Reading** Recognize new sight words.	**Revision Receptive** Colours Parts of the body, eg *fins, body, face, lips, tail* **New sight words** (words in written form) *fins, body, tail, lips, face*	/f/ *fins, face*

References

1 Hutchinson, T. 1985 *Project English 1*. Oxford: Oxford University Press
2 Halliwell, S. 1992 *Teaching English in the Primary Classroom*. Harlow: Longman

Chapter 9 What's your topic?

Using a cross-curricular approach for organizing language learning

Miss, this is for our topic on wild animals.

Children learn most effectively when they are involved. They become involved when they are interested, as the cartoon above suggests. One way of organizing language learning which builds on pupils' interests is through topic work. In this chapter, we will consider:

1 **What is topic work?**
2 **How topics can be used as a basis for planning and organizing language learning**
3 **How to organize topic work**
4 **The benefits and problems of using topic work**

The aim of this chapter is to enable you to decide on the relevance of topic work for your own context, to provide you with ideas on implementing topic work, and to encourage you to reflect on your own approach to teaching young learners.

1 What is topic work?

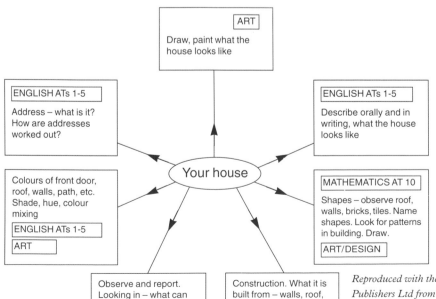

ART
Draw, paint what the house looks like

ENGLISH ATs 1-5
Address – what is it? How are addresses worked out?

ENGLISH ATs 1-5
Describe orally and in writing, what the house looks like

Your house

Colours of front door, roof, walls, path, etc. Shade, hue, colour mixing
ENGLISH ATs 1-5
ART

MATHEMATICS AT 10
Shapes – observe roof, walls, bricks, tiles. Name shapes. Look for patterns in building. Draw.
ART/DESIGN

Observe and report. Looking in – what can be seen through a window
ALL CORE SUBJECTS

Construction. What it is built from – walls, roof, etc.
SCIENCE AT 6

Topic work is a way of organizing children's learning and language learning around topics or themes of interest to the children. When teachers plan for topic work, they often make a topic web first. This is like a spider's web with the topic in the middle and linked to the topic are examples of the different subjects and activities which are related to it. Here is an example[1].

Reproduced with the permission of Stanley Thornes Publishers Ltd from THE REALLY PRACTICAL GUIDE TO THE NATIONAL CURRICULUM *first published in 1989*

The activities linked to the topic help children to learn and practise language, concepts and skills related to subjects across the whole school curriculum, eg maths, science, art and so on. In the process, children are using English in a purposeful way to find out things and do things which have meaning and interest for them and to communicate the results to others. For example, Jairo, a Colombian primary teacher, carried out topic work on bicycles with his ten-year-old pupils. As part of the project, children designed a bicycle for the future and then communicated their ideas to other classmates by displaying their designs.

Topic or theme-based work integrates language learning with children's subject learning across the curriculum in a way which takes account of how they learn. It does this through involving them in activities which focus on meaning, in which they experience things at first hand using many senses, eg seeing, hearing, touching, and which capitalize on their desire to socialize and communicate with others.

However, it is not easy to plan for full integration of subject and language learning unless you are the class teacher or you can collaborate with the main class teacher. So in this chapter, we are going to consider topic work mainly for language learning. We will consider how to make use of activities from a wide range of subject areas related to the topic area, which can be exploited for their language learning and communication potential. In the process, we will be practising many of the skills and concepts which pupils need in their subject learning as well.

2   How topics can be used as a basis for planning and organizing language learning

In the next sections, we will work through an example of how to plan for topic work. This is not the only way to proceed but it gives you a framework to start from, which you can try out in your own situation. In Chapter 8, we looked at planning individual lessons, but in this chapter we will consider how to organize and plan for a whole series of lessons all linked to one topic. Here are some of the planning decisions ‹‹ Chapter 8 you need to go through.

Choosing a topic

You may be able to choose your own topics or you may need to follow those recommended in your syllabus. Whatever your situation, there will always be some decisions or choices that you can make, eg the order in which to do topics, what activities to include, how long to spend, deciding how to involve children.

Task 1   Choosing a topic

■ How would you choose a topic and what factors would influence your choice of topic and activities?

■ Which age and language level do you think the topic and activities below would be suitable for?

■ Which language-learning activities based on the topic below would be suitable for the learners you have in mind?

■ Do all the activities in the web involve children in using language?

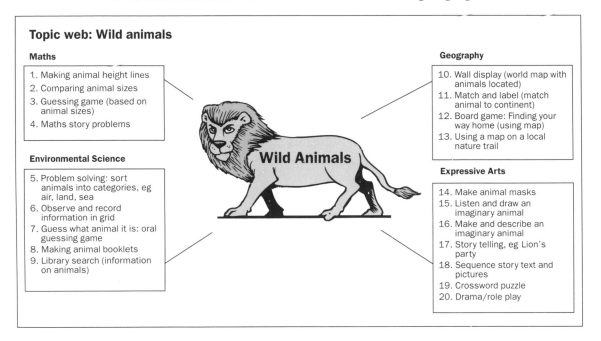

Topic web: Wild animals

Maths

1. Making animal height lines
2. Comparing animal sizes
3. Guessing game (based on animal sizes)
4. Maths story problems

Environmental Science

5. Problem solving: sort animals into categories, eg air, land, sea
6. Observe and record information in grid
7. Guess what animal it is: oral guessing game
8. Making animal booklets
9. Library search (information on animals)

Geography

10. Wall display (world map with animals located)
11. Match and label (match animal to continent)
12. Board game: Finding your way home (using map)
13. Using a map on a local nature trail

Expressive Arts

14. Make animal masks
15. Listen and draw an imaginary animal
16. Make and describe an imaginary animal
17. Story telling, eg Lion's party
18. Sequence story text and pictures
19. Crossword puzzle
20. Drama/role play

Commentary ■ ■ ■

You could choose a topic by

– asking children's opinion, which would be a way of involving them in the learning process

– consulting your syllabus and textbook for ideas

– asking other teachers

– consulting books or magazines with ideas on topic work[2].

The example above is quite a broad topic, which is useful if you want to have plenty of choice of activity and you plan to spend a few weeks on topic work. If you only have a short time available, you might narrow down your focus and choose just one type of animal.

Here are some of the factors which may influence your choice of activities:

● pupils' interests, eg what kind of wild animals are they interested in?
● pupils' conceptual level, eg measuring activities involving non-standard measurement like finger spans can be carried out with quite young children (age five to six) but making model animals to scale would be suitable for older children (nine upwards)
● time available to do the topic work
● level of language needed for the topic or to do the activity – does it contain the right balance of new to familiar language?

- level of cognitive challenge, ie will the activities challenge pupils mentally?
- potential for encouraging pupil involvement and participation, eg 'observe and record' activities involve seeing and hearing, 'making an imaginary animal' involves manipulation, collaborating, talking together
- pupils' language needs, ie does it help pupils to develop the language and skills they need to form a basis for communicating effectively?
- resources available to do the activity
- syllabus, eg does the topic enable you to practise the language structures, skills, functions, attitudes, etc required by your syllabus?
- potential for linking with other activities, ie can the activity be linked meaningfully to another activity so it makes sense to children?

The topic *Wild animals* is suitable for almost any age of learner but you would need to adjust the concepts included to match the cognitive level of the children. For example, one of the activities is a maths story-problem involving addition and subtraction, and another involves children using a map to identify the continents different animals come from. You would need to ensure that children were familiar with these concepts from their general primary curriculum. I am assuming that they would be suitable for a group of children aged nine to ten. Several of the activities involve reading and writing simple texts, so they would be suitable for children who could read and write in their own language and had already been learning English for two to three years.

Other activities linked to the topic could include, for example, crossword puzzles, word mazes, card games (collecting sets of animals or categories of animals), making clay or paper animals, writing animal poems.

All but one of the activities involve children using language. *Making an animal mask* involves important skills like observation and manipulation *but* does not seem to involve language work. However this activity could be used as the basis of other activities so that it *would* involve language work, eg children choose a character from the story of Lion's party, learn the vocabulary for the materials they will need in making the mask, make the mask, describe their animals to the class and then use them in a drama. Alternatively the teacher could give children instructions to make the mask which would involve them in listening. ■

Once you have chosen your topic, you can make a topic web like the one above. Break the topic down into the related activities under the curriculum areas they represent. This will make it easier for you to think about the resources needed, the language, skills, concepts and attitudes you want to develop and revise. You do not need to use all the activities in your web. It is a source of ideas which you can expand or leave as you require.

Analysing language/skills/attitudes in learning activities

Here is a checklist of things you can do once you have selected a range of activities. You can:

« Chapter 8 and p122
- analyse them to see what language structures, skills, attitudes, etc they involve
- identify which language structures, skills, etc will be new for pupils and which will be familiar and can, therefore, be recycled through the activity
- check with the syllabus and textbook to see what language structures, skills, vocabulary, etc need to be covered
- adapt activities in order to ensure that they do provide practice in using some of the language you want to focus on.

The planning sheet below can be used for analysing the activities. Other headings can be included, depending on the requirements of your teaching situation, eg types of text (story, invitation, etc), attitudes (towards learning foreign languages), moral values (helping others, etc). Two examples have been completed based on the topic web.

Once you have analysed the activities, you are then in a position to choose which ones you want to use with your pupils. But at this point you may want to think about how to sequence the activities you have chosen so there are meaningful links between them from the pupils' point of view.

Sequencing activities

Task 2 Sequencing activities

■ Activities 1 and 16 are taken at random from the web on page 120. They are not directly linked to each other. Choose two other activities from the web or think of two more activities which could be directly linked to (precede or follow) either Activity 1 or Activity 16.

■ What are the advantages of linking activities?

Planning sheet

Topic: Wild animals   Class: 3 (age about 9–10)

Activity 1: Recording animals' height

Objectives and activity	Language focus: vocabulary and structures	Skills and functions	Pronunciation	Notes
– To find and interpret information on animals' sizes from books – To measure and record the height of animals on paper or the wall – To develop confidence in getting information from books in English	**Receptive (recycled)** Vocabulary related to size, height, length, numbers in metres and cm *deer, wolf* **New vocabulary** Unfamiliar animals' names, eg *camel, zebra* **Structures** *It is 2 metres tall.* *Its tail is 50 cm long.* *Its neck is … long.*	**Reading skills** – Finding appropriate books – Finding key information about animals' sizes/heights in library books – Recording the information about sizes on a grid **Measuring skills** Using a measuring rod/tape measure to record the heights of animals on paper and label with the sizes	Final consonant clusters, eg in *length*	Links with maths – estimating and measuring skills Organization: in pairs and then compare answers with other members of the group before recording animals' heights on paper or on the wall Children can help teacher later stick them on the wall

Activity 16: Make and describe an imaginary animal

Objectives and activity	Language focus: vocabulary and structures	Skills and functions	Pronunciation	Notes
– To make an imaginary animal from given body parts – To describe your animal orally to the group or class – To identify the animal described	**Productive (recycled)** Names of animals: *deer, tiger, eagle, fox, bear, elephant* Names of parts of animal's body: *ears, tail, legs, fur, head, horns, trunk, tusks, feet* Tenses: present simple, eg *It lives in a jungle.* *Its name is ...* *It has a tail.* **New language** *It has an elephant's tail.* *It has an eagle's legs.* *Who is it?*	Manipulation skills Decision making, eg choosing body parts Oral skills, eg describing Listening skills, eg listening for key points Collaborating with other pupils, eg choosing relevant animal from a set of pictures **Functions** Describing what an animal looks like	Pronunciation of possessive *'s*, eg *deer's, elephant's* Revision of /ɔː/ as in *horn*	Art work, eg make an animal by sticking together different parts of different animals Organization: work in small groups

Commentary ■ ■ ■

If you chose Activity 1, you could precede it with an activity where children had to first estimate the heights of a chosen group of animals. In Activity 1, they could then check if their estimates were correct or not. After they had completed Activity 1, they could practise making oral or written comparisons (Activity 2 in the web) between the animals on the height line, eg *A zebra is taller than a deer.* They could then play a problem-solving game in which they had to work out the animal from the description, eg *It's shorter than an elephant. It's taller than a deer. What is it?*

If you chose Activity 16, you could precede this with Activity 15 which introduces the idea of an imaginary animal through a listening activity and so provides a model of how to describe it. You could then follow Activity 16 with guided written descriptions of the imaginary animals. These could be later used as a game in which pupils had to match written descriptions to the pictures of the animals.

If we create meaningful links between activities, the purpose of doing the activities will seem clearer and may make more sense to pupils. For example, if children estimate animals' heights first, this then gives them a reason for searching through library books to find out if their guesses are correct. This may lead to greater involvement and understanding.

Guidelines for sequencing

Our decisions about how to sequence activities are based on assumptions about how children learn. So the way we sequence activities may affect the way children respond to and process information in the activities. The criteria used in sequencing above include:

- moving from receptive to productive skills, eg listening to speaking
- activity dependency, eg pupils need to predict the heights of the animals before they can check the heights in library books; in other words, one activity depends on the outcome of the previous activity
- cognitive complexity – simple to more complex, eg guessing to problem solving
- moving from linguistically controlled to more free, eg from writing a description using given vocabulary to writing without any language help
- going from concrete (hands on) to abstract, eg making something and describing it then imagining something and describing it. ■

Outcomes of activities for pupils

« Outcomes p89 In carrying out different activities, children will produce different kinds of outcome, eg a story, a drawing, a play, a correct guess. These products or outcomes are records of the work carried out and they provide a way for children to communicate ideas to others.

Task 3 Identifying outcomes for activities

Below there are two different products or outcomes created by pupils for the topic on wild animals.

- What was the activity which led to the outcomes? (Check the topic web on page 120)
- Who could be the audiences for the outcomes?
- Suggest some more possible outcomes from each activity.

Name of animal	What is it like?			Can it				
	Colour	Size	Body	run?	jump?	walk?	swim?	climb trees?
giraffe	brown with spots	5½ metres high	long legs, long neck, horns	✔	?	✔		
tiger	brown, black + white stripes	1 metre high, 2 metres long	long body, long tail, whiskers	✔	✔	✔	?	
elephant	grey	3½ metre high	big body, big ears, trunk	✔	–	✔	?	

It's got a tiger's head. It's got a giraffe's body, a bird's wings. Which one?

Commentary ■ ■ ■

Outcome (product)	Activity	Possible audience
Animal pictures made up of different parts Correct guesses (guessing which animal is being described by the other group)	Make imaginary animals from different body parts and then each group takes it in turns to describe an animal orally looking at all the animals produced. Other pupils then have to guess which animal is being described. (Activity 16)	Other pupils in the class are the audience for the descriptions. Also pupils in other classes.
Grids of information on animals seen in zoo, park or wild-life video	Pupils observe and record information in grids while at zoo or park. (Activity 6)	Other pupils in same class or school; parents on Open Day

The activities in the topic web could all lead to different outcomes. For example, the drama could be produced as a written play and the zoo visit could lead to the development of stories or poems or reports rather than grids. It is also possible to vary the nature of the outcome for the class. Instead of all the pupils producing the same outcome, eg one grid, each group could produce their own, which would give you several different wall charts, or each group could produce a different *type* of outcome, depending on their choice. This gives pupils more choice and responsibility. ■

In topic work, pupils learn how to work together, how to find out information, how to manage their work and present it. The emphasis is on the process of learning and so we could say that one outcome is the development of *process* skills. For example, in Activity 1 it may lead to increased confidence in finding information in English. But it is also important for pupils that there are some definite end *products* or *outcomes* of the topic work. They will have a record of their work for their own satisfaction. They can also present their work publicly for others to see, which provides a real stimulus for checking and putting effort into the presentation. This is very important for language learning because it encourages close attention to language, in particular, accuracy. Outcomes also provide you with an indication of pupils' performance, which is a record of progress and can be used for assessment purposes.

>> Chapter 11

Starting points for topic work

If you can think of an interesting way of beginning your topic work, you will arouse pupils' curiosity and make them eager to take part. The frogs, for example, that the children brought into the classroom in the cartoon at the beginning of the chapter would make an excellent starting point for discussion.

Task 4   Choosing starting points

Below are three starting points for the topic work on wild animals.

■ Consider the advantages and disadvantages of each one.
■ Which one would be most suitable for your learning situation?
■ What questions could you ask pupils to stimulate discussion for starting point **A**?

A A visit to a zoo or park during which pupils observe, draw and make notes of animals they see, using a grid for recording. If you have no access to a zoo, you could focus on local wild animals, eg mini-beasts (beetles, snails, worms, woodlice, etc).

B The teacher tells a story about a wild animal, eg *The Enormous Crocodile* by Roald Dahl[3].

C A display of a jungle scene with different animals

Commentary ■ ■ ■

Advantages	Disadvantages
A Provides pupils with first-hand experience of wild animals. Gives pupils the opportunity to develop observation skills and find out things for themselves. Is likely to be very memorable and exciting for children. The experience is likely to encourage pupils to raise questions, which provides a good lead-in to the topic.	**A** There may be no zoo or park within easy access. It requires a great deal of organization to be successful. There is a large amount of information for pupils to take in. There are many opportunities for distraction and children getting noisy. Teacher may need help in escorting children. Much of the discussion between children may be in L1.
B Stories are very meaningful and enjoyable for children. It is easy to set up and organize. A well-chosen story can stimulate and arouse pupils' curiosity. It gives plenty of opportunities for language exposure and use.	**B** The story is chosen by the teacher. Questions to stimulate curiosity and thinking need careful preparation.
C Colourful displays attract children's attention. Children could easily be involved in helping to make the display. The display could be developed gradually over a period of time.	**C** It means a great deal of initial work and preparation by the teacher with perhaps limited opportunities for language use. It may not generate many questions from pupils unless there is something to stimulate their thinking. It may be difficult to organize for teachers who do not have their own classrooms or who share classrooms. Children lose interest in displays after a while.

In deciding which would be the most suitable option for you, there will be a number of things to consider. For example, although you may be attracted by the idea of taking pupils to a park or zoo, it may not be practical in your situation. However it is always possible to focus on what are sometimes called 'mini-beasts', the small animals which can be found around many school gardens, eg worms, snails, woodlice, etc. You have to weigh up the advantages and disadvantages of each option: the amount of time available; the number in the class; who would be available to help in taking the children on a visit; the amount of language practice it would provide and so on. It may be that in terms of opportunities for language exposure and practice, you can achieve more by telling pupils a story. The important thing, however, is to know why you have chosen a particular option and to be able to justify it in terms of your overall goals.

To stimulate discussion for the zoo/park visit, here are some suggested questions. These are not the only possible ones. If you know your class well, then you can relate your questions to their specific interests and experiences. The questions are designed to stimulate thinking and to draw on children's background knowledge and experience. If children have limited English, accept answers in the L1 and then rephrase them. Highlight key words you want them to learn. Before the visit ask:

> *Have you been to a zoo before? What animals did you see? Big/small?*
> *Which animal did you like best? Why?*
> *What does it look like? What does it eat?*
> *Where do the animals live in the zoo? Is that their real home?*
> *Why are the animals in the zoo? Are they happy/sad?*
> *What animals will we see in the zoo tomorrow?* ■

3 How to organize topic work

There can be a lot of work involved in organizing topic work. So it is best to start small. Begin with a small project that takes only two or three lessons, perhaps linked to your coursebook. If it is successful, this will give you confidence to try a slightly longer project.

In the following section we will consider some of the important things you need to decide or organize in planning for topic work.

How much time do I need?

- Plan how long you want to spend on topic work.
- Prepare an overall plan of activities in sequence.

Task 5   How long does it take?

Here is an example of a set of activities for one week based on zoo animals. It assumes that children will visit a zoo and that the class will have three or four lessons a week.

- How long would you need to do these activities?
- Which of these activities would you keep and which would you change?

Week 1
– Visit to zoo. Observe and record information on animals in grids.
– Make class grid with information collected.
– Play 'Guess what it is': oral description of animals based on grid information.
– Make animal masks based on animals seen in zoo and described in the game above.
– Create role plays or mini-dramas using masks.
– Sing *The Lion King* song.

Commentary ■ ■ ■

How long you would need depends on whether you have special lessons for English, how long they are and how many you have a week. If you only have two or three non-consecutive lessons per week, each lesson will need to be self-contained, as children may not remember activities if you carry them over from two or three days ago.

Which activities you do will depend on the level of your pupils, their needs and interests and your teaching/learning goals. For example, your pupils may have well-developed reading and writing skills and so you may wish to include activities which use reading and writing, eg make class booklets about animals. ■

What materials do I need?

- Decide what materials you need to carry out the activities.
- To reduce the burden of making materials, think about how the children can help. What can they make or bring to class?

Activity	Resource	Where from?
Tell Lion's party story (Activity 17)	Pictures or models of wild animals	School library, magazines, or ask children to bring in pictures or model animals.
Make an imaginary animal from parts (Activity 16)	Paper, glue and scissors	Draw one set of six different animals and photocopy it to make six sets. Children can colour them. Alternatively children can draw different animals and then cut up the parts.

- Make a similar chart and complete it for some of the other activities in the topic web above.

Monitoring and recording children's progress

» Organizing assessment p157

- Keep records of *how* children work (the learning process) as well as of the outcomes of their work during the topic. If time is limited, just monitor a few activities closely and keep brief notes on each child. Alternatively, focus on four or five children in each lesson so that by the end of the topic you have notes on each child's performance in some activities.

Activity: Make and describe an imaginary animal   Organization: Group

Name of pupil	Evidence of learning	Comments
Carla	Did not say much in English but clearly understood what to do. Helped to make an animal. Laughed a lot.	Lacks confidence to express herself. Has limited productive language. Needs more language preparation and a supportive partner for next oral activity.

Classroom organization

- Decide how you will organize pupils for each activity, remembering to vary ways of working in a lesson, eg whole class>pair>group>individual>whole class.

Here are some suggestions on the type of organization that may be suitable for particular procedures or types of activity:

Organization	Procedures/types of activity
Whole class	starting things off setting tasks demonstrating giving feedback story telling getting opinions
Pairwork	communication games oral practice activities paired reading helping a partner joint writing
Groupwork	problem-solving tasks discussion/planning making things group writing surveys communication games
Individual work	thinking activities independent writing copying drawing and observing reading a book

Task 6   How shall I organize children for these activities?

- How would you organize children for the following activities, taken from the topic web?
  Listen and draw an imaginary animal (Activity 15)
  Make and describe imaginary animals (Activity 16)

Commentary ■ ■ ■

Here are some suggested ways of organizing children for two of the activities from the topic web. These are not the only ways and you may have good reasons for arranging children differently.

Listen and draw imaginary animals (Activity 15)

This could be done as a whole-class activity with children working individually to listen and follow instructions. After they have finished they could compare answers in pairs. The reason for this type of organization is because children need to concentrate quite hard on listening in order to get the information. This is best done individually, without any distractions.

Make and describe imaginary animals (Activity 16)

Children could be organized as a whole class first as the teacher demonstrates how to make the animals. They could then work in small groups to make their animals, but later return to the whole-class organization so that the teacher could demonstrate the next part of the activity. Children could then move back into their groups and take it in turns to describe one of the animals they had made while other children guessed which animal it was. This could be followed by a whole-class activity where a group has to describe an animal chosen from any group and the group which identifies the animal first gains a point. So the organization would be: whole class>group>whole class>group>whole class.

The reason for this type of organization is that children all need to understand what they are going to do and how to do the activity. Whole-class organization enables the teacher to give instructions and demonstrations to all children at one time. It also enables the teacher to control the class more easily and ensure that children are attending. Children who may be slow to understand can be supported by seeing their peers taking part in demonstrations. However opportunities for children to practise are limited in whole-class organization. They need to move into groups so that they get the chance to carry out the activities themselves. This also encourages collaboration among pupils. In this activity, I suggest breaking down the teacher's instructions into two stages, ie the making of the animals and then describing the animals, to make it easier for pupils to remember. They might otherwise have difficulty remembering all the instructions as the activity has two parts. I suggest a return to whole-class organization at the end of the activity as a useful way of getting feedback on children's performance. It also allows the teacher to end the activity or lesson in an orderly and focused way, which is particularly important with younger children who may not yet be able to regulate their own behaviour. ■

How to group children?

- For group work, you need to think about *how* to group children. This can be according to:
  - friendship
  - ability
  - mixed ability
  - shared interest

« Chapter 3
- Change your groupings from time to time so children get a chance to work with different children and are not labelled as belonging to a weak or strong group.

Task 7 Grouping children

■ How would you group children for the following activities?
Observe and record animals (Activity 6)
Make and describe an imaginary animal (Activity 16)

Commentary ■ ■ ■

For *Observe and record*, you could use friendship pairs, as children are more likely to co-operate. You don't want to have to deal with discipline problems when children are out of the classroom in a zoo or park and less easy to control.

For *Make and describe an imaginary animal*, you could use mixed-ability groups so that children with stronger oral skills could support those who are weaker. However you would need to consider ways of ensuring that each group member contributed to the activity so that one or two did not dominate. For example each child might have to choose an animal part to contribute to making the animal.

There is no simple solution to grouping as a lot depends on the way particular children relate to each other and friendship patterns can change. However you can train children to work together in more co-operative ways provided they understand the purpose of working « p53 with others. ∎

If you have already used topic work before, plan a topic, but introduce some change in the way you do it based on any new perspectives you have gained from this chapter. If you are new to topic work, try out the task below with a friend.

Action plan

Aim: To try out topic work in your class.

Procedure

- Try to find someone to work with or share your ideas with.
- Make a list of possible topics. If you use a textbook, choose a topic linked to your » Display p146 textbook, eg at the end of *Bravo Book 1*[4], there is nice picture of the seaside. This could lead in to a topic on *holidays* or *the seaside*.
- Think of an interesting starting point to introduce the topic to pupils, eg Anna Mousou writing in JET magazine[5] got children to bring in their animal toys and books with animals as a way of starting a project on animals.
- See how pupils respond and what ideas they generate.
- Plan a few linked activities based around the topic which practise the language and skills needed in your textbook. Give children the opportunity to use the language they already have in less controlled activities.
- Plan one major outcome, eg making story books or putting on a drama or puppet play.
- Evaluate it by asking children's opinions, eg
  - *Did you enjoy it?*
  - *What did you like best? Why?*
  - *What did you learn?*
  and by asking yourself questions such as
  - *What went well and why?*
  - *What did not work well and why?*
  - *What would you change for next time?*
  - *What have you learned about topic work?*

---

4   The benefits and problems of using topic work

In Chapter 1, we looked at a list of conditions which are needed in order to create the kind of learning environment where children can make use of their natural abilities to learn English. Let us see which conditions are particularly supported by topic work and let us also look at some of the problems which may prevent topic work from creating these conditions.

Task 8   Identifying conditions supported by topic work

∎ Decide which of the following conditions for creating a good learning environment can be strongly supported through topic work.
  - create a real need and desire to use English
  - provide sufficient time for English
  - provide exposure to varied and meaningful input with a focus on communication
  - create a friendly atmosphere in which pupils can take risks and enjoy their learning
  - provide opportunities for children to experiment with their new language
  - provide plenty of opportunities to practise and use the language in different contexts
  - provide feedback on learning
  - help children notice the underlying pattern in language

Commentary ■ ■ ■

Create a real need and desire to use English

Topic work can do this. It is usually based on things which interest children, it provides experiences which involve them physically and mentally, and provides real reasons for communicating their ideas.

Provide sufficient time for English

Not necessarily. It depends on how much time is allocated for English lessons

Provide exposure to varied and meaningful input with a focus on communication

Topic work does this through providing a variety of activities based on the topic and through the emphasis on using English in a purposeful way to find out, do things and communicate the results to others.

Create a friendly atmosphere in which pupils can take risks and enjoy their learning

Yes, but only if the topic is one that really interests pupils, and the teacher shows genuine interest in children's ideas and supports their attempts to communicate.

Provide opportunities for children to experiment with their new language

Yes, because of the focus on communicating and sharing ideas which encourages children to express their meaning using whatever language they have.

Provide plenty of opportunities to practise and use the language in different contexts

Yes, through the large variety of activities based on the topic.

Provide feedback on learning

Plenty of opportunities are available but it will depend on the teacher making use of these. Feedback is not automatic.

Help children notice the underlying pattern in language

Plenty of opportunities are available because of the varied input, but it will depend on the teacher explicitly drawing children's attention to language. It will not happen automatically because of the heavy emphasis on communication. ■

Topic work seems to supply many of the conditions needed to enable children to make use of their natural learning abilities in learning English. However, it does depend on the way in which it is implemented.

You need to look critically at any new approach so that if you decide to adopt it, you do so in a clear and informed way. This means understanding the benefits and problems from an educational and practical point of view as well as from your personal perspective.

Here are some problems commonly voiced by teachers who are unsure about introducing topic work in their situation, together with some possible solutions.

Problems	Suggested solutions
I am a specialist English teacher with no knowledge of the general primary curriculum.	Try to plan together with the class teacher or subject teachers. If class teachers are too busy to plan jointly, get their advice on what skills and concepts children have already developed and what activities to use. Alternatively use a story as the basis for your topic work and develop a set of activities around the main theme of the story, eg vegetables in *The Great Big Enormous Turnip*.
My pupils cannot work independently.	Plan for gradual independence. Introduce them to decision making gradually once they have got used to the idea of topic work.
It does not allow systematic coverage of the basic English syllabus.	To avoid this problem combine topic work with the use of a coursebook which will provide coverage of a basic vocabulary, structures, functions, etc. Do topic work once a month or once every two months as a way of recycling language already introduced to children. This is an interesting way of revising core items in the syllabus and can easily be justified to the school.
Children get so involved and excited in the activity that they tend to use the L1 to communicate.	Build in different stages to the activity: the initial stage will involve children finding out / exchanging ideas (focus on fluency where they may naturally use L1 or a mixture of L1/L2); later stages could involve children in planning how to present their ideas (attending to the language) and then presenting to an audience (focus on careful presentation and accuracy).
I have limited resources.	You don't need vast resources. Get children to bring things in, eg pictures, postcards, objects. Ask factories, shops, printing works for spare materials, eg paper, adverts, boxes.

>> See Chapter 12 for ideas on developing independence.

In general, there are more advantages than disadvantages in using topic work. Its main value is that it enables teachers to plan for learning in ways which support and build on how children learn in general and how they learn languages.

Summary

In this chapter, you have considered:

- *what topic work is:* a way of organizing children's language learning based around topics or themes of interest to children. Activities linked to the topic can help children to develop their language, skills and concepts across all the subjects of the curriculum.
- *a framework within which to plan and organize for topic work.* This includes different aspects such as choosing a topic, selecting activities, sequencing activities, analysing the language/skills, etc in activities, identifying outcomes and starting points for topic work. For each aspect, you were encouraged to consider factors which might influence your decisions and to think about reasons for choices made in planning.

- *how to organize topic work*. Careful organization is crucial in order for topic work to be successful and this involves decisions about time available and time needed, resources needed, ways of monitoring progress, organizing children for learning and grouping children.
- *the benefits and problems of topic work*. Topic work has the potential to create many of the conditions needed to support children's language learning, though this depends on the way it is implemented. Common problems teachers face in using topic work include lack of knowledge of the primary curriculum and difficulties in getting children to work independently. Possible solutions include collaboration with class/other teachers and learner training. A deeper understanding of the benefits and problems of topic work will help to make the decision to adopt topic work a principled and not merely an enthusiastic choice.

An important implication which arises from this chapter is that topic work has considerable potential as an approach to teaching young learners. However, its effectiveness depends on the way you put it into practice in the classroom. This, in turn, depends on your understanding of and belief in the principles which form the basis of topic work. You can develop your own understanding of these principles if you constantly make active links between them, your teaching and your beliefs about children's language learning. By making these connections you will be able to identify both the benefits and problems of using topic work, and so make principled changes to your teaching. You will not be doing topic work just because other teachers or professionals tell you it is a good thing, but because you believe it is an appropriate choice for your learners and you know why.

References

1 Clemson, D. and Clemson, W. 1989 *The Really Practical Guide to the National Curriculum 5-11*. Cheltenham: Stanley Thorne
This is a practical book with a useful section on topic work (based on the British primary curriculum).
2 A group of Hungarian primary teachers have produced a set of topic-based materials for 7–11 year olds. *Theme Pack: Islands; Theme Pack: Growing.* Swan Communications/Max Hueber Verlag.
3 Dahl, R. 1980 *The Enormous Crocodile*. Harmondsworth: Puffin Books
A delightful story about a very nasty crocodile.
4 West, J. 1993 *Bravo Book 1*. Oxford: Heinemann
5 Mousou, A. 1994 'Learning about animals.' In *JET* vol. 4, no. 3

Chapter 10 Can we make a spinner?

Involving children in making and using resources

As we discussed in Chapter 1, children learn directly through first-hand experiences, such as observing and recording information about wild animals, and through practical activities like action games and making things. Language accompanies or grows out of the experience or activity. This enables children to associate meaning with the words used. The focus is on meaning, and there is rich input for language learning and many opportunities for communicating in English. But this kind of activity requires resources. We need to consider the type of resources which will enable children to learn in this way and how we can organize and use them most effectively. In this chapter, we will consider:

1 **What are teaching/learning resources?**
2 **Making and using your own resources**
3 **Using pupils as resources**
4 **Organizing resources in ways which involve pupils**
5 **The use of classroom display to create an attractive and dynamic learning environment**

The aim of this chapter is to think about what resources are, why you use them and how you can involve children not just in using them but also making and managing them. It encourages you to reflect on the way you use resources which provides a means of examining your beliefs about children and their learning in relation to your teaching.

1   What are teaching/learning resources?

I shall take a broad definition of resources in this book and consider them as anything which can assist the teaching/learning process, either human or material. This would include: pupils themselves, adults, equipment, objects, manufactured materials (eg paper, erasers, glue), text-based materials (eg textbooks, readers) and visuals (eg charts, pictures). If we take a narrower definition, we might focus on what are traditionally known as teaching/learning aids, ie visuals, objects, realia or mainly non-text-based materials which support the learning process.

Resources can be:

- bought by you, the pupils or the school, eg glue, pencils, coloured pens
- made by you or your pupils, eg flash cards, pictures, puppets
- collected by you or the children from nature, eg leaves, pebbles, sticks
- donated free by companies, eg posters, advertisements, empty boxes, containers, pieces of wood (from saw mills)
- people – you yourself, other people in school or invited to class, pupils.

Consider what effect it has on pupils if they are involved in making and managing resources. They are likely, for example, to feel more interested in using the resources and to have more concern for looking after them. They will also get more opportunity to practise their English, for example, when you instruct them how to make the resources or they read the labels on storage jars and tins in order to put a 'resource' (eg a spinner) away at the end of a session. Even in a teaching situation which does not allow much freedom to experiment, there are many simple ways in which pupils can be involved, eg in colouring in the pictures to be used as flash cards.

Here are some questions which you could use to check on how far children are involved in

« Chapter 7 materials

making and managing resources in your classroom.

- Who normally makes the resources you use?
- Are children consulted about how resources are used and where they are stored?
- Are all or some of the resources accessible to children at any time?

The theme of pupils' involvement in the making and use of resources will run through this chapter.

2   Making and using your own resources

Resources which you make cost money, time and effort so make sure they are worth the effort you and your pupils may put into making them. Let's consider why we should go to the trouble of making a resource and what sort of resources we might make rather than buy.

Task 1   What type of resource should we make?

- What type of resource would you be likely to make yourself or with pupils' help and why?
- Below are two examples of teachers using resources they have made (a worksheet and a spinner). For each lesson, decide:
  – Why is the teacher using the resource in her lesson?
  – Is the resource really needed in the lesson?
  – Can the resource be re-used? If so, how?
  – Can the resource be made by children?
  – How would children benefit from making and using the resource?

LESSON A: Worksheet

Below left is a worksheet made by a primary teacher for a lesson on everyday activities for (eight-year-old) children in their second year of learning English.

Here is how the worksheet fits into the lesson plan:

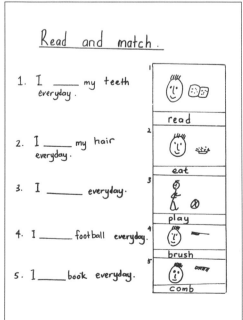

Activity	Resources
1 Introduce everyday activities, eg *I brush my teeth.*	Calendar, picture cards to show everyday activities
2 Group drill	Pupils
3 Number pictures. Pupils call out the number of the picture when the teacher describes an activity.	Same picture cards (numbered)
4 Choose an activity and mime it. Pupils have to guess the activity.	Pupils
5 Pupils match pictures and sentence strips.	Sentence strips and pictures (as above)
6 Song about everyday activities.	Pupils
7 Worksheet – read and fill in the blank with the correct word.	Worksheet

LESSON B: Spinner[1]

Another primary teacher is planning to finish a topic on domestic animals. In this lesson, she plans to introduce and model some descriptions. In the last part of the lesson, she wants children to practise in small groups. Each child will take a turn to spin the spinner. He/she has to say three true things about the animal which the spinner points to, eg *It has a tail. It likes milk. It has whiskers.* If a spinner lands on the same animal twice, the second child must not repeat what has been said before.

Commentary ■ ■ ■

Your previous experience may affect your choice. If you have taught children before, then you may have made a large number of concrete things which allow children to do 'hands on' practical activities, to use their bodies, to manipulate, to imagine. If you have taught adults before, it is likely that your range of resources may be more limited and perhaps be more text-based. Though adults may enjoy learning with a variety of resources, they are more capable of learning with the help of purely text-based resources than children.

One reason that teachers make their own resources is that resources they make themselves are designed for their particular pupils, to suit their needs and interests at particular points in the learning programme. In Lesson A, the teacher is using the worksheet to help pupils consolidate the language they practised earlier in the lesson. In Lesson B, the teacher is using the spinner to provide a stimulus for freer practice of oral descriptions.

In Lesson A, the worksheet may help to reinforce the vocabulary and structures practised earlier, and it gives each child a chance to do this individually. However it does not seem strictly necessary, as the teacher could write the work on the blackboard or on a chart for children to copy into their books. If we consider that the teacher may have taken 30 minutes or so to complete the worksheet and then needs to photocopy it, it does not seem worth the effort and cost.

In Lesson B, there is a much clearer justification for the spinners, particularly if pupils could be involved in making them. It introduces a game-like element into the practice which makes the activity more purposeful and enjoyable for the pupils.

The worksheet is only useful for this particular lesson and once it has been completed there is not much further use for it, apart from as a record for the children and maybe their parents. The way in which the worksheet has been designed makes it fixed, which limits its flexibility as a resource. A creative teacher can probably find more uses for it, eg *Guess which picture I am thinking of* but, on the whole, it has restricted use in its present form.

The spinner, on the other hand, is much more flexible and can be re-used many times.

- Children can help in planning how to use them.
- Even with a fixed content, eg animal pictures, it can be used for many different activities with the same pupils, eg *Mime the animal. Say the noise of the animal. Describe the animal.*
- If numbers or colours are used on the spinner, then it can be used for an even greater variety of purposes. The numbers or colours can then refer to sets of cards which contain questions, sentences, instructions words, pictures related to what the teacher wants pupils to practise.
- It can be used with a variety of different age groups.

Here are some examples of activities that can be used with a spinner.

Story telling (spinner with pictures of six different characters on it, eg *a monster, a dog, a boy, a girl, a bird, a woman*)	Pupils take it in turns to spin. They have to make up a story which includes whichever character the spinner indicates. The next pupil continues the story and introduces the character the spinner indicates and so on.
Question words (spinner with a question word written on each section, eg *What, When, Where, Why, Where, How, Yes/No*)	Teacher either tells pupils a story or they read a story first. Then they take it in turns to spin. Pupils have to make up a question based on the story starting with the question word the spinner indicates. For *Yes/No* they have to make up a question to which the answer is *Yes* or *No*.
Parts of the body (spinner with pictures of parts of the body, eg *leg, hand, arm, head, finger, eyes*)	Each pupil in the group has to make up an instruction related to the part of the body the spinner indicates, eg *Raise your leg. Put your hand on your ear.* Other pupils carry out the instructions.

Both resources could be made by children. A worksheet could be produced by children provided they had a model to work from. In fact, this would make the use of worksheets much more dynamic and productive. For example, you could add a second part to the worksheet such as this: *Now in pairs make up some more examples for your friends to do.*

By doing this, you have given children a model or pattern in part 1 of the worksheet, and then asked them to produce their own examples in part 2. So you are encouraging them to use their thinking skills to work out the pattern, eg to make up a sentence which describes an everyday activity and to leave a gap for the verb; to pay attention to language (how the sentences are formed); to develop productive skills, ie writing. By getting them to produce their own examples for friends to do, you are giving them a reason for completing the worksheet, ie they have to find out not just how to complete the sentences but how to make their own. You could also build in a feedback stage so that children have a chance to correct any mistakes in the worksheets they produce for their friends.

Making a spinner is a 'hands on' practical activity and therefore ideal for language learning provided it involves using language. If children have to follow instructions in order to make them, this creates a real purpose for listening or reading and they are getting meaningful input for language learning at the same time. If children have been involved in making the spinners, they will be very excited to use them. ■

The two examples above suggest that it is helpful to think about what sort of resources are most productive in terms of their range of uses and which are most likely to create the kind of conditions which stimulate children's language learning.

Here is a checklist of questions you could ask yourself when selecting or making learning resources.

- Do I know why I am using the resource for teaching?
- Is the resource appropriate for my purpose?
- Is my time in making the resource justified?
- Is it easy to store?
- Will it engage the children for a sufficient length of time?
- Is it cheap to buy/make?

- Is it productive, ie can it be used for many different purposes?
- Can children be involved in making or preparing it?
- Will children's language learning benefit from making or using it?

Action plan

Aim: To find out if you are making the best use of resources.

Procedure

- Identify a lesson you plan to teach which uses several resources.
- Apply the checklist above.
- Teach the lesson.
- Reflect on how the lesson went, focusing on your use of resources:
  - Which resources did children respond to best? Why?
  - Which resource was most useful for language learning?
  - Which resource worked least well and why?
  - What changes would I make in my use of resources if I taught this lesson again?

Thinking about why you used particular resources and whether they had the desired effect can provide you with a useful way of being thoughtful about your teaching.

Here are some reflections made by Zsuzsa Kuti, a Hungarian primary English teacher, on the resources she used in the first lesson of a series based on the life cycle of the butterfly. Her pupils are eight to nine years old.

LESSON OBJECTIVES (English):

- *to provide information about the life cycle of the butterfly*
- *to activate children's knowledge on the above topic*
- *to develop children's reading comprehension by completing a worksheet*
- *to develop children's comprehension through shared reading*
- *to improve children's oral fluency in a role play*

Which resources did children respond to best? Why?

The most popular teaching materials in this lesson I consider to be the chart of pictures, the worksheet, the story book and the puppets.

PUPPETS

This time the children were especially interested in playing with the caterpillars as they were slowly pulled out from a magic bag. They all appreciated my home-made puppets and had a good laugh when they were revealed from the bag. This initial fun element seemed to help to reduce the pressures of real-time communication so when it came to the children's turn to play with the puppets they were all eager to take one of the roles. They seemed to be very happy to use the puppets, which reduced the linguistic demands which the role play placed on the learners.

In one of the following lessons the puppets were used again in another role-play activity with an extended version of the dialogue which seemed to please the children a lot.

Which resource worked least well and why?

There was maybe only one area which seemed to me a bit problematic. In the last activity the children were invited to take part in an action song which was accompanied by body movements. Some of the children (more mature boys) appeared to be reluctant in using their hands to do some actions first. This was not the first time that it happened so it did not take me by surprise. When I asked for the reason on a previous occasion they claimed that this was 'too childish' and they would rather just sing along. In this lesson, though, as they saw the others having fun they joined in and took part in the action song voluntarily.

What changes would I make in my use of resources if I taught this lesson again?

To provide more opportunities for individual learning, I would probably prepare more sets of pictures and wordcards for the stages of the life cycle of the butterfly next time. This way children could work out the order and the labelling in pairs and checking could be done together as a whole-group activity. I think this would be particularly useful since the children found this task so challenging that on the following day one girl came up to me to ask whether the stages (caterpillar–cocoon) were really correct the previous day or it should be the other way around (cocoon–caterpillar).

When a child brought in an encyclopaedia about animals (in the mother tongue) the following day it occurred to me that some scientific background would have been also useful at this stage to back up our learning. Building on the child's initiative I immediately set a project for the children to collect more information about butterflies from various books on nature which they did eagerly. When the children had discussed their findings in English, these books were displayed in the classroom….

Reflecting explicitly about our use of resources is not something teachers have time to do very often. But Zsuzsa Kuti's comments show how helpful this process can be for teachers' own development. The process involves putting into words (articulating for yourself) what we are trying to do, why we are doing it, then using feedback from our lesson to consider how we might do it differently. These help to reshape and extend our own knowledge. Either writing down our ideas, as Zsuzsa Kuti did, or telling them to someone else brings them out into the open so that we or others can consider them. In the process, they may get modified in some way. For example, if Zsuzsa Kuti had not asked herself which resources did not work so well, perhaps she would not have remembered the incident with the two boys. Now that she is aware of some pupils' sensitivity, she may have modified her ideas of what may be suitable for her age group or may be more alert to differences among pupils. So the process of articulation has helped to change her knowledge about resources.

3   Using pupils as resources

What is under our noses and under-used as a resource for teaching English? The answer is, of course, children. They are there all the time which is why we may not think of them as a resource. There is a double benefit in making use of children as resources: you benefit from the use of a resource which costs nothing and is constantly available; children benefit from being more involved in the language-learning process and having more chances to practise English. Here are some of the roles they can play in the classroom:

1   they can act as partners for other children to practise language
2   they can act as tutors to help each other learn English
3   they can act as models or demonstrators to help you show other children what to do
4   they can act as makers of learning resources for other children to use
5   they can use their bodies as resources.

We will now look at examples of how children can act in these roles.

Task 2   Using children as a resource

■ Match each of the five roles (1–5) above to an example below. Think of another example for each one.

A Here is an example of an instruction card which 12-year-old pupils have made for 10-year-old pupils to read and carry out.

> Tshering pelden ①
>
> Thursday 20 August.
>
> Draw two witches in the cave.
> Draw witches eating bones and
> drinking mens bloody. It is very bad

B Two children, Françoise and Pierre are seated side by side reading a book. Pierre is reading aloud while Françoise listens carefully. When Pierre pauses or gets stuck she prompts him, eg

> **P** And Father Bear said, 'Who's been eating my ...?'
> **F** Read the sentence again.
> **P** And Father Bear said, 'Who been eating my p...?'
> **F** Look at the picture. What is in the bowl?
> **P** *Porridge.*

C Françoise and Pierre are seated facing each other. They are carrying out a pairwork activity from *English Club*[2]. They have drawn a suitcase on their papers and six items of clothing in it. They are now asking each other questions to try to guess what their partner has in his/her suitcase. They have eight guesses.

D The teacher is in front of the class giving instructions to the pupils, such as *Make your body like a pair of scissors.*

E Françoise has been called out by the teacher to demonstrate a role play on shopping. The dialogue is on the board.

> **T** Can I help you?
> **P** Have you any eggs?
> **T** How many do you want?
> **P** Six please.
> **T** Here you are.

Commentary ■ ■ ■

Example A   Role 4. Here children are creating resources to be used by other children. There are many other ways they can help you in creating resources, eg drawing and colouring pictures, helping to collect things for and make displays.

Example B   Role 2. Here Françoise, who is a stronger reader, is helping Pierre with his reading. She is prompting him when he gets stuck. In a class of 25–30 pupils you would never have time to give such individual attention to each child. Pupils can help each other in many ways provided the task you give them to do is not too difficult.

Example C   Role 1. Here children are working in pairs to find out what items of clothing they each have. By acting as partners, they are providing practice opportunities for each other.

Example D   Role 5. Pupils are playing the machine game in which they have to make their bodies act like an object or part of a machine. In the scissors example, each pupil tries to make his/her body act like a pair of scissors. If machines are chosen, eg *car* then pupils act in groups to form the parts of the car. They are using their bodies as a resource.

Example E   Role 3. The teacher is using one pupil to demonstrate to others what to do in the activity. This gives children a chance to see how to do the activity.

Action plan

Aim: To extend pupils' roles in the classroom.

Procedure

- When you plan your next lesson, check which of the above roles you are giving to pupils.
- Plan to get pupils to carry out a role you do not normally use, eg child as peer tutor.
- Ask pupils what they liked or disliked about it.
- Monitor the effect on their performance.

---

4   Organizing resources in ways which involve pupils

The way we organize our resources and equipment in the classroom may seem unimportant. But, in fact, it reflects our beliefs about the role of resources in the teaching and learning process and about how they should be managed. Where do we store our resources? Are they kept in locked cupboards and brought out when needed, or are they accessible to pupils? Of course, it is not quite so simple as that because we do not all have our own classrooms and may need to carry our resources around with us. Nevertheless, even if we do not have our own classroom, the way we organize resources says something about our beliefs and assumptions about children's capacity to learn.

Much of what has been said in other chapters emphasizes the need for a variety of resources in the primary classroom. But this can pose a problem in terms of organization and storage of materials and equipment, and in terms of managing children's use of all these materials. It can be daunting to face clearing up at the end of a session which involved children in the use of lots of materials. So one solution is to train children to become more independent in getting out and putting away materials so that they assist you in managing the classroom, which gives you time to pay more attention to individual children[3].

Simple ideas to start with could include:

- giving different children responsibility for giving out and collecting pens, pencils, crayons and other equipment
- asking children how and where to store things in the classroom
- getting children to make boxes or decorate tins and label them for storage of pens, pencils, etc
- involving children in making a display of their work and getting them to think of a caption to go underneath.

Task 3   How do teachers' beliefs affect classroom organization?

- Read the examples below and compare the way Bijay and Mohan have organized and stored resources.
- Which classroom is more likely to encourage pupils' involvement in managing resources? Why?
- What are the problems in trying to encourage children to take more responsibility for managing resources?

Classroom A

This is Bijay's classroom. He is very well organized and has everything neatly arranged. He does not have many resources so he is careful to look after them by keeping them in his cupboard. He has many pictures and displays on the wall to make the classroom look attractive. Bijay says:

A nice clean and attractive environment is very important for children. I always make sure I have lots of colourful pictures and charts on the wall. My pupils are from poor urban areas and they are not used to handling books at home. For that reason I keep the books in a cupboard which I open at reading time so they won't get dirty or lost.

Classroom B

Here is Mohan's classroom. It is similar in size and layout to Bijay's. He has a book corner at one end of the classroom, a display of children's work and all the materials needed for each day's lessons stored and labelled on open shelves. Mohan says:

I believe that pupils are strongly affected by their environment so I want to make sure that our classroom is a happy, productive, attractive environment for them to study in. Most of my children come from poor urban families. I want them to feel that it is their classroom as well as mine. I want them to learn to look after and use the resources in the classroom as if they belonged to them. This will be a useful skill in later life as well.

Commentary ■ ■ ■

Both classrooms have pupils sitting in groups. However Classroom A is organized to suit the teacher while Classroom B is designed to be a comfortable place for both pupils and teacher.

In Classroom A, the display of pupils' work is high up on the wall, above their eye level, so they may have difficulty seeing it. In Classroom B, pupils' work is at pupil level so they can see it and relate to it more easily.

In Classroom A, reading books are kept in a locked cupboard to which the teacher controls access. Similarly, all the resources are kept in a cupboard marked *Teacher's*. The teacher also controls access to the materials. In Classroom B, there is a reading corner where pupils can freely go in and take out a book. Similarly the resources are arranged in labelled boxes and shelves along the side of the classroom so pupils can gain access easily.

Both teachers care about their pupils and want them to learn in an attractive environment. However they differ in their way of achieving this aim, which reflects differences in their beliefs about children and their capabilities. Bijay's organization suggests that the classroom can only be kept attractive if he protects it from children and what damage they might do to it. Mohan's organization suggests that children are capable of learning how to look after and manage resources. His classroom is organized in a way which will give them opportunities to do this. Resources are arranged at pupils' level so the classroom allows pupils access to them. It assumes that pupils will be involved in selecting, organizing and putting them away. The resources in Classroom A, by contrast, are organized in a way which protects them from children and allows Bijay to keep complete control over them.

Mohan and Bijay teach in similar situations and have access to similar facilities but what makes a difference to their approach is their beliefs about children's capacity to learn.

Possible problems in trying to encourage children to take more responsibility for managing resources could include:

Pupils don't have their own classroom and so resources can't be left there.

This certainly makes it more difficult, but you could develop a mobile kit of resources which children help you to set out for each class, eg sets of crayons, scissors, rulers, paper.

It takes time to train children to manage resources.

This is not so much a problem as a reality we need to accept. I have come across several teachers in circumstances similar to Mohan and Bijay's who managed to train children to look after and manage their classroom resources. It might help if you can work together with the class teacher or other teachers who teach the children so you can plan a joint approach to training them in the use of resources. This means children would be getting a consistent message from all those who taught them.

There is no support for your approach from other teachers/the school.

You could invite other teachers or the head teacher to visit your classroom so you could demonstrate what you are trying to achieve. It may take time to win them over. Try to work with one or two teachers who are interested in doing the same. You can then give each other mutual support. ■

5 The use of classroom display to create an attractive and dynamic learning environment

All learners appreciate a physically attractive learning environment. Children are particularly sensitive to their environment because they learn through all their senses. So classroom displays create a stimulating environment which attracts and motivates them for learning. But display does not just mean putting up a few pictures or posters on the wall to make it look nice. It is an attractive collection of things which are arranged in a meaningful way with a clear learning purpose. Displays can:

- provide information or language input for pupils, eg days of the week, numbers, or facts about a topic to stimulate children's interest such as a variety of clocks when teaching about time
- reinforce language learning taking place in the classroom, eg an alphabet chart when learning the letters of the alphabet, words of a song you are teaching
- encourage high quality work by displaying pupils' work and showing it is valued
- act as a stimulus for topic work, discussion or exploration of ideas
- stimulate pupils' interest or curiosity.

Task 4   Making and using classroom displays

Below are two examples of displays.

- What do you think is the teacher's main reason for making each display?
- How do the displays contribute to children's language learning?
- How could pupils be involved in making such displays?
- Which of the displays provides opportunities for pupils to interact with the display?

Display 1

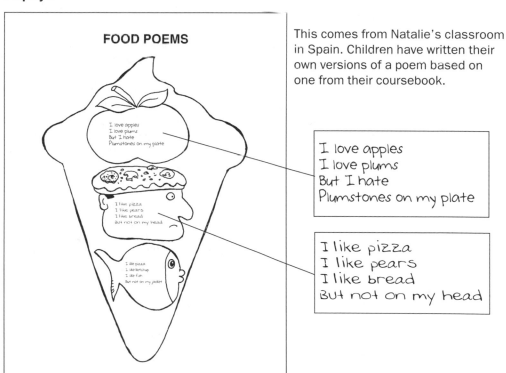

FOOD POEMS

This comes from Natalie's classroom in Spain. Children have written their own versions of a poem based on one from their coursebook.

I love apples
I love plums
But I hate
Plumstones on my plate

I like pizza
I like pears
I like bread
But not on my head

Display 2

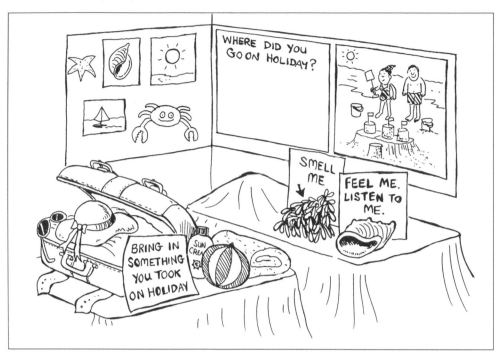

This display is one that Audrey plans to use in her classroom in Mexico. The display invites pupils to engage with it in different ways. Can you find examples of how pupils are engaged?

Commentary ■ ■ ■

The purpose of Display 1 is to encourage pupils to produce good quality work by displaying it publicly. The purpose of Display 2 is to act as a stimulus for class discussion leading to a project on the topic of holidays.

The food poem display gives children a real communicative reason for writing in English. In addition, if they know that their work is going to be displayed, they will be more willing to take care with the presentation work; in other words it can motivate them to revise and to pay attention to language details. The holiday display helps to create a desire to talk. It encourages children to draw on and share their own experiences which you can exploit for language practice. However, it is unlikely that all children will react in the same way to a topic so it is important to find ways of including the interests of those children who may feel excluded by a topic like holidays. In addition children may learn from these displays that their work is valued.

Children may not notice displays unless they are given a reason for doing so. One way of getting their attention is to involve them in both making the display and using it. Otherwise your work may be wasted, and you may be giving them the message that only displays made by the teacher are important. In Display 1, pupils could make the backing for their poem and could write their names on the bottom. They could also help in putting it on the wall. In Display 2, they could be involved in bringing things in for the display and in arranging them and labelling them.

Both are attractive, but it is Display 2 which tries to engage pupils in an interactive way. It encourages them to write down where they have been on holiday and bring in examples of things they took with them. It also gives them a chance to feel the shells, listen to them and to smell the sea weed. Pupils are much more likely to pay attention to the display if they have to do something with it, rather than just looking passively. ■

Summary

In this chapter you have considered:

- *what teaching/learning resources are.* A broad view of resources means that virtually anything can count as a resource as long as it assists the teaching/learning process. If you allow children more involvement in the making and management of your resources there are many benefits for language learning.
- *the reasons for making resources* and whether they justify the effort. We considered how productive resources were in terms of their range of uses and whether learners could make them so as to increase their involvement and opportunities for language learning. We also considered the value of reflecting on how you use resources, and we saw from the example of one teacher how this reflection can help to change our knowledge about teaching.
- *how children can act as resources for language learning:* as partners for others, as tutors in helping others, as models or demonstrators, as resource makers, by using their bodies as a resource. The benefits of using children in this way are enormous both in terms of increased pupil involvement, interest and also language practice.
- *ways of organizing your resources to involve children.* The way you organize your resources reflects your beliefs about children and their capabilities as learners. So if you believe children are capable of learning how to manage resources in the classroom, then you will organize your classroom in a way which encourages this. If resources are accessible to children and they are trained to manage them, you will have more time to spend with individuals and children will benefit by developing greater independence.
- *the purpose of displays:* they provide language input for pupils, reinforce language learning, demonstrate that pupils' work is valued, provide stimulus for topic work, arouse pupils' interest or curiosity. Children can gain important messages from displays. But this is only likely to happen if it is *their* work which is displayed or they have been involved in creating the display. Although displays need to be planned carefully so that they attract children's interest, they also need to be designed so they engage children in an interactive way. Otherwise children will soon lose interest.

The implications I would like to draw from this chapter are, firstly, that resources have the potential to create the kind of learning environment which supports children's language learning: an environment which is attractive, stimulating and involves children through a variety of senses in meaningful language-learning activities. But in order for this potential to be fully realized, children need to be involved in making, using and managing resources. Secondly, reflecting on the way you use resources can give you a way of examining your beliefs about children and their capabilities which may encourage you to rethink some aspects of your teaching.

References

1   Phillips, S. 1993 *Young Learners.* Oxford: Oxford University Press
    On p121, there are instructions on how to make a spinner. This book has some useful suggestions on the use of resources like puppets, games, etc and a selection of ideas for activities.
2   Read, C. and Salaberri, S. 1992 *English Club Student's Book 1.* Oxford: Heinemann, p38
3   For many practical ideas on storage, record keeping, classroom behaviour and display, see Montgomery, D. and Rawlings, D. 1986 *Bright Ideas. Classroom Management.* Leamington Spa: Scholastic Publications

Chapter 11 Learning to see

Assessing learning and teaching

Teacher:	Listen to what you said. *(pupil has tape recorded his answers)*
George's voice:	*(on tape)* No she got none brothers.
George:	None. *(sounds surprised)*
Teacher:	None. *(agreeing)* Now we don't say 'none', we say 'She's got no brothers.'
George:	No ... no *(practising for himself)*

The example above comes from a classroom where seven-year-old George is learning English as a second or additional language[1]. The teacher is drawing attention to a particular error which has occurred in George's taped answer of which he is unaware. She is giving him feedback about an aspect of his language which may help him to modify his internal rule system. She has also learned something about this pupil's language which may help her to adjust her teaching plans in the future.

As teachers, we have an important role in setting up and managing the conditions which enable pupils to learn effectively in classrooms. But how do we know whether learning is taking place and whether pupils are developing and making progress? To what extent are we achieving our teaching goals or intentions? As in the example above, we need feedback on our teaching and pupils need feedback on their learning in order to develop further. This is an important function of assessment which is the topic of this chapter.

In this chapter, we will consider:

1 **What is assessment?**
2 **Pupils' views on assessment**
3 **The difference between on-going and overall assessment**
4 **How to carry out on-going assessment**
5 **Ways of getting pupils to assess themselves**

The aim of this chapter is to consider how assessment can help you and your pupils, and what changes you may need to bring about in pupils' beliefs and your own beliefs and practice to enable both you and your pupils to benefit more fully from assessment. In this chapter, I will use the word *assessment* rather than evaluation. Evaluation is a broader term and includes formal and informal kinds of assessment and testing.

1   What is assessment?

Assessment seems to be something that most teachers spend a lot of time doing. So it is important to consider what it is, why we do it, what kinds of information it provides, and the decisions that might be taken based on that information.

What is assessment?

The term 'assessment' is used in different ways in different situations, which can make things confusing, especially when a group of teachers from different countries meet together. In this chapter, I am going to use the term assessment to mean: a way of providing feedback on learning and teaching.

Why do we assess pupils?

We may have several purposes for assessing, eg to identify pupils' progress, to check on pupils' achievement, but our priorities will be affected by our particular teaching situation and school policy. For example, in a school which requires the teacher to provide regular reports for parents it will be necessary to monitor and record pupils' progress fairly frequently. In a system which uses assessment results to decide if children are to be moved to the next level it will be necessary to find out how far children have achieved the goals of the programme using a particular set of criteria.

How do we use the information obtained from assessment?

The information we collect will be determined by our purpose. For example, if our purpose is to check achievement, the information may be in the form of test results, whereas if the aim is to monitor progress, the information may be in the form of comments or samples of pupils' work. Once the information has been collected, either the teacher or someone else can make decisions based on this information. For example if you have collected information about a pupil's progress, you might decide to talk to the child about strengths or problems, you might give him/her extra work to do, or you might place him/her in a new group. The decisions you make will be influenced by your own aims, your knowledge of the pupils, the context and your beliefs about children's learning.

Think about your own reasons for assessing pupils and what decisions you might make based on the information you obtain. Compare your answers with the possibilities below.

Reasons for assessment	How to use information obtained
To identify a pupil's progress in learning English.	Adjust learning tasks to suit his/her needs. Move him/her to another group. Give feedback on strengths and problem areas to work on. Help child make an action plan.
To identify what pupils have learned, ie achievement over a term or year.	Move pupil to the next class. Adjust yearly teaching plans. Change learning materials.
To check pupils' use of a particular skill or language structure in a lesson or unit.	Give further practice. Change your lesson plan for the next day. Give special help to some pupils.
To find out whether you have achieved your teaching objectives.	Adjust your future teaching plans. Try out new methods or techniques.
To identify the skills / language /attitudes, etc pupils have developed already.	Use it to plan the new term's work.
To find out whether pupils like/dislike particular activities and why.	Make changes to your activities. Involve pupils more in choosing activities.
To diagnose problems and/or strengths pupils have in a particular language area, eg writing, reading.	Prepare learning materials based on the problem areas. Give individual help to particular pupils.

How do children benefit from assessment?

The table shows that children may benefit from assessment in various ways. For example, they may benefit indirectly from the changes you make to your teaching plans based on the information you gather and benefit more directly when you give them individual feedback on their progress. However this still leaves them outside the system where things are done *to* them rather than *with* them.

2 Pupils' views on assessment

Let's consider some children's views about assessment and see what we can learn.

Margaret Prosser, a primary teacher in England, asked her eight and nine-year-olds whether a teacher's assessment of children's learning should be shared with them[2]. They were unanimous that this should be secret and the reasons they gave included:

To save embarrassment.
So people's feelings aren't hurt.
It might be unkind to tell someone they aren't very good at something if they think they are.
Supposing it's someone who is a slow learner. Think how they would feel if you said so.

The surprising thing about the comments is that these children all seemed to believe that the results of assessment would inevitably be negative. Does this mean that they have never experienced positive assessments? Margaret Prosser was so concerned about children's responses that she continued her investigations further to try to understand children's beliefs and how these seemed to be affecting their ability to benefit from the results of assessment.

In a different context, Sonia, a Colombian teacher trainer, asked a group of primary school children how they would like to be assessed. Here are some of their answers:

Through songs.
In groups.
Don't let the teacher come to school angry on that day.

Their answers suggest that they would like to be assessed:

- in enjoyable and non-threatening ways
- with their friends, rather than individually, perhaps so that they can gain support
- by a teacher who is always fair, not influenced by his/her moods or feelings on a particular day.

Their answers tell us what they would like in an ideal classroom and hint at previous experiences they have had. They suggest that some pupils may have negative feelings about assessment, like the British pupils mentioned above.

Though it would be unwise to generalize from these two examples, the children's comments highlight the power of children's beliefs and the way these beliefs may determine whether children can learn from assessment. They indicate that pupils may not always feel involved in the assessment process – it is something that is done to them by adults. Perhaps as a result of this lack of involvement, children feel it is something arbitrary that they have no control over. This may contribute to a lowering of self-esteem in some children and the development of negative attitudes about assessment. This in turn can affect their ability or willingness to benefit and learn from the information given by the results of assessment.

« Self-esteem
pp48–9

So what can we do to ensure that children can perceive the benefits of assessment? We can help children by:

- asking about their views on assessment
- developing their awareness of the purpose of assessment and how they can gain from it
- providing more information about their progress and how they can use this information to improve
- encouraging them to assess themselves, thereby involving them more fully in the assessment process
- examining our own beliefs about assessment and how these may affect the way we represent assessment to our pupils, ie do we present it as something beneficial for them or something to be endured?

Assessment does not have to be a negative experience for children. I hope that this chapter will help you to develop ways of making assessment a positive and enriching experience for them so that they feel more involved and more in control of their own learning.

3   The difference between on-going and overall assessment

Task 1   Different sorts of assessment for different reasons

■ What is the difference between the two assessment situations below? Think particularly about the reason for the assessment in each case.

A The teacher has carried out a writing activity with children. She has collected in their work and interpreted it. Here is her response on one of the pupil's work, showing the result of her assessment.

B It is the end of the year. The school requires the teacher to test children in English to see whether they have achieved the aims of the coursebook. Pupils have taken a short oral test and a small written test. They receive a report from the school which includes a list of all their marks in all subjects.

A

Friday   1-9-1995

In the Train

Last Sunday I went to Puloy Pinong buy a train. In the train they were many passengers. Suddenly a loud music come from at the back of the train, the passengers were angry because a boy called Ali is playing disco very loudly. A big, fat and fierce woman was staring at the boy. The woman wanted to Ali follow her- But the boy were very surprised. Ali did not know what to do. The lady took the boy and pulled him in to the toilet and locked the door. After the passengers were happy. And the passengers and I can relax peacefully.

I'm happy she did that.

Ramesh, this is really an interesting story! It must be exciting to travel in a train with so many people and with the loud music on. What were the passengers doing? Can you describe some of them to me? The disco music was loud. What were the words like? I admire that big, fat, fierce woman. She has guts! I wonder what she said to Ali. I'd like to know.

B

Subject	Grade	Comments
History	C	Satisfactory
Mathematics	C	Could try harder
English	D	Little progress this term
Science	B	Good work

Commentary ■ ■ ■

In the first example, the teacher has read the pupils' work and interpreted it according to her objectives for the writing activity. She has identified in what ways the child has been successful and in what areas he needs to improve. The results of her assessment are shared with the child and provide concrete suggestions for action. In the second example, the child's work has been assessed according to particular criteria and a marking scale. The grade shows the results of the assessment, ie how far she has met the objectives for her English class. The difference between the situations is that in the first, the child has the opportunity to make immediate use of the information from the assessment to improve, whereas in the second she does not. In the second situation, the result is final and the child does not have the chance to try again. The information is also less comprehensible to the child, eg what does Grade D mean?

On-going assessment (often called formative) is what we do on a daily basis – continuously, when we intentionally look for information which will help us to see how far a pupil is making progress in line with our objectives. **Overall assessment** (often called summative) happens only periodically, eg at the end of a term or year or period of study. It takes place when the teacher or someone else wants to check whether pupils have achieved certain goals or targets, usually through a test or exam.

On-going assessment is most important for both teachers and pupils. Teachers use the information gained to help pupils by building it into their teaching or by providing them with specific help. So pupils benefit immediately from the results of the assessment. The information gained day by day builds up a picture of the pupils' progress and language development.

Overall assessment gives information about what a child has achieved at the end of a particular period of study. This information does not always directly benefit the teacher or the pupils, though it may affect them. For example in some countries, pupils may have to repeat a class if they do not pass in subjects like English. Overall assessment provides a photo of the pupil at that point in time. It is a quick and efficient way of giving information to schools about pupils' achievement. However it is not useful on its own because it may not show pupils' full potential or the progress they have made. It will only show what they can do at that point in time. So this suggests that both types of assessment are needed as one complements the other. ■

Assessment is a very large and important topic and it isn't possible to discuss all aspects of it in one chapter. So I am going to deal only with on-going assessment. I believe that this needs to be given priority in a primary classroom as it is most helpful in supporting children's development and in informing our understanding of children.

4   How to carry out on-going assessment

Mary Drummond[2] has suggested that there are three important questions teachers need to ask themselves when they assess children's learning:

- What is there to see? (Evidence)
- How best can we understand what we see? (Interpretation of evidence)
- How can we put our understanding to good use? (Outcomes)

In other words, we need to think about what information will provide evidence of pupils' learning and how we can collect this information. Once we have collected the evidence, we need to try to make sense of it – to explain and interpret it within the context of a particular child's learning and what we know of that child. Finally we need to consider how we can make use of what we have learned from examining the evidence and interpreting it. Let's apply these questions to a real situation.

Assessing children's writing

The examples of writing that we will discuss below come from a class of 10 to 11-year-old Bhutanese children who are learning English as a second language. They liked stories very much and their teacher, Yenti, frequently read stories to them. They had written stories before but on this occasion he wanted to find out whether children were able to draft their stories, ie to use a process by which they produce several attempts, each one improving on the one before. In a preceding lesson, Yenti drew children's attention to story endings and how to make them interesting. He then asked pupils in friendship pairs to write a story with an interesting ending. After draft one, children were asked to comment on each other's stories, particularly the ending. They redrafted them, making the ending more interesting. Finally Yenti underlined simple surface errors in their second drafts, eg spelling, tense, punctuation and asked children to correct their own work and write a final version ready for publication in a class story book. Below is part of the first, second and third drafts of a story called *Cat and Rats Story*, written by two children: Chenco Pem and Deki Dem.

1

Wednesday 15 July
Cat and the rat story
Once upon a time there was an old cat called pussy. One day pussy cat was very hungry and the cat went to forest to look a food And he started crying. Then he slept under the tree. Then he saw a small house. Then he run inside the house. There are some rats. Then the cat was very happy. Then he run after the rats. He run first, He got one rats. Many years ago the cat was very old cat he cannto catch the rat. And he had old wife. They had five child One big boy was in class seven. The small boy was in class six.

By Chenco Pem and Deki Dem

2

Cat and the rats
Once upon a time there was an old cat called Pussy. One day Pussy cat was very hungry and the cat went to the forest to look for food. And he started crying ~~to cry~~ and ~~cride~~ crying and he was very thirsty. Then he slept under the tree. Then he saw a small house. Then he ~~run~~ ran inside the house. There ~~are~~ were some rats. Inside the house there was one pipe and he drank the water. Then he ~~find~~ found some rats .in the house. He got near the corner, There ~~are~~ were some rats. He got one rat, two rats, three rats, four rats and he ate ~~old~~ all the rats. He was very happy. Then he went home. There was a beautiful ghost girl. He ~~marriyed~~ ~~marryed~~ married with her. They ~~are~~ were very happy At night the ghost girl Killed the pussy cat.

by Chenco Pem and Deki Dem

3

Cat and the rats.
Once upon a time there was an Old cat called Pussy. One day Pussy cat was very hungry and the cat went to the forest to look for food. And started to cry and cried as he was very thirsty. Then he slept under the tree. Then he saw a small house. Then he ran inside the house. There were some rats. Inside the house there was a pipe and he drank some water. Then he found some rats in the house. He got near the corner. There were some rats. He ran after the rats. He ran very quickly. He got one rat, two rats, three rats, four rats and he ate all the rats. He was very happy. Then he went home. There was a beautiful ghost girl. He Married with her. They were very happy

by Chenco Pem and Deki Dem

Consider each of the questions for yourself before you read the comments below them.

What is there to see?

In this context: *What can we learn about the product and process of children's writing from examining the children's drafts above?*

When we observe children's language as if we were interested visitors from outer space rather than judges or inspectors, we are sometimes astonished and excited by what we find out. From these children's writing, their teacher learned many things about both the process and product of their writing. For example, the children:

Process
- were able to create a plan for their story and hold it in their heads across three drafts
- could create drafts which included deliberate and purposeful changes, eg *He got one rats* was changed to *He got one rat, two rats, three rats*. These were not just random changes.

Product
- produced a story which contained a number of events in sequence
- could successfully self-correct limited types of surface errors, eg *are>were, old>all*
- made the story more interesting for readers by making stylistic changes, eg use of repetition: *He got one rat, two rats, three rats, four rats and he ate all the rats.*
- produced a final version which was more interesting and accurate than the earlier draft.

How best can we understand what we see?

In this context: *How can we interpret our findings about children's writing? What can these two children do well and what do they still need to learn?*

When you interpret the evidence, you think about your teaching purposes – what you want children to achieve in their writing and to what extent they are able to do this. However you may also take account of your knowledge of each individual and what you think they are able to manage. Based on Yenti's teaching goals for writing, let's identify some particular strengths and areas where the pupils need to develop.

Strengths *The two children can …*	Points for development *They need help to …*
produce a set of simple logically connected events	develop a more complex story structure where there is a definite motive for events which take place
produce grammatically correct sentences	use more complex sentence types
use simple punctuation, eg full stops	use more complex punctuation devices, eg speech marks, commas
use simple connectors, eg *and, then*	increase their range of connectors, eg *therefore, so*
show some awareness of their audience, eg use of repetition to create effect, inclusion of ghosts to make the story more exciting	increase audience awareness, eg use a greater range of adjectives, adverbs, and a variety of verbs to create interest
produce a story with a definite beginning and ending even though the ending is not closely linked to the story	make the ending more closely integrated with the story

How can we put our understanding to good use?

In other words: *How can we use the information from our assessment to move children forward?*

You may have identified many aspects where children could develop further. I shall take one example here, eg the story structure. The children's story above is based on a set of loosely connected events. One way of helping them to improve their story writing is to develop the structure of their stories so they create a clearer plot with definite characters who have motives for what they do. For this you could use a story frame to make explicit and draw attention to the structure of their story as below. To begin with, you could get children to fill in the frame with details from their own story. Then you could get them to complete the frame with an alternative version of the same story and discuss the link between the problem and the solution. Later they could write up their new version of the story. However, it is important that children do not get the idea that there is only one way of writing a story. The frame is merely a tool to support them initially.

Title
Cat and the Rats

Authors
Chenco Pem and Deki Dem

WHO?	Old cat and rats
WHERE?	Small house in a forest
WHEN?	One day
PROBLEM	Old cat – hungry and thirsty
SOLUTION	Went to forest to find food. Saw house. Went into the house and drank water – ate rats
END	Old cat was very happy – married a beautiful girl

Observing with an open mind what children are capable of doing with language can be tremendously rewarding. It helps you to see children's potential and enables you to adjust your own planning and teaching to children's learning. So assessing pupils' progress and assessing your own teaching are closely linked. However if you are just beginning to teach children or if you need to provide regular reports to parents, you may feel the need for a little more structure in the way you carry out your assessment. Some textbooks offer frameworks for doing this. Let's look at an example of a system taken from *Fanfare 1 Teacher's Book*[3] and consider how helpful it may be for your situation.

Pupils' language profiles

Collecting, recording and interpreting information

The teacher records pupils' progress on a profile sheet as shown below. He/she uses a simple key with four bands (levels) to assess pupils' achievement for a set of attainment targets (objectives) in five skill areas. For example, if Peter is able to use some social expressions, eg *Hello* and *Goodbye*, but not all the time, then he might be assessed as which indicates he needs more experience/practice. This profile is designed for pupils in their first two years of English.

The Teacher's Book recommends that the profile is completed for five or six children at a time so the teacher can focus on them for several lessons. This means it might take two to three units of the book to complete the profile for a whole class.

Here is an example of the profile:

Teacher _____

Class _____

Date _____

Unit(s) _____

Teacher _____

Class _____

Attainment targets	1	2	3	4	5	6	7	8	9	10	11	12	13	14	15	16	17	18	19	20	21	22	23	24	25
Listening																									
1 Recognizes the phonemes, rhythms and patterns of English																									
2 Can grasp the overall sense of simple messages in context																									
3 Can follow simple oral instructions in context																									
4 Can identify simple details in oral texts																									
5 Can grasp the overall sense of less contextualized messages																									
Speaking																									
1 Can reproduce brief messages with appropriate pronunciation and intonation																									
2 Can use simple social expressions																									
3 Can produce short, modelled oral messages and descriptions																									
4 Can produce original oral messages																									
Reading/Writing																									
1 Can interpret the written code 1) at word level, and 2) at simple phrase/sentence level																									
2 Can grasp the overall sense of brief written texts																									
3 Can extract specific information from brief written texts																									
4 Can follow simple written instructions																									
5 Can produce modelled written information 1) at word level, and 2) at phrase/sentence level																									
6 Can produce original written messages																									
Learning Skills																									
1 Can work independently of the teacher																									
2 Can select and carry out own work activities																									
3 Can reflect on and assess own performance and progress																									
4 Can make use of reference sources																									
Social Skills																									
1 Shows interest in learning English																									
2 Shows interest in and respect for other lifestyles																									
3 Is able to co-operate with others in pair/group work																									
4 Shows appropriate leadership skills in pair/group work																									

For the attainment targets, the Teacher's Book suggests that decisions about whether children have reached a target in language learning and social skills will be based on:

- the teacher's observation of the way that the child behaves in class
- the teacher's lesson records and notes made on each lesson
- the child's own diary.

So the assessment will be based on several sources of information.

Sharing information and taking action

With regard to sharing the information in the profiles with children, the Teacher's Book advises:

The Pupils' Profile itself should not be given to parents and children, but should form the basis of a written comment by the teacher which can then be given to the parents of a child.

The teacher's lesson record enables the teacher to keep a note of pupils' problems so that these can be taken account of in future planning.

Task 2 Pupils' language profiles

Look at the example of a pupil's profile above.

- Where does the teacher get information to use in the profile? Where else could the teacher get information from?
- How is the information for each pupil recorded on the profile?
- What different aspects of language is the teacher assessing through the profile?
- How does he/she actually interpret the information and assess a pupil?

Commentary ■ ■ ■

The teacher collects information by observing and listening to children while they are doing class activities, by keeping notes of how children respond in class in a daily lesson plan and by reading their diaries. Alternative sources of information could be children's written work, information from the class teacher (if the English teacher is not the class teacher) or from parents.

The numbers 1–25 along the top of the profile represent the number of children in a class (space for 25). The small boxes under each number are completed with the appropriate symbol (see key) to show a pupil's attainment in a certain target area.

The profile enables the teacher to assess different aspects of the four main language skills (listening, speaking, reading and writing). Each skill is broken down into a smaller sub skill, eg *can produce original oral messages*. The teacher can also assess pupils' learning skills, ie how effective they are as learners, and social skills, ie their attitudes to learning English and how well they work with others.

For each individual skill (called attainment targets on the profile), the teacher has to decide at what level the pupil is performing. There are four main levels in the key provided:

- not yet covered
- child needs more experience in this skill area
- has secure understanding
- can apply and extend his/her skills or knowledge.

However it is clearly not easy to decide the level at which a pupil is performing on the basis of one observation. You would probably need to make regular notes of children's performance over a period of time to support your more formal observation for the profile. ■

Organizing assessment

Fanfare 1 Teacher's Book suggests that you can observe several children at a time over several days in order to complete the profile. However that might be difficult to do with lively or large classes, and you might need to organize it more formally. Here is a suggestion:

Divide pupils into groups. Observe one group at a time and set written or art work for the other pupils. This would enable you to observe each pupil properly though it may limit the number of observations you could make.

Day	Observation group	Work set for other groups
Mon	Red	Silent reading
Tues	Blue	Crossword puzzles Word games in groups
Wed	Green	Read and draw/colour

There are various problems in using a profile like the one in the example. Firstly, the profile may have too many items to consider and you may find it too complicated for daily use. If this is the case, then you could focus on those areas you think are important for your pupils at a particular period. On the other hand, you may find the detail very helpful as a way of thinking about all the different areas in which children need to develop their language. Secondly, if, as suggested in *Fanfare*, you complete the profile for groups of five or six children at a time, groups of children assessed later will have had more practice than groups assessed first, and may therefore achieve a higher level on the scale. It might be fairer to use a system where you plan to assess all pupils on specific targets on a week-by-week basis until you have completed them. Thirdly, there is the practical problem of how much time you have for observation. The more times you observe a child, the more confidence you will have in your assessment. But you also have to be realistic in how much time you can spare.

When you have collected the information, you need to decide what to do with it. The school may require you to keep records of children's progress over the year. If parents require you to produce some kind of progress record, you could convert the information from the profiles into a written progress report in which you highlighted strengths and identified areas for further work. You could illustrate this report with samples of children's work over the term, chosen with each child, to form a portfolio for each one. The profiles are also a useful reminder to you of areas where individual children may need help or of areas where you might want to challenge children further. For example, if most of your class can read simple written instructions at a level where they can apply and extend their understanding, the instructions may not be challenging enough. It may be time to provide them with more complex written instructions so they can develop further.

Using pupils' profiles

Before trying out a profile, it is useful to think through some of the potential problems. Try using it yourself to assess the work below by a ten-year-old Spanish pupil in his second year of English. He has written a short description of a monster based on one modelled by the teacher. He has drawn and coloured the picture.

Task 3 Assessing a piece of work

Use the *Fanfare* profile sheet to assess the piece of work below.

- What can you learn about the pupil's writing from looking at his work?
- How would you interpret the information? ie Which attainment target(s) would you use to assess the piece of work?
- What action would you take based on the information you got from assessing his work on writing? How can you share the information with the child?
- What problems did you find in using the profile?

Draw and colour:

Write:

He has a green body.
He has a red eyes.
He has a red teeth.

Commentary ■ ■ ■

From this piece of work, you can learn that the child is able to create his own interesting drawing of a monster and write simple appropriate sentences to describe it, using a model. He can use some adjectives of colour. He seems to have a problem knowing when to use the indefinite article in a noun phrase (*a* red eyes, *a* red teeth).

You could use attainment target no 5 under Reading/Writing, eg *can produce modelled written information at sentence level*. Although he can reproduce the basic pattern of the description, his problems with the use of the indefinite article in noun phrases suggests he cannot yet fully apply his language knowledge to writing his own description. Is this just a slip or a recurrent problem? It is difficult to know without looking at more of his work.

There are various steps you could take in helping him to make further progress. The decision would depend partly on what you know of his needs in other areas of his work. You could:

- help him to become aware of how singular and plural are signalled in noun phrases, eg *large hands* but *a large hand*
- introduce him to different kinds of adjectives, eg size (*large, small*), shape (*round, square*) appearance (*fat, thin*), etc
- give him more experience of writing descriptions of people/animals in varied situations, using a wider range of adjectives
- encourage him to increase the length of his text by building in more parts to the description.

If the problems identified are common to many children, you could put some (anonymous) examples of children's work on the blackboard and encourage children to identify the problem and ways of solving it, eg (using the description above) *Here is a description of a monster. Tell me all the good things about it first. Is there anything we can improve?*

Completing the profile uncovers some of the dilemmas in carrying out on-going assessment. If we assess a child on only one piece of work, we do not know if this is representative and shows his/her full capability. We need to sample across several pieces of work before we can get a realistic picture. The other difficulty is that children are developing all the time in leaps and starts. They sometimes fall backwards and then move forwards rapidly. It is important to gather information regularly because the situation can change. The task also shows that when assessing progress, we need to make a personal judgement based on the evidence available. There is no purely objective way of assessing. But the more evidence available, the more likely that we will make a balanced assessment. ■

There is no perfect procedure for carrying out on-going assessment. All of them have their advantages and disadvantages, and so it is best to use more than one procedure so that you gain different perspectives on children's progress.

Action plan

Aim: To try out a system of on-going assessment.

Procedure

- Try out the *Fanfare* system in your own classroom for a period of time.
- To begin with, focus on a small number of children (three or four) and focus on three or four attainment targets which you feel are relevant.
- Find out the problems in using the system and adapt it to suit your needs.
- Try out the new profile system with your whole class for a term.

Think about what you learned about your pupils' language and about carrying out on-going assessment.

---

5   Ways of getting pupils to assess themselves

As a busy teacher, you may feel that involving the pupil in the assessment process sounds fine in theory, but is difficult to do in practice. Where could you find the time to give individual feedback? One solution to the problem is to encourage and train pupils to assess themselves. This means teacher and pupils are working in partnership. If pupils can learn to

>> Chapter 12

monitor and assess themselves, they will be more receptive to feedback and more aware of their own needs. Their assessments can also provide useful information for your records. They could also be included as part of a folder of work which could be presented to parents at intervals to show the child's progress. A child's self-assessment could be put together with your own assessment to form a portfolio.

Children do not automatically assess themselves, but they can do it with support from the teacher. One way of helping them to learn to assess themselves is through a process like drafting which we discussed earlier. At each draft, they are prompted to focus on one aspect of the writing and revise. Through this support, the teacher is helping to make them aware of the criteria that are used in assessing writing so that children will eventually internalize and use them independently.

Drafting is relevant for writing, but what other ways are there of encouraging children to assess themselves? Below are three examples of procedures developed to encourage pupils' awareness of learning and ability to assess themselves. The first one was completed by an eight-year-old child. The second one was completed by a Danish learner[4] in the third or fourth year of learning English. The third one is a diary entry completed by a ten-year-old child learning French.

Task 4   Can children assess their own learning?

- Compare the self-assessment forms. What are the differences and similarities?
- Would you use any of them for your pupils?

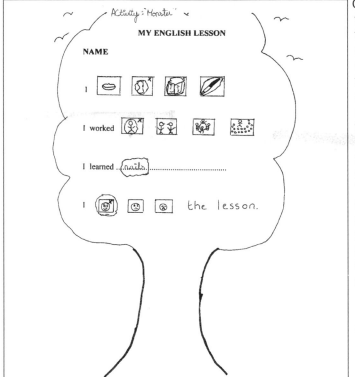

Children completed this tree after they had finished the lesson. They had to choose which pictures applied to the lesson and then tick or asterisk the pictures. The first line shows the different skills they were practising. The second line shows different types of classroom organization. The third line asks them to say what they learned in either the L1 or L2. The fourth line has three faces which show how they may feel (happy, sad and neither happy nor sad).

Example A   Tree

Example B   Questionnaire

Evaluationsheet for November/December

Name: __Tomas Larsen__ Working with: __Martin Tine Dorth__

Subject/Areas __Making Newspaper__

Materials used: "Allan Simansen" Vi unge "Times" Danish newspaper

Good things (remember why):
We were a good group and worked very good, because we were all
at the same level. We helped each other very much all though we
splitted up in two groups. We learned also a lot of good words and
sentences. We was very concentrated and this was very
important. I think our newspaper was very good one that was
maybe because we was so concentrated.

(well written above "good"; were written above "was")

Bad things (WHY):
In the beginning we wasn't very concentrated

(weren't written above "wasn't")

What do I know now that I didn't know before:
I know that English isn't that difficult to translate to Danish
and Danish isn't that difficult to translate to English. It helps a
lot

Plans Suggestions for the future:
I'd like to make a group out of the four of us again. And we can
discuss what to do

Example C   Diary

Friday 31st March
I learn french easier if the
English word sounds like the
french word like brun and brown
and bleu and blue. And it helps
me if mrs Bean points to something
like if it was vert she points
to something green. It would
help if Mrs B uses some
English.

Commentary ■ ■ ■

Each child shows an ability to carry out self-assessment at his/her stage of development. The younger child is able to state what she has learned and to indicate whether she enjoyed the lesson. The diary entry and the questionnaire show that the older children can reflect on their own learning in quite sophisticated ways.

Tree	Questionnaire	Diary
Suitable for young children or beginners as there is little writing involved. It is conceptually simple. It is structured, ie focuses on specific aspects of learning, eg what they learned, their feeling about the lesson, how they were organized.	Suitable for older learners as it is conceptually more complex. It is semi-structured, ie it gets pupils to analyse their strengths and weaknesses and how they worked, to identify what they have learned and to plan for the future.	Suitable for any age as long as the child can write. Younger children can write in the L1. It is unstructured. The child can focus on any aspect of learning but it may help to give some key questions or headings initially, eg *What English did you learn today?* *Which activities do you like/not like? Why?* *Which activities are difficult/easy and why?*

Which, if any, of the above procedures you would use with your pupils will be influenced by a number of things, including the age and conceptual level of the pupils. The first involves using pictures or symbols which attract younger or less motivated children and make the assessment seem fun. If you want to use diaries, you will need to consider: whether pupils can already write and enjoy writing; what preparation they need so they understand what a learning diary is for; how much time you can give to responding to diaries. Questionnaires may be too complex and formal for use with younger children, but even older children can be reluctant to use them if they are very complicated. So they need careful designing and pupils need to be involved in developing them. ■

The benefits of self-assessment

Pupils will not always have a teacher to assess and provide feedback. Ultimately they need to learn to assess themselves and identify their own needs. Forms such as these assist pupils to think about their own learning and become aware of their strengths and weaknesses. This may encourage them to monitor themselves more carefully and make better use of opportunities for learning. These forms also provide very useful feedback to the teacher on what pupils have difficulty with, how they like working and what type of learning activities they prefer. For example, Ricky's diary entry gives a lot of helpful information about how he likes to learn. This could be used as a basis for discussion with Ricky or even the whole class about ways of learning.

Summary

In this chapter you have considered:

- *what assessment is* (ie feedback on teaching and learning), the reasons for assessment (to check achievement in teaching and learning, identify progress and needs), the kind of information obtained (marks, observations on progress, etc) and how this can be used (to modify your teaching, to provide extra help). We also considered how assessment can benefit children.
- *pupils' views on assessment.* Pupils may have strong beliefs and feelings about assessment which prevent them from fully benefiting from the results of assessment. I suggested

various ways you could help to change such beliefs: by making them more aware of the purpose of assessment; providing more information about their progress and how they can use this to improve; by helping them to assess themselves; by considering the effect of your own beliefs about assessment on the way you represent it to children.

- *the differences between on-going and final (overall) assessment.* On-going assessment is a continuous process of providing feedback to children on their progress in order to help them to develop. Overall assessment in contrast provides an overall picture of children's achievement at a certain point in time, often for official reasons. It does not directly contribute to children's learning. However these two types of assessment are best seen as complementary rather than in opposition.

- *three aspects you could use to guide on-going assessment:* finding evidence of children's learning; interpreting the evidence; using the findings to help children develop. Two methods of assessing children were analysed: an informal method based on the teacher's own objectives using the questions on p152 and a more structured method using a profile and attainment targets. Through examining the use of these, we uncovered some of the benefits, eg it can enable you to see a child's potential and to adjust your teaching to children's learning on the basis of the information you collect, and some of the dilemmas, eg the difficulty of ensuring that any assessment is balanced and fair to the child. Assessment needs to involve continuous sampling of children's work in order to get a realistic picture of their strengths, weaknesses and achievements.

- *different ways of encouraging children to assess themselves,* eg through the use of drafting, questionnaires and diaries. The aim is to help children to become aware of their own strengths and weaknesses and to learn to monitor their own progress through gradually internalizing the kind of criteria used to assess achievement. The process of self-assessment also has the added benefit that children feel more involved in the learning process and may be more receptive to your feedback. From your point of view as their teacher, you learn more about your pupils and their language learning.

There are two implications which arise from this chapter. Assessment is a tool which has the potential to help pupils make progress in their learning. In fact, if we think back to the learning contexts in Chapter 1, this is one advantage that classroom learning can provide over learning in a natural environment. The feedback which assessment can provide may make children more aware of their language and their learning process, and so help them to reach higher levels of achievement in the long term.

Assessment can also be a powerful tool in your development as a teacher. It can help you to see with new eyes. It can make you more aware of pupils' learning and capabilities as we saw with the drafting in Yenti's class. Through monitoring pupils' learning and checking this against your teaching intentions, you may become aware of gaps which develop. This then helps you to adjust your teaching in a way which enhances and supports pupils' learning.

References

1 This excerpt is taken from the video called *Language in the multi-ethnic primary school*, produced by the ILEA (Inner London Education Authority).

2 The study by Margaret Prosser is reported in Drummond, M. 1993 *Assessing Children's Learning.* David Fulton

3 McHugh, M. and Occhipinti, G. 1993 *Fanfare 1 Teacher's Book.* Oxford: Oxford University Press

4 This example is from a pupil in Leni Dam's classroom and is reported in the article 'Developing Autonomy in Schools: Why and How?' In *Language Teacher (Munintor Teanga)* Vol. 1, no. 2, Dublin 1989 pp22–3

Chapter 12 How can I be a better language learner?

Learning how to learn

Most classes are likely to contain children with different abilities, different styles of learning and with different attitudes to English as we have seen in some of the earlier chapters. How can we respond to their different needs and interests? It may be difficult to do this effectively and still have time left for all the other things we need to do. One solution is to help children to become more effective learners and take more responsibility for their own learning. This will help us as teachers and will also benefit children. In this chapter we will consider:

1 **Teachers' views about successful language learners**
2 **Pupils' views about successful language learners**
3 **What does 'learning how to learn' mean?**
4 **Ways of developing pupils' capacity to 'learn how to learn'**
5 **Teachers' concerns about implementing 'learn how to learn' goals**

The aim of this chapter is to raise your awareness about the importance of helping pupils to become more effective language learners. But it may be difficult for you to help pupils to become more effective learners unless you understand yourself what it means to be an effective learner/teacher, and have attempted to develop and improve your own practice. Though the focus of the chapter is on helping children to become more effective learners, it will encourage you, at the same time, to reflect on how you can develop further as a teacher.

A constant theme of this book has been the need to help children to become more effective and more independent language learners. This chapter focuses on this theme more explicitly, but there are several references in other chapters which you could refer to as well. These are mentioned on p167.

1 Teachers' views about successful language learners

Imagine a class of primary children who have started English this year. Alexis is quick and active, always ready to take part in activities and readily volunteers answers. Irene is quieter but is quick to pick up things and obviously understands what is said. Peter is very shy and withdrawn and does not say anything. By the end of the year, some of these children will have made great progress; others may have made little or none. By looking at those who are successful, can we identify what helps them to be effective learners?

Task 1 What do successful language learners do?

■ Think about two pupils in one of your classes who are successful language learners. Write down the things they do which make them effective.

Commentary ■ ■ ■

Did you find that your two pupils were similar or different to each other? Maybe like Lily Wong Fillmore[1], you found that there was not one single type of successful learner. She observed young children learning English as a second language in America for several years. She found that half of the most successful pupils were:

> *sociable, outgoing, talkative, eager to communicate with anyone who was receptive to them, highly verbal; several had mouths that seemed to 'operate non-stop round the clock'.*

But not all the successful learners were like this. Some of them:

> *had little to say, rarely spoke unless the teacher urged them to; worked hard; were shy; were analytical and curious and were able to make good use of situational cues in interpreting messages.*

This shows that successful learners vary. The most outgoing children are not necessarily the most successful learners. Quieter pupils can also be successful. The pupil who says the most and is the most active is not always the most effective, though these pupils often gain our attention most frequently. Pupils may benefit from knowing more about how other pupils in the class work so that they understand that there are different ways of learning language.

Compare your list with the following points made by a group of Spanish primary teachers. You would not expect to find all these qualities or characteristics in one learner but they do provide a useful checklist.

A successful learner is one who:

- *is prepared to take risks*
- *is motivated to learn English*
- *is creative*
- *is well organized*
- *pays attention*
- *has concentration*
- *is curious*
- *is confident*
- *does not give up*
- *is keen to communicate*
- *participates actively*
- *corrects own mistakes*
- *takes every opportunity to use English*
- *is willing to plan and review work.*

If we look closely at learners who are successful, one of the things which distinguishes them from other learners is not so much the difference in characteristics or in personality but their ability to manage their own learning flexibly. ■

2 Pupils' views about successful language learners

As we have seen in other chapters, pupils' beliefs and attitudes play an important part in influencing their responses in the classroom. So it seems important to find out their views about language learning and what they think makes a pupil successful. If they have very narrow or fixed views about what is possible in language learning, this may block their own potential for developing. For example, this 13-year-old Spanish pupil, when asked what type of pupil makes a good language learner, said:

All types of pupils regardless of their character.

whereas another pupil in the same class answered:

Someone who is shy will have more difficulty because he/she doesn't dare ask.

The first pupil's comment suggests that he/she believes that everyone has the potential to be a good language learner, whilst the second pupil's comment implies that only certain types of pupil will be successful. If this second pupil is, in fact, a shy person, he/she may approach language lessons believing that success will not be possible. So if we find out and discuss pupils' views with them, it may help them to develop more realistic views about language learning and to realize how much their own efforts can contribute to their success.

Task 2   What can you do to be a good language learner?

■ Ask some of your pupils what kinds of things they can do to help them be more successful in learning English.
■ Three groups of Spanish children were asked this question. Compare their views with your pupils' views.

What kinds of things can you do to help you be successful at learning English?

13-year-olds	10-year-olds	7-year-olds
practising at home	practising it	games and songs
songs	studying	books
books with examples	paying attention in class	tales
listening to tapes	making an effort	playing
watching films	completing your homework	paper
reading books	translating a bit of text each day	teacher
	travelling abroad	writing
		reading
		video/TV

(comments in translation)

Commentary ■ ■ ■

These Spanish pupils' views give us an interesting insight into their ideas about language learning. The seven-year-olds have an activity-oriented view which is strongly related to their experiences in the classroom. Learning in their classroom sounds varied and enjoyable. The ten-year-olds have quite a formal view of language learning which seems to relate to their classroom experience. It sounds quite a serious process involving lots of effort. However one child also connects language learning to the world outside through foreign travel. The 13-year-old pupils' views also seem to relate to their experiences at school, but several of their suggestions also link to out-of-school activities, eg watching films, listening to songs. These are the opinions of a particular group of children in a particular context, and so it would be dangerous to over-generalize. You need to find out about your own pupils and whether there are differences between age groups and why.

Children's views are heavily influenced by the experiences they have at school. But as children mature they begin to see a need for learning language and connect language learning with the outside world. They realize that language learning does not just have to take place in classrooms with a teacher. You could encourage this realization and so help to make pupils more aware of the possibilities. There are an enormous number of things pupils could do quite creatively. An Indonesian teacher reported that when he was a child studying English at school, he used to have conversations with himself in English in a mirror. Encouraging out-of-school learning will help pupils to become more independent. ∎

3 What does 'learning how to learn' mean?

We have identified the things that successful learners do. But the question is how we can help our learners to be more successful. I suggest that we need to help them to learn how to learn.

Here is an analogy:

Penny was a teacher. She was helpful and friendly to others. But she had one big fault. She never listened to what other people said. She always interrupted them before the end of their conversations or even tried to talk while they were talking. Consequently other staff were polite to Penny, but they tried to avoid spending time with her. She became unhappy and went to see the head teacher about a transfer. The head teacher asked, 'Why are you unhappy in this school, Penny?' Penny explained that the other teachers were not friendly to her and she did not have any close friends at the school. 'Do you know what the reason is, Penny?' said the head teacher. Penny shook her head despondently. 'I am going to give you a word of advice. Try talking less and listening more to others. Keep this in mind over the next few weeks and then come and see me again.' Penny was puzzled and slightly offended. But the next time she was talking to someone, she remembered the head teacher's words. She slowly became aware that she was talking a lot and not listening. A year later, Penny was still in the same school but she had more friends. She had become a much better listener now.

How does this story relate to learning to learn? The point of the story is that Penny was only able to change her behaviour when she became aware of it. You can apply a similar analogy to your pupils.

Think of your pupils in their school and classroom. They are busily engaged every day in their classroom learning English. Once involved in their daily language-learning activities, they are not normally aware of how they are learning. They may work together in pairs or groups and sometimes individually. They help each other by practising together, prompting and correcting each other. Not all pupils, however, like working together or sharing. Some pupils seem to be very active about using the language in class and will often spontaneously use it with their friends. They have all kinds of feelings and attitudes towards English, but they are not usually aware of them. Some of them are also doing a lot of other things which help them to learn a language. For example, they may be repeating new words to themselves to help remember; they may be comparing new words or patterns and noticing differences or similarities; they may be guessing by using context clues. However pupils are usually not aware that they are using these strategies.

In the story, Penny was only able to change when she became aware of the way she communicated with others and of the effect on them. And it is the same for your pupils. In order to become more effective learners, they need to become aware of their learning. It is only when they are able to stand back from their activities and become more conscious of what they do when they learn that they will be in a position to change, control and manage it. This awareness involves understanding how they learn and what will help their learning. Here is a set of questions which learners gradually need to learn to ask themselves with your help.

>> (this chapter)

- **How do I learn?**
  They need to become aware of the strategies they are using and how effective they are.

« Chapter 2
pp21–2

- **What are my goals?**
  They need to know why they are learning so they can set their own goals and plan their learning.

« Chapter 4
pp47–8, 53–8
« Chapter 10
pp142–4

- **How shall I manage my learning?**
  They need to manage their learning, their feelings about learning and make choices so that they are using their time and their skills in the most appropriate way.

« Chapter 11
pp159–61

- **How am I getting on?**
  They need to be able to monitor their learning and evaluate their progress so that they can take appropriate steps to improve it.

Making the pupils more aware of their learning is not an end in itself. It is designed to develop their ability to regulate their own learning. By modelling and making explicit the processes needed to carry out activities and why/when to use them, we hope that children will gradually internalize this understanding. A few pupils seem able to do this on their own, but the majority do not. However they can reach this awareness and learn to control their own learning with support from their teachers and other adults.

4 Ways of developing pupils' capacity to 'learn how to learn'

In this section, we will consider some ways of putting these ideas into practice. We will focus on the first of the questions above: how to raise awareness of the learning process, as this is the most challenging for teachers.

There are many ways in which you can raise pupils' awareness about language learning. However you will need to judge what is appropriate for your learners, given their age and interest in learning English. Younger learners (five to eight-year-olds) will be less able to reflect on their learning in a conscious way as this ability to reflect consciously and to analyse is linked to children's level of cognitive development.

Raising pupils' awareness about the language-learning process

Task 3   Raising pupils' awareness about learning

- Tape record the first part of one of your lessons and listen to it. See if you can answer questions **a–d**.
  a Do the pupils know what activity they have to do? Give the actual words which indicate this.
  b Do they know why they are doing it?
  c Do they know how they are going to work, eg in pairs, groups, etc?
  d Do they know how their performance will be evaluated? (Underline or write down the words which tell you.)

- Then read the lesson transcripts below and consider questions **a–d** in relation to them.
- Do you think that pupils benefit from getting this type of information?

Transcript A

This is taken from an actual lesson. The teacher is beginning her lesson with (seven to eight-year-old) pupils in their second year of learning English.

T OK, today we're going to learn something new. I'm going to tell you ... I'm going to give you riddles. Do you know what riddles are? *(writes word on the blackboard)* Do you know what riddles are, class? Yes or no?

Pps No.

T No. OK, riddle is *Teka teki. (writes Malaysian word on board)*

Pps Teka teki.

T Riddle is teka teki. Now do you know what is riddles? Yes or no?

Pps Yes ...

T OK, I tell the riddle. You all answer. I tell. You give me the answer.

Transcript B

This teacher has planned a lesson based on the book *Whizz Kids*[2]. Here is how she plans to introduce pupils to the relationship quiz which will be the main focus of the lesson. She has written down her imaginary dialogue with pupils. Most or part of the discussion will be in the L1 as children have limited English. The children will be seven to eight-year-old beginners.

1   **T**   Has anyone heard or seen a quiz?

    Pps Yes.

    T   Which ones have you seen?

    Pps *Mastermind. (etc)*

5   **T**   What happens in a quiz? What do people do?

    Pps *(pupils answer in L1)* People have to answer questions.

    T   What else, Simon?

    P   The person who gets the most correct answers is the winner.

    T   How many people take part?

10 **P**   Many.

    T   Do they play by themselves?

    Pps Sometimes they are in teams.

    T   Do you like TV quizzes?

    Pps Yes.

15 **T**   Why?

    P   Because they get prizes and it's fun.

    T   We are going to do a quiz today on family names.
           Can you think of any family names we learned yesterday?

    Pps Sister, brother ... *(pupils mention a few)*

20 **T**   That's right. Where can you find them in your book?

    Pps Page *(indicate page in book where relationship terms are given)*

    T   You are going to play in two teams. *(shows with her arms)* Each time I will call out two pupils and they have to spell a word correctly. There are ten words. If you spell one correctly you get a point for your team. *(shows how points are given on the board,*

25   *demonstrates the game with pupils)* The team with the most points is the winner. This game will help you to remember the family words and to learn to spell them. Is there anything else you can do to remember the words? *(T uses a mixture of English and L1 as children have limited English. Pupils suggest various possibilities)*

    T   OK, now let's do the quiz.

Commentary ■ ■ ■

Transcript A

a In Line 1, the teacher tells pupils what activity they are going to do, ie riddles. As pupils do not know the word 'riddle', she gives them the word in their mother tongue. It is not clear, however, whether pupils know what a riddle is even in their mother tongue. It would have been helpful if she had given an example first so that pupils would be able to draw on previous experience and make sense of the activity.

b She does not indicate why they are doing the activity.

c She briefly explains how they will do the activity, ie as a whole class with pupils listening and then giving an answer: *OK, I tell the riddle. You all answer. I tell. You give me the answer.*

d She does not indicate how their performance will be evaluated, ie are answers in the mother tongue acceptable, are one-word answers acceptable?

Transcript B

a The teacher tells the pupil what activity they will do (line 17 *a quiz on family names*). The initial discussion helps to draw on and activate pupils' background knowledge about quizzes. This will help to make the activity more meaningful to them.

b She tells them why they are doing the activity (line 26 *This game will help you to remember the family words and to learn to spell them.*) However she does not touch on the wider reasons for doing vocabulary activities linked to learning English, maybe because she feels children are too young to understand.

c She tells them how they will work, ie in teams.

d She explains that success means getting the most points for your team by getting the spelling correct (lines 23–25 *If you spell one correctly you get a point for your team. The team with the most points is the winner.*)

There are many reasons why it may be beneficial to share information with pupils that enables them to answer these questions:

What activity am I doing?

If pupils know what learning task they are going to do, they can make use of their previous knowledge about such tasks. For example, if pupils know that the learning activity is a quiz, they will be able to draw on their previous experience of quizzes from TV or radio. This may help them to understand how to do the activity and find it more meaningful. Even quite young children can understand this kind of information, provided it relates to familiar types of activity.

Why am I doing it?

Your immediate reaction to Transcript B above may be that it is a waste of time to tell pupils this information. However, even quite young children are able to understand such information if it is explained simply and it makes sense to them in human terms, eg *You remember Carlos has a friend in England. How can he keep in touch? He can write to him, can't he? Today we are going to practise writing letters in English and so this will help Carlos when he writes to his friend.* Pupils are often quite puzzled why they have been asked to do something and try to guess what is in the teacher's mind. Initially you may need to give some of this information in the L1 and to create a purpose which makes sense to them and relates to everyday experiences. But with older children (aged ten upwards) you will be able to help them understand the wider purposes for learning English. If pupils understand the significance of what they are doing, they can co-operate in working towards a particular outcome. They are also in a better position to monitor whether their work is relevant to the goal that has been set. If you always start the lesson in this way, pupils will get used to it and gradually work out the reason for doing things themselves.

How shall I do it?

If pupils know exactly how you expect them to work and how long they have to do the activity, they have a better chance of carrying it out effectively.

How do I know when I am successful?

If you tell pupils how you are going to assess their performance, eg *find six differences between the pictures*, then they will know what to aim for. They will also be able to monitor more easily when they have been successful. ■

Action plan

Aim: To help pupils to know what is expected of them.

Procedure

- Choose a lesson you are planning to teach.
- Plan how you would share some of this information with pupils:
  - What are pupils going to do? (Activity)
  - How are they going to work? (Organization)
  - Why are they going to do the activities? (Reason)
  - How will their performance be judged? (Assessment)
- Write down what you will say, to give yourself confidence.
- Focus on one or two items in your first lesson, eg on what activity pupils are going to do.
- Begin with a class you feel comfortable with, maybe a class of older pupils.
- If it works, add in another item, eg how pupils will be organized or why they are doing an activity.
- If it does not work, simplify or change the way you do it.
- Later try it with a more difficult or a younger class. Notice how you need to change the way you present the information with younger children.
- Reflect on what you have learned from trying out these ideas.

But if you are going to assist children to answer these questions, it helps if you are clear about them yourself. So let's see if you can apply these questions to one of your own lessons.

Putting it into practice for yourself

Think about the questions in relation to your next lesson.

What activities am I using in the lesson?

This refers to the learning activities you have planned. Are you clear about what they are and how you are going to refer to them with the pupils so they understand and find them meaningful? For example, you could say *Today we are going to practise prepositions* or you could say *Today we are going to play a guessing game*. The second example is expressed in a way that makes sense to your learners.

Why am I using these activities?

This refers to your reasons for choosing these activities, what you want pupils to achieve through the activities in terms of your goals for language learning, eg if you give a crossword puzzle you may want to develop pupils' vocabulary. If you do a circle time activity on how pupils can help each other, you probably want to develop positive attitudes

« Chapter 4
pp49–50

towards helping one another. But younger pupils will not necessarily be able to make sense of your goals. So how are you going to create a purpose for the learning activity which makes sense to them? You will have to create reasons that are meaningful to them, perhaps by drawing on their interest in games and puzzles. For example, to practise prepositions you might play a game which involves hiding a toy dog and pupils trying to guess where it is. *Let's see if you can guess where Spot, the dog, is hiding.*

How shall I organize pupils for learning?

This refers to the way you manage the classroom activities and the pupils to enable them to learn most effectively, eg for a particular activity, do you think it is best for pupils to work individually, in pairs, in groups or in what way? How long do they need for this activity?

How shall I know whether pupils achieve my intended outcomes?

This refers to the outcomes you expect – the evidence you need to tell you and the pupils how far your goals have been achieved. If you don't tell pupils what counts as a successful outcome or performance, they have no way of knowing whether they have achieved success.

Raising pupils' awareness about learning activities

Pupils are very familiar with learning activities as they do them every day. They make a big difference to pupils' enjoyment. They are, therefore, a good starting point for raising awareness about learning. Here are some suggestions which you could try over a period of time with your class, from the beginning of a term or year.

1 Your textbook may have small picture symbols which represent different types of activities. These are taken from *Big Red Bus*[3].

If not, develop some simple ones like the ones below which were designed by a group of Spanish teachers.

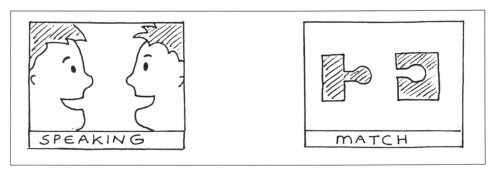

2   Point out or show the picture symbol to the pupils and discuss what it represents, eg

T   *(shows picture of a child's ear)* What's this?
Pps An ear.
T   Yes. What do you do with your ears?
Pps Listen.
T   That's right. And what is this? *(shows picture of a child drawing)*
Pps Drawing.
T   Yes, draw. Today you are going to listen and draw.

3   Do the activity, eg listen to instructions and draw the balloons.
4   At the end of the lesson, show the picture symbols and remind pupils of the activity they have done.
5   The next time you do a 'listen and draw' activity, show the symbols and ask them to tell you what activity they are going to do.
6   After a few weeks get pupils to tell you what activity they did in the lesson by pointing to the symbol for the activity or drawing it. You can stick the symbols up on the wall to be easily referred to.
7   Begin to introduce pupils to other symbols from the textbook or new ones you have prepared.
8   As pupils get more familiar with the idea of talking about what activity they will do, get them to suggest or draw symbols for activities in the textbook which have no pictorial symbol, eg story telling. Older pupils may like to invent some more exciting symbols like this one suggested by Spanish teachers.

9   Later, set aside one lesson a week for pupils to choose which activities they would like to do. Each group could choose one activity. This begins to involve pupils in managing their learning in a very simple way.

Raising pupils' awareness about strategy use

Pupils do activities every day, usually without awareness of the way they do them. Their focus is on the activity itself and the end product, eg finishing a crossword puzzle or filling in the blanks. One of the ideas behind learning to learn is that pupils need awareness of how they carry out learning tasks (of the strategies they use) in order to improve and develop more flexible ways of working. If this information is shared with other pupils, they can benefit by extending their range of strategies.

Here is an example of how you can raise children's awareness of strategy use through modelling. The lesson is designed to help (eight to nine-year-old) pupils learn to use a wall dictionary. The wall dictionary consists of words which children have learned to recognize by sight and to use in their own writing. New words are added to the dictionary as they are learned. Children have already learned how to place words in alphabetical order.

Task 4   Modelling language-learning strategies

- What is the teacher's main aim here?
- Does she make it clear to the children why they are doing the activity?
- How does her modelling raise children's awareness about the kind of procedures and strategies needed in carrying out the activity?

(Teacher gets children to sit in a semi-circle close to the wall dictionary.)

1   **T**   What do you think we are going to do now?

P1   Dictionary.

T   Yes, a good guess. Today we are going to learn how to use our wall dictionary.

T   You know the stories we are writing. I am writing a story about a witch and a cat. But
5   I'm not sure how to spell '*witch*'. What can I do?

P2   *(spells)* w–i–t–

T   That's super Chandra. You can spell it. But maybe some pupils can't spell. Maybe there is no friend like you to help me. What can I do then?

Pps   Look in dictionary.

10   **T**   Yes, we can use the dictionary to help us when we don't know how to spell a word. So help me to use it. Where do I look?

Pps   There, there. *(pointing to W section)*

T   How do I know where to look?

P3   *(in L1)* Find the first letter.

15   **T**   Yes, that's a good start. What's the first letter of 'witch'?

Pps   W.

T   OK. So where do I go to find the word?
(Pupils all bid to answer)

P1   There. W words. *(Pupil points to the wall dictionary)*

20   **T**   Yes, Deepak? You help me. Show me what to do.
(Deepak goes to the W section and points to the word)

T   Thanks. How did he find it? There are lots of words under W.

P1   *(in L1)* I knew the second letter was 'i' so I went down the list of words till I came to *wi*. Then I found it.

25   **T**   Well done. Why do we put words in the dictionary in a special order like this?

Pps   Easy to find them.

T   Yes, it's quicker, isn't it? Shall we do some more examples? You can tell me how to find the words.
(Pupils volunteer)

30   *(After several examples, T sets a writing task)*

T   Now you are going to carry on with your stories. If you find any words you can't spell, what will you do? Chandra?

P2   Use the dictionary.

35   **T**   Yes but why is that a good thing to do?

P2   *(in L1)* We won't bother our friends and the teacher.

T   Yes. It helps you to learn how to work by yourselves – to be independent.

Commentary ■ ■ ■

The teacher's main aim is to help children to learn how to use the wall dictionary and understand the reasons for using it.

The teacher makes it clear to the children why they are doing the activity by eliciting the reason from the pupils themselves, by creating a problem situation they can understand and respond to. She then highlights the reason to make sure all pupils have heard it (line 10: *Yes, we can use the dictionary to help us when we don't know how to spell a word.*).

Modelling does not mean telling pupils what to do. The emphasis is on getting

173

them to work out for themselves with the teacher's support what they need to do – a kind of guided discovery. The teacher draws on their recent story writing to highlight a situation where they need to use the dictionary. The need for help with spelling is one they have recently experienced, and so this makes the situation more real and meaningful to them. This helps them to feel more involved and because they are involved it is more likely they will understand and remember. With the teacher's help, children talk about how to use the dictionary, eg *So help me to use it. Where do I look? How do I know where to look?*, they actually use it (children go across to the wall dictionary and find the word) and they think about the reasons for using it. In effect, the teacher is externalizing the kind of processes which someone might draw on automatically in using the dictionary. But for children, it needs to be made explicit in the beginning so they can understand, practise and eventually internalize those processes. Children need to be reminded frequently of relevant ways of working and of strategies they can use when they do related activities, so that they transfer these to new situations. ■

If you were going to use this technique with your pupils you might create a different context for introducing the use of dictionaries, one that is relevant to your pupils' interests. If your pupils have limited ability to express themselves, you could carry out the initial part of the discussion in the L1, using English wherever you think they could understand. This is not a waste of time if it helps them to use the dictionary or do other activities more effectively. It is an investment in the children's future.

5   Teachers' concerns about implementing 'learn how to learn' goals

At this stage, you may feel interested in the ideas on learning to learn but have doubts about whether you can actually implement them. Or you may feel doubtful about the value of the ideas themselves.

Task 5   What are the problems and how can you solve them?

■ What difficulties might you find in trying to implement learning to learn ideas?
■ What solutions can you suggest?

Commentary ■ ■ ■

In a seminar in Madrid, a group of Spanish primary teachers were asked to list any worries or problems they might have about trying to implement 'learning to learn' ideas in their classroom. Here are some of their responses:

Problems

- Use of mother tongue (needed for younger children when reflecting on learning or in raising awareness activities)
- Colleagues don't work like this in their other subjects
- Parents' attitudes – 'wasting their children's time'
- Takes time / Lack of time to finish work
- Mixed-ability classes
- Bad behaviour
- Constraints of textbooks/curriculum – textbooks are not 'learn how to learn' oriented

In discussing the problems, we all agreed that there were no easy solutions. However, we felt that it was important not to give up, but to keep 'learning to learn' as a goal which we worked towards step by step. Here is a list of the solutions, many of which were discussed in the seminar. I have also added other ideas.

Use of mother tongue

Set aside five minutes at the beginning or end of lessons for reflection on learning which requires the use of L1. Separate off the use of L1 from the rest of the lesson.

Colleagues – they don't work like this in their other subjects

Convince other teachers by being open about what you are doing. Invite them to observe. Ask their advice and try and involve them. Convince the head teacher to develop a whole-school policy.

Parents' attitudes – 'wasting their children's time'

Send a letter to parents. Invite them in to see what you are doing at a parents' evening.

Takes time / Lack of time to finish work

Develop a systematic programme through the year. Have a special focus, eg giving children more choice/responsibility in selecting partners or in choosing activities one day a week.

Develop re-usable materials, eg use of symbols, or work with another teacher and share ideas.

Use stronger pupils to help/explain/demonstrate to other pupils.

Integrate it with your usual teaching. (See Gail Ellis[4] for a suggestion on how to do this.)

Mixed-ability classes

« Chapter 3 Encourage pair and group collaboration and peer tutoring.

Bad behaviour

« Negotiating rules pp47–8 Negotiate classroom rules/procedures at the beginning of term. Reinforce and praise positive behaviour.

Constraints of textbooks/curriculum

Adapt them to fit your needs. Build in an explicit 'learning to learn' focus.

Summary

This chapter has explored in detail how to help pupils to become more effective language learners, a theme which has been emphasized throughout the book. In this chapter, you have considered:

- *teachers' views about successful language learners.* The most interesting finding is that successful language learners vary widely in behaviour and personality, but what may distinguish them from other learners is that they tend to be more effective and flexible at managing their learning.
- *pupils' views about successful language learning.* It is important to find out their views as pupils may have misconceptions which prevent them from fully realizing their potential as language learners. Pupils clearly do have views about language learning, strongly influenced by their school learning. This suggests you can begin to develop and extend these views of language learning and can influence their approach to language learning. With maturity, pupils increasingly become aware of the use of English in the outside world which you can exploit to encourage more independent out-of-school learning.

- *what 'learning how to learn' means.* It involves becoming more aware or conscious of how you learn language, what will best assist your language learning and how to take greater control over it. This awareness and control are related to four key areas: increased awareness of the process of learning; creating your own reasons for language learning and planning for language learning; managing language learning and feelings about language learning; monitoring and evaluation of language learning. Pupils do not automatically develop this awareness and control but can do so with your help.
- *ways of developing pupils' capacity to 'learn how to learn'.* You could begin to raise pupils' awareness about language learning through what you do every day when you begin your lesson: by drawing attention to what they are going to do, how they are going to work, why they are doing the activity and what outcomes are expected. You can also make children more aware of the strategies and procedures needed for doing activities by modelling the processes and making explicit what is involved.
- *teachers' worries about 'learning how to learn'.* The main problems relate to the time it takes, colleagues' and parents' attitudes, lack of suitable materials, children's reactions and behaviour and the need to use L1. Solutions include convincing and educating parents and colleagues, adapting materials, training children to become independent and setting aside a special time for using the L1 to reflect on learning.

There is one suggestion and one implication I would like to end with. You may feel that making pupils more conscious about learning will prevent them from learning or will take the fun out of learning. Or you may have worries about the practicality of learning to learn for the classroom. In my experience, primary teachers are torn between feelings of excitement at the possibilities and worries about whether they can actually make them work. These feelings are natural and you should acknowledge and express them. Sometimes ideas make more sense after they have had time to sit in your head and after you have had time to try them out for yourself.

Helping pupils to learn how to learn should form the basis of your teaching if you want pupils to develop their full potential as learners and language learners. But you need to start with yourself. You need to become aware of your own development as a teacher and apply the same questions to yourself as you applied to pupils' learning above. You will then have a greater appreciation of what it means and feel more confident to help your own pupils. Ask yourself:

- Am I aware of the way I teach and my attitudes/beliefs about teaching/learning?
- How can I plan my own development as a teacher?
- How can I manage the process of my professional development better?
- How can I monitor and evaluate my own development?

Becoming more aware of the process of your own development will make you better able to understand how to help your pupils to learn how to learn.

References

1 Wong Fillmore, L. 'The Language Learner as an Individual: Implications of research on individual differences for the ESL teacher.' In Clarke, M.A. and Handscombe, J (eds) 1983 *On TESOL '82*. Washington: TESOL, pp162–3
An interesting study with much of interest for teachers in foreign language contexts.
2 Concari, I., Hirsch, F., Krieger, U. and Urrestarazu, J. 1994 *Whizz Kids Pupil's Book 1*. Oxford: Heinemann, Unit 1 lesson 3, based on Activity 2 and 3.
3 Lobo, M.J. and Subira, P. 1993 *Big Red Bus 1*. Oxford: Heinemann
4 Gail Ellis's article is in Brumfit, C., Moon, J. and Tongue, R. (eds) 1991 *Teaching English to Children*. London: Collins ELT, pp191–200

Looking forwards

I would be interested to know why you chose to read this book.

- Was it because you had an assignment on young learners to do for a course?
- Was it because you are new to teaching children and wanted some survival ideas?
- Was it because you wanted some new ideas or perspectives on teaching children?
- Was it because you wanted some ideas for designing an in-service course for teachers?

I hope that you found something of relevance to your purpose. More importantly I hope that perhaps you were intrigued, challenged or even puzzled by something you read. Perhaps you will take away an idea or view which will not fit readily into your existing scheme of ideas, which challenges your own views or extends your own view in some way.

Meeting new ideas or different ideas often leads us to question and rethink what we do. It may give us confidence to try out new ideas. This encourages change. 'Why is this a good thing?' you may ask. Once we have been in teaching for some time and developed a set of routines that we can rely on, one of the dangers is that we become settled. We depend on well-tried procedures so we do not need to make too much effort. Maybe we don't want challenges – we had lots of those earlier on and now we want some peace. Routines, of course, are a good way of reducing stress and anxiety but there is a danger of getting stuck in a rut. This is what Mary Drummond[1] calls a model of inertia. I have adapted her model below and called it the *Cycle of Standing Still*.

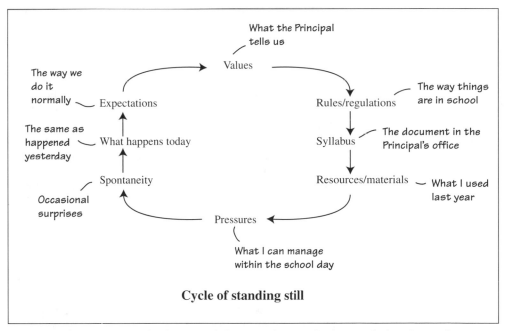

Cycle of standing still

The cycle develops as we begin to settle into routines and rely on tried and tested procedures. This is not in itself a bad thing. It can be negative, however, if it encourages unquestioning acceptance of the way we have done things before. In the cycle, each day's teaching is not a new experience, but the same day's teaching repeated many times. We rely on things that work in our classes; we make use of what we did last year; we accept the rules and regulations as they have always been and so it goes on. In other words, everything in the teaching environment contributes to making things predictable, safe and routine. Fine! But the more this happens the less likely it is we will feel any need to change. Security is very comforting.

Moving forwards

We don't have to get into a cycle of standing still. One way is to start asking questions about what we do and why we do it. That makes us think about our teaching rather than merely accepting it. Try this with some of the items in the cycle above:

Rules/regulations, *eg What are the rules for? Why do we have these particular rules? Are they all necessary? Who makes the rules? Could children also be involved?*

Resources/teaching materials, *eg Why am I using this activity? Why is it designed like this? Could I improve it in some way?*

We can't necessarily answer all the questions but the effort of trying to ask and answer them may begin to awaken our interest. Asking ourselves questions is at the basis of change because we stop accepting things as being inevitable and become aware of other possibilities. eg *I don't have to do it this way every time. I could try it like this for a change,*

Why move forwards?

Why should we create anxiety for ourselves by abandoning routines and security in order to develop and move forwards? Maybe we feel quite comfortable as we are. But that does not always last. I believe that developing professionally is the main way of making our jobs really involving, satisfying and worthwhile. It helps to lift our work out of the merely routine and mechanical and can help to sustain us through the ups and downs of daily teaching. It also makes us better able to respond positively and flexibly to external demands such as, for example, the introduction of a new curriculum or new textbooks.

Getting to know yourself

When we observe some teaching or some children learning, we may believe that other people will see exactly what we see. This is not the case. What we see and how we interpret what we see is affected by all our previous experience, by our beliefs and assumptions, ie things we take for granted are true. This is why discussions about videos of teaching can be very heated indeed during in-service courses. Everyone assumes they are watching the same bit of teaching, but in reality they are not. They are watching as many bits of teaching as there are teachers. Each teacher interprets it in line with his/her beliefs. These beliefs and assumptions which underlie our actions and opinions are rarely brought out into the open or examined. And yet if we want to develop as teachers, we need to understand ourselves, our attitudes and beliefs. In Chapter 12, I suggested that if we want children to become more effective learners, they need to become aware of their feelings and attitudes and ways of learning in order to be able to make changes in the way they learn. The same applies to teachers' development. We need to become aware of the link between our beliefs and what we do in the classroom. Let's use the analogy of a plant to make the points clearer.

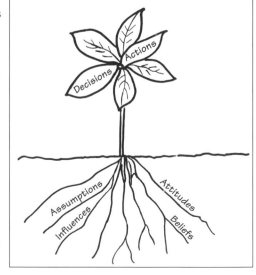

The part we see above the ground – the stem, leaves and flower – represents our practice, what we do in the classroom. The part we can't see is the roots which go down very deep into the soil. They help to anchor the plant and allow it to get nourishment from the soil. The roots represent our unseen beliefs and assumptions which nourish and sustain our classroom practice. As they are hidden, we take them for granted. Change in our practice can only occur if we become explicitly aware of those beliefs and begin to question and challenge them. If we are not aware of our underlying beliefs and values, then we will take our practice for granted and it will remain unquestioned.

How to move forwards?

Maybe you are wondering how you can develop yourself while working on your own in your classroom. In fact the classroom and your own teaching provide you with many opportunities to develop as some of the action plan tasks in the book suggest.

It is useful to have some guidelines or a framework to work with. We will use the three questions from Chapter 11 as a guide for working in the classroom.

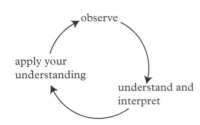

What is there to observe?

We tend to see and observe things in our classrooms in the way we have always seen them. Previous experience colours what we see. But if we want to change, we need to see in new ways. So how can we distance ourselves from our experience so we can see with new eyes? Here are some ways that might help:

Observing children

Observe a child in a friend's house or in a relative's house. Describe what you see. Try to avoid interpreting or making any judgements of what you observe at this point, eg *Franco sees a slug – watches as the slug moves slowly – touches it and the slug stops. Pokes it to make it move but the slug gets smaller. Stops poking and picks up his toy car. The slug begins to crawl again. Franco notices and again comes back to look. Pokes it again and the slug stops.*

Observing others' classes

Ask a friend or an experienced teacher if you can observe. It is easier to be detached in someone else's class. Make notes on one or two events which you think are interesting. Try to describe exactly what happens without judging them as good or bad.

Observing your own class

Give the class some written work for a short period and observe some of the children. Note down exactly what they are doing and saying. Tape record them if you can.

Peer observation

Ask a friend to observe your class or part of a class and make notes. Write up your own notes about the same lesson and later compare notes with your friend, eg:

Took children to the vegetable garden rather than bringing vegetables to class. Thought they would be more interested. Gardener warned us about stepping on the vegetables. Divided them into three groups of ten children and elected a group leader for each group. Gave out a set of blank card strips and a pencil to each.

Told children in their groups to discuss and then identify the vegetable names, write each name and then place it near the vegetable. Patrick's group finished quickly. So I showed them some other vegetables they had not looked at so far. Felt that groups are too large so individual children are not so involved.

Learning how to detach yourself from what you observe is not easy, but it may help you to see things in new ways.

How can I understand what I see?

Once you have collected information, you want to understand and interpret it.

It is hard not to be influenced by our own beliefs and assumptions when trying to understand and make sense of what we have seen. So one way of helping ourselves to see things in new ways is to get other perspectives.

Asking children

If you have been observing children, for example, Franco in your friend's house, ask the child, eg *What were you looking at? What was the slug doing? Why? Do you like watching the slug? Why?*

If you have been observing in a friend's classroom, talk to the children you observed after the lesson. Get their opinion of what they were doing and why, eg *I noticed you were talking together in English. What were you doing? Why? Did you like it? Did you find it hard or easy? Will the teacher be happy with your work?*

If you have been observing an activity in your own class, eg writing a letter to a penpal, ask pupils what they thought about it afterwards, eg *Are you happy with what you wrote? Why?/Why not? Will I be happy with what you wrote? What did you think about the activity? Was it clear? Did you like it? Did you find it easy/difficult?*

Asking others

If you have observed a child in your friend's house, ask the child's mother or older brother/sister for their understanding of what you observed. If you have observed in another teacher's class, ask for their interpretation of what you observed children doing, eg *What was happening at the table in the corner? What were the children doing? What did you feel about the way the children worked?*

If you also make notes of what you have observed, and your interpretation of the event, you will have three different interpretations of the same event:

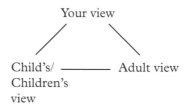

This will give you a much richer understanding of what you observed and also help to give you different perspectives. You may, for example, have interpreted a child as not doing his work when he chatted to his friend. But if you talked to the child, he might tell you that he and his friend were confused and were discussing how to do the activity. This gives you a different view of his behaviour.

How can I apply my understanding?

One way you can apply your understanding is in the way you plan your teaching for the future, and in the way you respond to learners based on your new understanding.

For example, Aishah from Malaysia had observed that her pupils were reluctant to write. She talked to other teachers about the problem. One teacher told her about diary writing and how helpful it was for motivating pupils to write. She and a friend decided to try the idea out. They prepared an action plan which they showed to their head teacher.

You don't need to make a formal action plan, but it is helpful to think about all the same questions as Aishah and her friend have done. It is also very supportive to have someone else to work with.

---

1 WHAT WILL YOU TRY OUT?

Diary writing

2 HOW WILL YOU DO IT?

Explain the idea to pupils and ask them to buy an exercise book to use as a diary.

Ask them to write something at least two times a week (more if they want).

We will read ten diaries a week and respond to pupils' ideas.

3 WHY DO YOU THINK THIS IS A GOOD IDEA?

Perhaps pupils will feel motivated to write if they see that we arc interested in their ideas, not whether the writing is correct. If they write more, their writing will improve.

4 WHO WILL YOU TRY IT OUT WITH?

We will try it out with Year 3 pupils first.

4 WHAT OUTCOMES DO YOU EXPECT?

We hope pupils will begin to enjoy writing.

We hope they will write something every week.

We hope that the amount they write will increase over the term.

5 ANY PROBLEMS EXPECTED?

Time to read and comment on the diaries. Some children may not be willing to write

---

Here is what Aishah wrote to me after one year of trying out the idea:

What I found is that this diary writing is an effective tool for the younger students (primary school children from seven to twelve years old). They have improved tremendously, especially in the area of putting their thoughts into words. They have developed from one-sentence entry to one whole-page entry. At times they can even write complex sentences. However their sentences are not always error free and sometimes they repeat the same error. But I guess at this stage I'm more concerned to develop their ability to put thoughts and ideas into words.

Aishah's enthusiasm is very clear in the letter. She has become excited by what she is doing. I hope that you will continue to develop and grow as a teacher, and that, like Aishah, you will feel inspired and excited by your teaching.

References

1 Drummond, M. 1993 *Assessing Children's Learning.* David Fulton

Glossary

ability this refers to a learner's underlying capacity to do certain things. It is usually demonstrated in performance though any single instance does not necessarily reveal a learner's full ability.

accuracy this refers to grammatically correct language in either speech or writing in the L2. It is often contrasted with *fluency*.

assessment the gathering and interpreting of information about a learners' progress in order to provide feedback to them or to provide feedback to teachers on their teaching. This is often referred to as *formative* or on-going assessment as it is aimed at assisting the learning/teaching process. Assessment may also be concerned to measure achievement as, for example in end-of-year tests or public exams. This is referred to as *summative* (overall) assessment. This does not normally contribute directly to the teaching/learning process.

attitude positive or negative feelings, beliefs, behaviour towards a person, object or event. Attitudes can't be directly observed but only inferred from a person's actions. For example, if a child tries to avoid speaking in English in class though he/she is quite happy to read, write and listen, you could infer that he/she has negative attitudes towards speaking in English.

approach the underlying theoretical beliefs about language and learning which guide the way someone plans and carries out his/her teaching. When we talk about using a communicative approach to language teaching, we mean that the teaching content and methods used will be influenced by a view of language which emphasizes communication and meaning and a view of learning which encourages active learner involvement and choice. However the way each teacher implements this approach will vary depending on his/her interpretation of it.

cognitive relates to the mental processes by which we acquire knowledge. Cognitive processes include perception, remembering, attending, classifying, etc.

concept the general underlying idea or meaning which is associated with a word in people's heads. For example, when we think of *a dog*, we would probably agree on some basic criteria which characterize it, ie it has four legs, a tail and it barks. However each one of us will also have our own concept of *a dog* which will vary in some details from person to person. Children, who are still developing cognitively, may have very different understandings from adults.

context language takes place in a particular situation for a purpose with specific participants with reference to events or topics – this is all part of the context and these aspects help to give clues to the meaning. So when we want to teach some new language, eg vocabulary, we often do it through a story, a song or a drama. We say that the story or song provides a context or situation for introducing the new vocabulary.

criterion a standard against which something can be
(pl criteria) evaluated. For example, if you take a driving test, you have to reach a certain standard in order to pass. If you take a test, your answer is evaluated according to a set of guidelines or criteria.

draft a rough or unfinished version of a piece of writing. If you are writing an application for a job you may produce several drafts before you are satisfied that it is ready to send off.

EFL English as a foreign language. This refers to situations where English is learned as a subject at school mainly for international communication. It is not normally spoken or used in that society for any purpose, eg English is a foreign language in France.

error the incorrect use of a linguistic item in speech or writing, due to lack of knowledge about the language. Many children make errors in the use of articles, eg *a/an* as these are quite complex aspects of language. It is often contrasted with *mistake*.

ESL English as a second language. This refers to situations where English is widely used in a particular society, eg for education, for trade, for business, but is not the first language for the population. An example would be South Africa, where English is used for education, business and other purposes.

exposure the opportunities for learners to hear, speak, read or write the language they are learning. In ESL situations these may be informal but in EFL situations they may need to be planned.

feedback information provided to someone on their performance. For example, if a teacher draws attention to a child's spelling mistake or to the way he/she pronounces a word, this is a kind of feedback.

fluency the ease with which learners communicate either in speech or writing in the L2. In speaking, it usually refers to lack of hesitation and pausing, and ability to express one's message effectively using all the language available. In writing, it refers to the ease and effectiveness with which the message is expressed. It is often contrasted with *accuracy*.

form   the actual words (written) or the sounds (spoken) which represent something in language, as contrasted with the meaning or use. If a teacher asks a question, eg *What did you do yesterday?* to check if the learner can produce the correct answer grammatically, then the focus is on the form of the language.

function   the purpose which a sentence can perform in communication. For example, the question form *Will you open the window?* can be used in some situations as a request. Any sentence can be described in terms of its form, eg an interrogative, as well as the way it functions in communication, eg a request.

grammar   a set of rules which help to explain how words or parts of words are combined to produce meaningful and acceptable units/sentences within a language.

input   the language that the child is exposed to through listening to the teacher, to peers, to tapes, to video or TV, or through written text. This provides the raw material for the child to work on and develop his/her internal language system.

interaction   communication with other people. Classroom interaction refers to the communication which takes place between teacher and pupils, and pupils and their peers.

interlanguage   the type of language produced by learners in the process of learning a second or foreign language. It refers to their underlying language system which is still in the process of developing.

L1   your first language or what is sometimes called your mother tongue. It usually refers to the language you speak at home.

L2   the second language or other languages you speak, ie not your first language.

mistake   a slip or an incorrect use of language during speaking or writing caused by carelessness, lack of attention or tiredness. It is often contrasted with *error*.

model   to demonstrate or provide an example of what is expected. For example, a teacher may show learners how to revise a piece of writing by doing an example on the blackboard for the whole class to observe. He/she may provide an example of the language they want learners to practise.

principles   in the classroom context, the set of rules or beliefs which underpin a textbook or guide a teacher's actions. These may or may not be stated explicitly. An example of a principle is 'In planning your teaching build on what children know already.'

productive   this refers to the language which learners are expected to produce either in speech or writing. It is often contrasted with *receptive*.

receptive   this refers to the language which learners are expected to understand either through listening or reading. It is often contrasted with *productive*.

recycle   to use again or to provide further practice of the language or skills which have already been presented to learners.

self-esteem   the value someone places on him or herself. Self-esteem can be measured by considering the degree of match between a person's self-image and his/her ideal self (the self they would like to be). If the match is strong, then there is likely to be high self-esteem. If there is a gap between the two, then self-esteem is probably low.

self-image or   a person's awareness of self – of his/her
self-concept   own characteristics, personality, etc. This awareness is developed through the responses and reactions of other people to that person.

skill   the knowledge or ability to achieve particular purposes through actions. Skills vary from complex ones like teaching to relatively simple ones like tying your shoes, which are more predictable. Well developed skill is fluent, automatic and takes little effort, eg after you have been driving a car for many years you stop being aware of how you do it. Reading, writing, speaking and listening are referred to as language skills.

strategy   a way of using skills in a purposeful way to achieve a particular goal. For example, it is like a tennis player who has many different skills in playing tennis, eg serving the ball to an opponent, returning a serve within the court, etc. When the player manages these skills in a flexible way so as to defeat his/her opponent, we can say he/she is using a strategy or using his/her skills in a strategic way. Whereas skills become automatic with practice, strategies are applied flexibly.

structure   a particular aspect or item of grammar. Some examples of structures include: the past tense, articles, the comparison of adjectives. Different languages may have different structures. For example, French, Italian, Spanish distinguish between masculine, feminine and neuter nouns while English does not.

Index